Jazz Noir

Jazz Noir

Listening to Music from
Phantom Lady to *The Last Seduction*

David Butler

 PRAEGER

Westport, Connecticut
London

Library of Congress Cataloging-in-Publication Data

Butler, David, 1974–
    Jazz noir : Listening to music from *Phantom Lady* to *The Last Seduction* / David Butler.
        p.   cm.
    Includes bibliographical references and index.
    ISBN 0–275–97301–8 (alk. paper)
    1. Jazz in motion pictures.   2. Film noir—History and criticism.   I. Title.
PN1995.9.J37 B88   2002
791.43'657—dc21   2001054596

British Library Cataloguing in Publication Data is available.

Library of Congress Catalog Card Number: 2001054596
ISBN: 0–275–97301–8

First published in 2002

Praeger Publishers, 88 Post Road West, Westport, CT 06881
An imprint of Greenwood Publishing Group, Inc.
www.praeger.com

Printed in the United States of America

The paper used in this book complies with the
Permanent Paper Standard issued by the National
Information Standards Organization (Z39.48–1984).

10 9 8 7 6 5 4 3 2 1

Copyright Acknowledgments

The author and publisher gratefully acknowledge permission to use the following material:

Chapter 3, script extract from *Young Man with a Horn*, courtesy of Warner Bros. Chapter 4, script extract from *I Want To Live!*, © 1958 Metro-Goldwyn-Mayer Studios Inc. All rights reserved. Chapter 5, Music Timing Notes for *Taxi Driver*, extracts from the Martin Scorsese Collection, Special Collections, American Film Institute.

Every reasonable effort has been made to trace the owners of copyright materials in this book, but in some instances this has proven impossible. The author and publisher will be glad to receive information leading to more complete acknowledgments in subsequent printings of the book, and in the meantime extend their apologies for any omissions.

*To Yana—for impoppable smiles, brilliant lines
and wonders I don't deserve*

Contents

Contents

Preface

This book developed from my Ph.D. thesis, which I undertook between October 1996 and January 2000. The support and assistance I received during my doctoral training was crucial in enabling me to write this book. I therefore want to first of all thank those individuals and institutions that helped me get to this stage.

I am deeply indebted to the British Academy and the Hulme Hall Council for the exhibitions that they granted me. I could not have completed my thesis without their support, which was more than simply financial. I am particularly thankful for the generosity of the wardens of Hulme Hall, Dr. Thain Flowers and Jacquie Wilson, who provided me with a perfect home away from home during the last four years. Special thanks must also go to my supervisor, Alan Marcus, for his encouragement, guidance and winning words in my application to the British Academy. I'd like to thank Emily and Tim, colleagues in the Department of Drama, for their solidarity; it has always been reassuring knowing that you were out there on the same journey. I owe a great deal to Susie Hird for her translation skills and for taking care of my room during my time in America. I am extremely grateful to Jessie Peramal for her paper and for being the perfect neighbor (if only you could say the same, Jessie!). I also want to thank the staff of the Department of Drama for their support, particularly Janet Jones, Estelle Gallagher, Ken Richards and Clare Whatling. I am especially grateful to Clare for unlocking concepts and ideas that I would never have considered and for giving me the opportunity to present aspects of my thesis in a lecture for her course, "Ideology in Film." Finally, I am still in something of a state of shock from the terribly nice things said about my thesis by Richard Dyer and Peter Martin during my final examination. I am grateful to both Richard and Peter for agreeing to read and examine my thesis and for offering constructive comments. On a hazy day in March 2000, we double-booked the exam room with a party of fifty Japanese students, and Richard and Peter instantly put me at ease and made me feel that the previous years had been worth all the work, something that I didn't always find easy to believe during the actual process.

When it came to developing the thesis into this book, two people deserve special mention for their incredible support and encouragement. First, David Mayer got everything moving by recommending that I submit my abstract to a friend of his at Greenwood Press. That person turned out to be Eric Levy who has proven to be a wonderfully supportive editor. There are few people who can out-strange me when it comes to writing e-mails, but Eric has a penchant for the obscure and quirky phrase that made communicating with him a delight. Similarly, David was last familiar with me in a previous incarnation when I wrote a lot of *very* strange plays, generally involving trans-dimensional killer sheep and a sentient mountain intent on whatever it is that sentient mountains are intent on doing. Needless to say, these tried the patience of the reader (who was often David), and he has shown either extraordinary vision or diplomatic memory loss in forgetting (or possibly forgiving) these oddities and supporting my academic writing. There are no sentient mountains in this book, I hasten to add.

One of the strengths of the book is its use of archival documents and primary sources. I would not have been able to include this material without the support and assistance of a group of individuals and institutions that immeasurably boosted my confidence in the book by allowing me to include citations from their archival documents. I am extremely grateful to both Martin Scorsese and Robert Wise for granting me permission to use their private documents, from the special collections held in their name at the American Film Institute and USC Cinema and Television Library, respectively. Mary Jane Miller, of MGM, was of great assistance in approving my use of several extracts from the screenplay for *I Want To Live!* (1958), and, equally supportive and courteous was Jeremy Williams of Warner Brothers in approving the use of Warner materials relating to *Young Man with a Horn* (1950). These materials appear courtesy of MGM and Warner Brothers, respectively.

I am also indebted to the librarians and archivists who have stopped me from getting swamped and lost during my researches. I would particularly like to thank the staff of the John Rylands Library, Andrew Simons of the National Sound Archive in London and those marvels who made my research in Los Angeles a pleasure: Scott Curtis and Barbara Hall of the Margaret Herrick Library, Ned Comstock of the USC Cinema and Television Library, Brigitte Kuepper and Julie Graham of the Arts Special Collections at UCLA and the staff of the American Film Institute. It was also a delight and honor to speak with Laurie Johnson, Lennie Niehaus and David Meeker—their generosity in sharing their insight and expertise was inspiring, and I hope my questions did not annoy them. Special thanks also go out for the generosity of Alain Silver and Robert Porfirio for sending me an advance copy of Bob's article "Dark Jazz: Music in the Film Noir." In the early stages of the project I was extremely grateful and relieved for the suggestions and encouragement of Catherine Constable and Peter Martin, as well as for their loan of vital books and videos, often returned unacceptably late.

I've drawn so much encouragement and heart from the friends who have come and gone since I began this project and I don't want to reduce them to a list—however, that's where you're going folks! There were days when the way seemed pretty uncertain, and the following people have never failed to clear the mists: Ismail Albyrak, Daniel Ardron, Teresa Bishop, Mata Boti, Won-Seok Choi, Marek Claussen, Itziar Crespo, Lincoln Dews, Matthew Edwards, Ahmed El-Mahdy, Jonny Gabbai, Wendy Hall, Daniel Hanlon, Kathrin Happe, George Hobbs, Waqar Khan, Denis Krivosheev, Susanne Lee, Tae Jin Lee, Yan Lim, Nadia Lisovskaya, Stephen Lock, Sylvain Louret, Sanne Maegaard, Francesco Negri, Vincent Penne, Pedro Reis, Paul Sabanskis, Catherine Sanson, Omokorede Senbanjo, John Shepherd, Yana Sotz, Ganga Tilakaratna and Gareth Williams.

Finally, the love and support of my family goes on and on, down from the door where it began. One day I hope to be able to explain to them what this Ph.D. thing is all about! Without them, however, I couldn't have contemplated undertaking this project, and so my deepest, dearest thanks go to my Mother, Father, Sister, Gran, Mollie and Mr. P.

Introduction

A tilted black-and-white shot reveals a woman in a long, slinky black dress walking toward the camera through a deserted bar. A series of shots objectifies her body and possessions (lipstick, coils of cigarette smoke, liquid pouring into a glass and a gun in her handbag), clearly constructing her as a femme fatale. The sequence is underscored by a theme for piano, bass, drums, tenor saxophone, harmon-muted trumpet and synthesized strings. Teddy Edwards, the tenor saxophonist, performs the theme with a strong feeling for the blues. The sequence appears to be from a film noir of the 1940s or 1950s. Except it isn't. What has been described is the opening to "Dead End for Delia," an episode from *Fallen Angels*, a 1993 series of short films noir for television.[1] It is a lavish recreation of the visual style of the classic film noir phase. Edwards, a black musician based on the West Coast, is a significant choice as the soloist. Considered the first to adapt the modernist jazz style of bebop to the tenor saxophone in the 1940s, Edwards represents a direct link to the music of 1940s California.[2] His presence lends *Fallen Angels* a historical musical accuracy to complement its visual recreation of film noir.

This sequence reflects a widely held assumption that jazz is the authentic sound of film noir. Yet, sociologist John Orr has suggested that jazz did not feature in the original noirs of the 1940s and 1950s. In his discussion of the film *Bird* (1988), which attempts to portray the life and music of the alto saxophonist Charlie Parker, Orr notes that film noir of the 1940s "consistently ignored black Americans" and that "*African-American music has been conspicuously missing from the soundtracks of noir movies*" (my emphasis).[3] Why should there be two conflicting opinions here?

As this book will discuss, Orr's statement does not conform to the claims of most writers and contemporary films about the involvement of jazz in film noir. His comment that jazz is "conspicuously missing" from film noir suggests, however, that one would have expected to find the music there. As a jazz fan and student of film, it is an expectation that I held myself when I first came to study film noir. Part of my interest in undertaking this project has been to determine how this "taken-for-granted" notion, to use Peter Martin's term, originated.[4] Orr does not discuss why jazz was largely absent from film noir. The inference is that jazz, as a black American music, was denied a greater presence in film because of the racism that was active in Hollywood. In this book, I seek to clarify the apparent confusion between the contemporary perception, expressed by texts such as *Fallen Angels*, of jazz as the sound of film noir and Orr's claim that it was absent from the very films it has been perceived to evoke. In the process, I intend to demonstrate the true nature and extent of the relationship between jazz and film noir. Would Teddy Edwards have been permitted to play his style of jazz in a film noir of the 1940s?

I am interested in the factors that have encouraged the association between jazz and film noir. Why should a particular style of jazz be chosen to underscore a film about the execution of a woman convicted for murder, as is the case with the 1958 film *I Want To Live!*? Such a question is concerned with the social and cultural associations attached to differing styles of music and the subsequent meanings that they convey to the listener. The work of Simon Frith and Peter Martin is crucial in this respect, and, in accordance with their arguments, I suggest that there is nothing inherent in jazz that necessitates that every listener associate it with the dominant noir themes of sex, crime and anxiety.[5] In this book I have adopted an interdisciplinary approach that combines aspects of film theory concerned with "race" and gender with music history and sociology.

It is not the purpose of this book to simply sift through films noir for those films that use jazz and then discuss whether the music is represented fairly or not. As Ella Shohat, Robert Stam and Lola Young have noted, analyzing images in terms of whether they are positive or negative has produced some important findings, but is not extensive enough in its considerations. For Shohat and Stam, in their discussion of ethnic and racial stereotypes, this approach to criticism can result in an essentialism that perceives stereotypes where a more complex representation is at work:

> Behind every Black child performer the critic discerns a "pickaninny"; behind every sexually attractive Black actor a "buck"; behind every corpulent or nurturing Black female a "mammy." Such reductionist simplifications run

the risk of reproducing the very racial essentialism they were designed to combat.[6]

In her study *Fear of the Dark: 'Race,' Gender and Sexuality in the Cinema* (1996), Young proposes a model that moves beyond the issue of positivity/negativity. She suggests that "critical accounts of the functioning of film representations should consider the social and historical context within which the textual practice is located."[7] Young's model provides a useful framework for this book. Much of the work in discussing jazz and film noir refers to these idioms in general terms. Yet, as will be outlined later, jazz and film noir are broad idioms that contain many distinct and often contradictory styles. Robert Porfirio's article, "Dark Jazz: Music in the Film Noir," one of the few pieces to focus on the relationship between jazz and film noir, is largely confined to film noir of the 1940s.[8] It would be misleading, therefore, to apply Porfirio's conclusions about the use of jazz to film noir per se. It is important to consider the use of jazz in film noir of differing periods, as it inevitably changes, rather than taking the standard practices of one decade as typical of the use of jazz in film noir as a whole. As Frank Krutnik has noted, it is unwise to generalize about film noir:

> Many crime-films produced from the 1950's to the present day have become incorporated within the "genre" of *film noir*. In this regard I would advise a certain degree of caution, for such films need to be considered not only in regard to the *films noirs* of the 1940's but also in regard to the cinematic and cultural-ideological contexts in which and for which they were produced. For the conditions which "germinated" the *films noirs* of the 1940's were, as I hope I have shown, specific to the 1940's. To generalise beyond this risks destroying the credibility of both the *films noirs* and the crime films *après noir*.[9]

This book does not attempt to discuss jazz or film noir as monolithic idioms. Beginning with early representations of jazz in the 1920s, I consider separately the changing use of jazz in films of the 1930s and 1940s before focusing on different phases of film noir in the remaining chapters. Much of the analysis in this book takes the form of case studies of specific films. I place each film in its historical context, contrasting its use of music with the contemporaneous jazz scene. A purely textual analysis of the films discussed carries the risk, referred to by Shohat, Stam and Young, of reaching a reductionist conclusion about their use of jazz. Through the use of archival sources, however, particularly for *Young Man with a Horn* (1950) and *I Want To Live!* (1958), the films I discuss most extensively, many of the tensions created by the involvement of jazz become more evident. I have made particular use of the archival holdings from the Margaret Herrick Library of the Motion Picture Academy in Los Angeles, the University of Southern California Cinema and Television Library, the Arts Special

Collections at the University of California at Los Angeles, the American Film Institute and the National Sound Archive in London.

The term "jazz" is used throughout the book. I am conscious that it is a label that many of its exponents resist. Duke Ellington, Ornette Coleman and Charles Mingus are only some of the major figures to express their dissatisfaction with the term itself. Ellington disliked the word because of its relationship with the seedy environments in which early forms of the music were often heard:

> By and large, jazz always has been like the kind of man you wouldn't want your daughter to associate with. The *word* "jazz" has been part of the problem. The word never lost its association with those New Orleans bordellos. In the 1920s I used to try to convince Fletcher Henderson that we ought to call what we were doing "Negro music." But it's too late for that now. This music has become so integrated you can't tell one part from the other as [far as] colour is concerned.[10]

As I will demonstrate, these associations encouraged the involvement of jazz in film noir. This book is not the place to devise a new term for jazz or destroy the existing one, however. In fact, not all those associated with jazz would feel the need to execute such a change. The jazz broadcaster Russell Davies has recently observed that "after a long period out of favor, the word jazz is no longer under threat of abolition."[11] As evidence, Davies includes the comments of the critic Stanley Crouch, who reflects a reclaiming of the word by black writers and musicians:

> The word jazz as a word spoken in the English language is unlike any other word. The very sound of it seems to me as close to anything Negro American, or African derived if you will, as you're gonna have for a music that's such a combination of European elements, African elements, Caribbean elements, some influences from American Indian folk sources. . . . It's good enough for me.[12]

Where appropriate, I have made the distinction between specific styles of jazz, such as swing, bebop, cool, progressive or free. Indeed, much of this book is concerned with the lack of specificity that Hollywood and critics and theorists of film have applied to jazz. The failure to take into account the diversity of jazz has often resulted in misleading generalizations about the music.

Chapter 1 establishes the key areas of discussion, including film noir, film music and the use of jazz in film. I begin by considering film noir and note its initial emergence in the 1950s as a French critical term applied to certain American films of the 1940s. This is followed by a discussion of the constitutive features of film noir. I then discuss the increase in the last ten years of critical literature to study film music. The work of feminist theorists and their critique of the conventions of traditional Hollywood scoring practices are of particular interest to this book. There has been little critical writing about the use of jazz in film, beyond articles in jazz journals such as *Down Beat*, but in recent years some significant work has come forth.[13] These recent texts do not accord the association between jazz and film noir much attention, however. A gap still exists for work considering the use of jazz in film noir.

In Chapter 2 I explore the racial myths and stereotypes that have influenced the use of jazz in film in general. I begin by considering the dualism of mind versus body and its origin in the Christian tradition, as Richard Dyer has demonstrated.[14] This dualism became firmly entrenched with racial significance in the eighteenth and nineteenth centuries and the imperialist ambitions of European nations. I then discuss a particular manifestation of the mind/body dualism in the form of the Eurocentric equation of rhythm with sex. I note applications of this dualism to the representation of jazz and its use in Hollywood films of the first half of the twentieth century.

Chapter 3 is concerned with the use of jazz in films noir of the 1940s, specifically *Phantom Lady* (1944), as a metaphor for sex and confusion. I suggest that although film noir offered an opportunity for Hollywood films to utilize jazz naturalistically, racism and the conventions of 1940s films meant that jazz could not appear in its most contemporary styles or have its intellectual aspects acknowledged.

Chapter 4 is devoted to the use of jazz in films of the 1950s. I discuss the emergence of the jazz-inflected soundtrack, the growing legitimacy accorded to jazz and how this acceptance enabled aspects of the music to find their way into the film composer's repertoire. The films that styles of jazz underscored were, inevitably, films noir or those with a crime element, however. I suggest that the most influential jazz musician on the jazz-inflected soundtrack during the 1950s was the white bandleader Stan Kenton and discuss how the "progressive" jazz he championed was echoed in the scores of Elmer Bernstein, Johnny Mandel and Henry Mancini.

The classic phase of film noir ended in the 1950s. Chapter 5 discusses the presence of jazz in modern noirs of the 1970s, 1980s and 1990s. I commence with a study of the rise of "crime jazz" and the music of Henry Mancini. I suggest that the jazz scores that dominated the soundtracks of television crime programs in the late 1950s and 1960s have contributed to a false impression about the extent of the use of jazz in the original films noir. Michel Chion's concept of "retrospective illusion" will be discussed in relation to the use of jazz in *Taxi Driver* (1976). When later noirs, such as *Body Heat* (1981) and *Blue Velvet* (1986), sought to re-create the world of their predecessors, they often utilized jazz as a means of suggesting the classic period of film noir. Through an analysis of *The Last Seduction* (1994), however, I suggest that it is now possible for jazz to be used to underscore contemporary film noir in ways and styles that would have been unlikely in the 1940s and 1950s. In *The Last Seduction*, sophistication and intellectual thought processes are underscored by jazz.

I conclude the book with Chapter 6, which briefly considers jazz projects that have drawn on film noir as a source of inspiration or means of packaging and promoting the music. The final section summarizes the main findings and issues discussed in the book before noting areas for further work.

NOTES

1. The sequence is altered slightly in other episodes, but maintains the same iconography and music.

2. Gioia, T. 1992. *West Coast Jazz: Modern Jazz in California, 1945–1960*. New York: Oxford University Press. p. 130. Ted Gioia notes that "no less an authority than [bebop] trumpeter Fats Navarro, citing Edward's early recording of 'Up in Dodo's Room,' credited the saxophonist with being the first bebop tenor player, the first to create an authentic modern sound freed from the models of Coleman Hawkins and Lester Young."

3. Orr, J. 1993. *Cinema and Modernity*. Cambridge: Polity Press. p. 179.

4. Martin, P. 1995. *Sounds and Society: Themes in the Sociology of Music*. Manchester: Manchester University Press. p. 60.

5. Martin, P. 1995. *Sounds and Society: Themes in the Sociology of Music*. Manchester: Manchester University Press; and Frith, S. 1996. *Performing Rites: Evaluating Popular Music*. Oxford: Oxford University Press.

6. Shohat, E., and Stam, R. 1994. *Unthinking Eurocentrism: Multiculturalism and the Media*. London: Routledge. p. 199.

7. Young, L. 1996. *Fear of the Dark: 'Race,' Gender and Sexuality in the Cinema*. London: Routledge. p. 37.

8. Porfirio, R. 1999. Dark Jazz: Music in the Film Noir. In A. Silver and J. Ursini, eds., *Film Noir Reader 2*. New York: Limelight Editions. pp. 177–87. Porfirio's work will be discussed more extensively in Chapter 1.

9. Krutnik, F. 1989. "In a Lonely Street: 1940's Hollywood, Film Noir, and the 'Tough' Thriller." Unpublished Ph.D. dissertation. The University of Kent at Canterbury. p. 329/6.

10. Kington, M. 1993. *The Jazz Anthology*. London: Harper Collins. p. 19.

11. Jazz Century. Part One: A Century of Jazz. Broadcast January 2, 1999. BBC Radio 3.

12. Ibid.

13. Gabbard, K., ed. 1995a. *Jazz Among the Discourses*. Durham and London: Duke University Press. Gabbard, K., ed. 1995b. *Representing Jazz*. Durham and

London: Duke University Press. Gabbard, K. 1996. *Jammin' at the Margins: Jazz and the American Cinema*. Chicago: The University of Chicago Press. Krin Gabbard has been the driving force behind much of this exciting development. Two anthologies edited by Gabbard were published in 1995 and were followed in 1996 by Gabbard's own text devoted to jazz in American films. As with Porfirio's work, this literature will be further discussed in Chapter 1.

14. Dyer, R. 1997. *White*. London: Routledge. pp. 14–18.

1

Kind of Jazz

Themes in the Study of Film Noir, Film Music and Jazz

On the 8th of May 1997, the Association of British Jazz Musicians held a one-day conference titled "Jazz in the Media," at the Queens Hotel in Leeds. It was not a well-attended event. Taking place on a quintessentially grim, rainy Yorkshire day beneath an oppressive sky, it was difficult at the outset not to feel that the atmospheric conditions reflected the uncomfortable position in which jazz in Britain then found itself. Virtually banished from the television schedules and receiving inadequate coverage on radio, British jazz could not be accused of being "media friendly." Presentations came and went, but although the prognosis was often poor—one speaker observing that the chances of jazz getting on television were so slim they were hardly worth considering—I somehow left Leeds with a renewed optimism and belief in the music. The final paper, "Exploiting the Technological Revolution," was delivered by Norman Rosenberg, a specialist in digital technology for the multimedia company Red Fig. Rosenberg sheepishly admitted that he had no real involvement with jazz, but was there simply to offer suggestions and generate awareness about the possibilities for jazz to interact with new technology. Bringing his discussion to a close, Rosenberg threw down the gauntlet to the attendees, suggesting that the jazz community had to start producing an emblem or identity and collaborate with the visual medium, possibly via a cable channel. A problem, concluded Rosenberg, should be an opportunity.

In fact, jazz *does* already have an established identity that has been generated through its collaboration with the visual media of film and television. Although "jazz," as a bewildering and seemingly impenetrable mass of styles that can easily terrify someone attempting to explore the music, has often been accused of possessing an image problem (esoteric/ stuffy/snobbish/weird/too much facial hair/not enough warmth/and above all, "nice," as the presenter of the affectionately lampooned jazz club in the British comedy series *The Fast Show* continually informs his audience), it does have at least one incarnation that has proven enduringly popular and attractive to filmmakers, advertisers and public alike. This image can best be described as "jazz noir."

It is not difficult to illustrate the prevalence of this image. The association of jazz with film noir can be found in all manner of media today, but is curiously not so prevalent in the actual original artifacts—the films noir of American cinema from the 1940s and 1950s. Despite this fact, the belief that jazz flourished in these films is commonly held and perpetuated. Consider the following examples taken from a variety of sources. The first comprises a series of messages posted to the jazzjukebox.com discussion board, during May 1999, on the subject of the music of film noir. The comments along this thread repeatedly referred to an almost symbiotic relationship between jazz, smoke, femmes fatale, stormy nights and weary detectives. For one poster, film noir and jazz seemed "to belong together," while another suggested that it was always the sound of an alto saxophone soloing on a mournful blues that could be heard in these films. Yet another commented that the films noir of the 1940s and 1950s would lose a lot without their jazz soundtracks.[1] It would seem from these messages that jazz was the inevitable underscore to film noir, at least in the memory of those posting the comments. But strangely, in a later message, one of the contributors admitted that among a list of classic film noir scores, few of the scores could actually be considered jazz.

For a second example of the perceived collaboration between jazz and film noir, I have chosen a brief sequence that was used to introduce the films and programs contained in BBC2's "Pulp Fictions" season of noir features, run throughout May 1996. This sequence is strikingly similar to the opening shots of *Fallen Angels* that I discussed in the Introduction (and in fact, one of the installments of *Fallen Angels* was included in the "Pulp Fictions" season). A shot of a portable fan against a wall, streaked with the chiaroscuro shadows cast from a blind, tracks to reveal the hand of a woman with red nail polish, a golden ring and a cigarette caught between two fingers—the trappings of the femme fatale—holding a detective novel titled "Pulp Fictions." The shadow of a man in the noir detective's uniform of suit and fedora moves across the wall and disappears. The woman lowers her hand out of shot, and the title "Pulp Fictions" is superimposed on the screen. The sequence is over quickly, but chooses, as the musical equivalent of its visual icons of film noir, an underscore of a solo saxophone playing in a bluesy post-bop fashion.

My third and final example is the packaging and accompanying book-let for the 1994 album *White Heat: Film Noir*, recorded by the Jazz at the Movies Band for Discovery Records. The album features cover versions of themes from classic films noir. With the exception of the themes from *Touch of Evil* (1958) and *Laura* (1944), all of these were originally performed by full orchestras in the symphonic tradition. The monochrome sleeve design incorporates, again, classic noir iconography: A silhouetted femme fatale stalks a cracked and steam-choked city street on the front cover and gazes at the camera through the mist on the back cover. The combination of jazz with film noir was clearly felt by Jac Holzman, who was responsible for the album's concept, to be a sufficiently strong one to justify a recording and release.

Each of these examples demonstrates a widespread belief that jazz and film noir were entwined during the 1940s and 1950s, that the shadows cast by one were inescapably echoed in the sounds of the other. I have to be honest that this is a belief that I also held when I first came to study film at university. For some reason, I had expected to find jazz in the example of film noir, *They Live by Night* (1948), which was included in an intro-ductory course to Hollywood film. In part, I was not disappointed. *They Live by Night* does indeed feature a sequence set in a club where a black band, fronted by a female vocalist, performs the blues song "Your Red Wagon." But this film was made in 1948, when the modern variant of jazz known as bebop was flourishing, and I had naively assumed that the soundtrack would have featured contemporary jazz more extensively. Why did I have that assumption? The music played by the band is not bop, and there are no soloists or possibilities for improvisation other than the vo-calist. In short, the band plays an extremely diluted form of jazz—music that is merely suggestive of jazz, but does enough for the audience to asso-ciate it with that idiom and the connotations related to it.

My "disappointment" at the jazz content of *They Live by Night* was also extended to the location in which the band performed. Again, I had come to the film with an assumption about film noir that was to prove, in this case, inaccurate. Fred Pfeil has cited "lurid jazzy bars" as being one of the iconographically constitutive features of film noir and, certainly, my expec-tation of *They Live by Night* was that at some point the film would present a dark and smoky nightclub in which a jazz band would be performing.[2] The nightclub in *They Live by Night,* however, is a deluxe, sanitized af-fair, hardly a "lurid jazzy bar." Significantly, Bowie and Keechie, the film's central characters, enter the club during the afternoon, a time in which, as the film's title states, they cannot exist. The club's interior is brightly lit, and the clientele appear respectable. Although appearing to break a per-ceived noir convention, this representation of the nightclub is entirely ap-propriate for the film and its story of doomed lovers on the run. Bowie and Keechie flee the city, the police and a gang of bank robbers that they have become involved with, in order to try to set up a "normal" married life. The two are not able to do so and are made to feel unwanted and hunted by society wherever they turn. The murky nightclub, which could have offered them a bolthole in which to hide, is not present in the film, and Bowie is openly told by a member of the local criminal community that they are not welcome there. The authorities have deemed that Bowie and Keechie are nothing more than criminals, but even "their own kind" will not harbor them.

The song "Your Red Wagon" heightens the message that Bowie and Keechie have to deal with their problem alone and cannot expect any help or respite in the nightclub. The singer approaches the couple, and even she hustles Bowie for money until he gives in. Notably, at a time when black actors were almost exclusively seen in demeaning and peripheral roles, the vocalist is black; this casting decision further demonstrates the couple's status as outsiders. Bowie and Keechie have even less power and control over their lives than the black singer. In this respect, jazz is used, through the blues lyrics, to underline Bowie's and Keechie's isolation and alienation from the world. The use of jazz as the music of the outsider is an area that I will discuss in greater depth, beginning with the section on *Young Man with a Horn* (1950) in Chapter 3.

With little previous experience of these films, why should I have expected to find jazz in a dark setting in film noir? As a child growing up in West Cumbria, I had precious little exposure to jazz. Live jazz was something I was not aware of and remains a rare event in the region today. Neither was my initial love for the music shaped by the radio or television. It was only when I had begun to explore jazz that I knew where to find it on the radio. Even then, the principal discovery was that media coverage of jazz in Britain is extremely poor. The greatest source of jazz in my childhood came instead from film and television soundtracks. The importance of film as a means of discovering jazz should not be underestimated, especially in a country where it is difficult in many areas to hear the music live. In the introduction to his directory of the use of jazz in film, David Meeker comments that he would eagerly attend film screenings in the 1950s simply to hear the music of trumpeter Shorty Rogers, who was featured in films such as *The Wild One* (1954) and *The Man with the Golden Arm* (1955).[3] Al Young, in an article addressing the portrayal of jazz in film, refers to the inspiring effect of *Young Man with a Horn*—a film that has usually been met with unimpressed responses from older jazz fans—on the South African-born jazz musician and composer Hugh Masekela:

> At school they showed us that movie, *Young Man with a Horn*, with Kirk Douglas. I saw him playing that trumpet and I said, "That's what I want to do—play trumpet, play jazz, and be a jazz musician."[4]

These beginnings fuel youthful imaginations and can lead to a life-long devotion to the music. Yet such an introduction to jazz does not necessarily result in an appreciation of its many forms, and jazz can be perceived as a specific style, rooted with its screen associations and thus deemed appropriate for a particular scenario, rather than an approach that can cross many stylistic boundaries and musical genres. This perception has implications both within and beyond the film industry. The jazz musician who attempts to develop a career as a writer of film scores can be discriminated against. Interviewed by Gene Lees in 1975, the composer Quincy Jones told how his reputation as a black composer and arranger in jazz resulted in assumptions being made about his versatility:

> When Quincy Jones was hired to write the score for one of his first movies, the producer had never met him. "And the cat . . . didn't know I was black until we came to face to face. Then he became concerned whether I could relate to a love scene between Gregory Peck and Diane Baker. And I remember that producer said, 'I don't want any blues or Count Basie in this picture.' Y' know, as if I hadn't put in my time with Bartok and Brahms, like everybody else."[5]

Jones expressed his frustration at being musically typecast as someone who could "do cop pictures," a reputation seemingly due to his skill in jazz and that was applied to the composer Lalo Schifrin, among others, for the same reason. It should not need to be said that the blues and Count Basie are only a small, however important, aspect of the range of jazz. Yet such assumptions about what jazz is and can achieve can shape the opportunities that are made available to its musicians. The combination of the audio and visual realms is a potent one, and a particular association, if repeated often enough, can become deeply ingrained until it is difficult to remove the image from its associated sounds, and vice versa.

The association of jazz with the world of film noir is a particularly appealing means of marketing the music. "Jazz noir" brings with it an attractive look of seductive femmes fatale, cynical private eyes, smoke and sophistication laced with an air of danger. This iconography provides an excellent set of "clues" for understanding what might otherwise be an unfamiliar music. What do jazz sounds mean? What is a particular improvisation about? Here again, I must admit that I've drawn upon the romanticized world of jazz noir in order to convince friends to accompany me to a jazz club, selling the gig on the idea that we can sit in the shadows like Humphrey Bogart and Lauren Bacall! Such a mythology offers a listener new to jazz a way of translating and making sense of an alien idiom. Words and images are important here. Descriptions of instrumental music are often provided, notes Simon Frith, to guide the listener, but this can become overbearing:

It may therefore be difficult to disentangle the way we interpret the meaning
of a piece of music from the way we interpret its title. This is, perhaps, most
intriguing for jazz, in which titles (*A Love Supreme*, *Sketches of Spain*,
"Misterioso") work like labels to supply interpretive information, an indication of how to listen.[6]

The description of a jazz performance as being evocative of film noir
conjures an immediate set of images for the reader or listener. As we shall
later see in this chapter, such descriptions have proven remarkably durable
and a convenient, if clichéd, shorthand. John Fordham, a writer and broadcaster about jazz for over twenty years, has commented on the difficulties
facing a writer trying to cover a jazz story for a British national paper.
During his paper at the first Leeds "Jazz in the Media" conference, Fordham
noted that the national distribution system is failing the jazz press, and that
some national papers do not have a jazz correspondent at all.[7] Fordham
observed that editors tend to prefer record reviews rather than accounts of
live performances. The tabloidizing or "dumbing down" of the press means,
however, that editors are often not interested in the niceties of jazz culture
and its influence on other musical styles. Instead, the central concern of an
editor is more likely to be "was it good or was it awful?" Stereotypes and
popular myths endured, the film noir connection no doubt being one of
them, and Fordham explained how he was only asked to write two articles
concerning jazz musicians in recent months (as opposed to him pitching an
idea) because the editorial interest was in "famous people with a dark side"
and there was no real interest in jazz at all. Fordham acknowledged that it
would be much harder to convince an editor about the worth of an article
that attempted to convey the music's undercurrents and vibrancy. Here
again, the attractiveness of jazz being linked with darkness and death, of
jazz being noired, proves a difficult link to break and stands in the way of
allowing the music to speak for itself; it is expressed instead through an
established and recognizable code.

   Two contrasting pieces of writing provided the spark for my interest in
this book. Both are brief, almost throwaway sentences that reflect the assumption about the involvement of jazz with film noir. The first was included in a promotional flier for a Contemporary Music Network (CMN)
tour of England led by the New York composer and drummer, Bobby
Previte, in February 1994. The flier referred to Previte's work as "'chamber music of film noir,' skillfully blending the improvisations of jazz with
the drama and textures of composed music."[8] I had no idea who Bobby
Previte was when I read the flier, but on its description alone I decided to
go to the concert, curious to hear "chamber music of film noir," but completely unsure as to what it might sound like. Previte's music was magnifi-
cent, and my first experience of live contemporary improvisation, but the
flier had been somewhat misleading in its description. In fact, the comment
on the flier was taken from Stuart Nicholson's 1990 study of contempo-

rary jazz, *Jazz: The Modern Resurgence*. Nicholson had applied his description of Previte's music to the albums *Bump the Renaissance* (1985) and *Pushing the Envelope* (1987), noting that:

> Both acoustic albums, they sound like chamber music for the film noir; the composition "Mirror, Mirror" from the latter album was taken from Previte's soundtrack for the film *Chain Letters,* while "Open World," from the same album, was a summation of his compositional style at that point in his career.[9]

However, the band that Previte brought to England for the 1994 tour was anything but acoustic. This group was Previte's Empty Suits unit, an electro-acoustic project and markedly different from the bands featured on his 1985 and 1987 recordings. It is unlikely that Nicholson would have defined the music played by Empty Suits on their CMN tour as "chamber music of the film noir." The inappropriate application of this comment to other examples of Previte's music is revealing. It demonstrates, in part, the tendency for critics to discuss jazz as a whole, without considering its wide range of styles. Previte's musical interests go far beyond jazz, as he states, "I'm not easily definable—I can't be put away and filed under this heading or that."[10] Nevertheless, it is in the field of jazz where Previte has tended to be conveniently categorized. The misleading use of Nicholson's noir description also underlines the appeal and widespread use of film noir as a means of describing and selling music classified as jazz. Yet what was it about the earlier albums that led Nicholson to liken them to the sound of film noir? Was it simply the balance between jazz improvisation and formal composition? More telling, perhaps, were Previte's own titles, which may have influenced Nicholson in the manner described by Simon Frith earlier in this chapter. *Pushing the Envelope* contains a track titled "Ballad Noir," which, unsurprisingly, is a beautiful ballad performed by a line-up of drums, piano, French horn, bass and tenor saxophone. Elsewhere, the album moves through a series of moods, at times dark, bright, rhythmic and sparse. Arguably, it is the album's darker moments that Nicholson is likely to have related to film noir. The final (title) track is an intense piece of music, almost dirge-like, as the saxophone and French horn improvise over sustained trills from the piano and Previte's crashing drums, until the end of the piece when the rhythm section cuts out leaving the horns free, hanging on their final notes as if sighing in relief at their release from the piano and drums. Whatever the reason for Nicholson's likening of Previte's music to that of film noir, it is certainly true that nothing like Previte's music on these two albums was actually used in the classic noirs of the '40s and '50s.

The second piece of writing that helped to instigate this project came in a discussion of film noir by John Orr for his book *Cinema and Modernity* (1993), which I referred to in the Introduction. Toward the end of the

chapter in question, Orr analyzes a number of contemporary films noir, including among these Clint Eastwood's 1988 film *Bird*, a biopic about the
alto saxophonist Charlie Parker. Orr's argument that *Bird* be considered a
film noir is not an implausible one. Numerous critics referred to the noir
stylistics and iconography in the film at the time of its release, and Orr notes
how *Bird* both perpetuates and recasts the noir tradition:

> Noir movies of the 1940s consistently ignored black Americans but the re-
> makes have done so equally. . . . Eastwood's movie . . . reminds us of what
> is missing from that earlier period of racial apartheid and prohibition. It is a
> retro-movie set in the noir period, told in flashback with a distinctly noir style.
> But included in its "blackness," for perhaps the first time, is something white
> film-makers have preferred to avoid, the question of pigmentation.[11]

Orr suggests that *Bird* has taken one of film noir's most recognizable
icons—the femme fatale—and updated it for modern audiences, but does
so in such a way that was all too relevant for the period of classic noir and
for Parker himself:

> The darkness of the streets in *Bird* also has a different connotation, because
> it evokes something else which went unspoken in films of the 1940s. The main
> threat to Parker's intense and anxious marriage is not one of his many pec-
> cadilloes, as melodrama would normally suggest. The femme fatale as female
> presence is finally buried, and in her place we have something very differ-
> ent. The femme fatale with whom Bird has a secret assignation on dark, wind-
> swept streets is heroin. It is the enemy of desire, not its lure, the white powder
> which destroys music as much as it destroys the man who makes it.[12]

But given the oft-repeated comment, by writers such as Nicholson, that
jazz is evocative of film noir, the most surprising assertion made by Orr is
not his recasting of the film noir, but his claim that the original cycle of
noirs did not make extensive use of jazz. As he writes, "it is also that
African-American music has been conspicuously missing from the soundtracks of noir movies."[13] This comment, as I will demonstrate throughout
the rest of this chapter, is a marked contrast to the claims of other writers
about the collaboration between jazz and film noir.

Without resorting to an extensive discussion of the literature, it is important and necessary to establish the current lack of texts to critically
consider the relationship between jazz and film noir. Although there is a
significant amount of literature concerned with film noir, little has been
written about the use of music in these films. Similarly, the number of studies devoted to film music has increased markedly in the last ten years, but
its focus remains on the dominant tradition of the symphonic score. In
recent years, however, there have been a small number of academic publications that examine the intersection of jazz and film. Despite this devel-

opment, the association between jazz and film noir remains largely unexplored. Often alluded to, the collaboration between jazz and film noir has almost been taken for granted. I close this chapter with a discussion of this literature and the gap for further work that remains. Before that, however, some of the key terms and themes that form the basis of this book, particularly film noir and the "classical Hollywood score," need to be introduced.

FILM NOIR

Film noir is a much-debated term in film studies. Fred Pfeil notes the fundamental areas of discussion as including:

What *film noir* is, which films the term includes, and what social or psychic processes it engages. Does *film noir* constitute a genre; or a style that can be deployed across generic boundaries; or a historically specific movement within Hollywood cinema?[14]

The excellent collection of essays contained within *Film Noir Reader* (1996), edited by Alain Silver and James Ursini, reveals a variety of critical positions on what film noir actually is. What is agreed upon is that film noir flourished in the 1940s and 1950s. The parameters of this "classic period" are generally held to be *The Maltese Falcon* (1941) and *Touch of Evil* (1958).[15] Often derived from the hard-boiled literature of writers such as Raymond Chandler, Dashiell Hammett and James M. Cain, the tales of crime, doom and despair favored by film noir are remarkably varied. The noir sensibility can be found in films that appear to belong to other genres, such as the science-fiction film *Blade Runner* (1982). Film noir has thus become established "despite the lack of any straightforward unity in the set of films it attempts to designate."[16]

The term itself originated in France in response to the wave of American films that became available after the Second World War had ended. Films such as *Double Indemnity* (1944) and *Murder My Sweet* (1944) pointed to a new trend in American cinema. This trend, or "series" as it was termed, received its first critical discussion in Raymond Borde and Étienne Chaumeton's 1955 book, *Panorama du Film Noir Américain,* which sought to define the film noir. As a result, much of film noir was, as Alain Silver has commented, "defined after the fact."[17] For Borde and Chaumeton, the defining characteristics of film noir were a sense of "anguish and insecurity" with the purpose of creating a "specific alienation."[18] Janey Place and Lowell Peterson acknowledge the anxiety referred to by Borde and Chaumeton, and note that it was best reflected through visual style, "the consistent thread that unites the very diverse films that together comprise this phenomenon."[19]

Many of the defining visual traits of film noir, such as chiaroscuro effects and low-key, high-contrast lighting, were developed out of necessity from budgetary restraints, as much as from the the artistic motives of directors like Orson Welles, Robert Siodmak and Fritz Lang. The film noir thrived in lower-budget "B" pictures where it was less scrutinized and constrained by the traditional conventions of Hollywood productions. In this sense, films noir remained a product of the Hollywood studios, albeit at times an anti-product, and, as Pfeil stresses, must still be "experienced and understood" in their relation to the Hollywood system of production, even if they broke many of its established conventions and expectations.[20]

The emphasis on the visual iconography of film noir may account for the lack of work done on the music and sound used in these films. Jazz is rarely discussed in the lists of features to be consistently found in film noir. When it is mentioned, there is seldom an accompanying explanation as to why jazz might be considered an important and recurring element of film noir. This absence reflects the general "ideology of the visual," which Caryl Flinn notes is typical of film studies.[21] Intriguingly, however, the Spring 1956 edition of *Film Music* contained an article by Roger Tilton that indirectly suggested the best way to visually represent jazz was through the same techniques that were a feature of film noir. Roger Tilton discusses the film *Jazz Dance* (1954), which, according to Bob Reisner, the film's associate producer, was conceived as a response to the fact that "so many films on jazz have been phony, plaster-of-Paris glamorizations of jazz. What is needed is a film which will let people experience *real* jazz!"[22] "Real jazz" for this film constituted an evening Dixieland jam session in New York. The intention was to capture the "overwhelming excitement of this event for the enjoyment of theatre audiences throughout the world."[23] Although seeking to emphasize the joy and exuberance of a jam session, moods that are difficult to find in film noir, Tilton's account of the genesis of the film's visual style significantly lists a number of features that are trademarks of film noir:

> Certain technical choices were instantly recognized to be most suitable for the pictorialization of jazz music. Black and white film was selected rather than color. Low key, high contrast lighting was favored over flat, high-key lighting. In the editing, sharp staccato cuts were used instead of long, slow dissolves. Finally, live, on the spot sound, filled with all the noises and echoes of the hall, was chosen for its feeling of presence, over the technically more polished alternative of a studio recording with dubbed-in crowd effects.[24]

Tilton does not say why these technical choices were deemed appropriate for representing jazz. Whatever the reasons, the result lends *Jazz Dance* a film noir look.

Sven Ahnert (1995) does offer a rare focus on the music of film noir that contrasts with Orr's claim that jazz was conspicuously missing from the original noir period. Ahnert suggests that jazz, specifically cool jazz, was a staple "requisite" feature of the film noir soundtrack as "atmospheric background" music that helped to give the "dark series its specifically sinister tone."[25] Ahnert's article promises much more than it delivers. He does not explain why cool jazz should contribute to a sinister mood. Ahnert argues that, from the early 1950s, American film music has been "increasingly oriented toward the expressive richness of modern music," particularly jazz and twelve-tone techniques.[26] For Ahnert, the reason these styles were chosen was simple: "What produces a sense of fear in an easily startled concert-season audience can also produce the desired cinematic horror."[27] Ahnert does not discuss how jazz produces a sense of fear, and, unfortunately, the remainder of his article does not include any examples of the sinister uses of jazz in a film noir. The article loses its focus somewhat by concentrating on a number of films—*Psycho* (1960), *The Spiral Staircase* (1946), *Dolores Claiborne* (1995)—that he acknowledges are not actually films noir. Instead, Ahnert's article is more a discussion of dark and sinister scores: noir music that does not necessarily accompany a film noir. What is evident from a study of film noir texts, therefore, is that it is difficult to reach a definitive conclusion as to how often and with what significance jazz has appeared in film noir.

STUDIES OF FILM MUSIC

The critical study of film music has expanded considerably in the last ten years. Most of these studies focus on the dominant tradition of Hollywood film scoring, which is rooted in the late nineteenth century romanticism of European "classical" music. As a result, there has been little attention given by these texts to jazz or jazz-inflected scores.

Roy Prendergast's *Film Music: A Neglected Art* (1992) and Royal S. Brown's *Overtones and Undertones: Reading Film Music* (1994) have provided two of the most thorough studies of film music. The bulk of Prendergast's work is devoted to mainstream Hollywood cinema and neglects important European composers such as Ennio Morricone and Nino Rota. Jazz is seldom mentioned with the exception of a number of pages discussing Elmer Bernstein's jazz-inflected score for *The Man with the Golden Arm* (1955). Prendergast acknowledges that, although *The Man with the Golden Arm* should not be considered a jazz score because of its lack of improvisation (Prendergast also suggests that improvisation is ill-suited to the demands of film music in general), "there can be little doubt that Bernstein's choice of the jazz idiom was the right one to make the story more absorbing and the social commentary a little less obvious."[28] Yet Prendergast does not attempt to provide an answer as to why jazz was the "right idiom" to express the film's themes of "hysteria and despair."[29] Instead, he concludes his discussion of the score by noting its success and the "immediate production of a host of imitative scores using jazz elements" for Hollywood films.[30] Similarly, composer and musicologist George Burt, in his 1994 book titled *The Art of Film Music*, briefly refers to bebop and progressive jazz as being appropriate idioms to suggest anxiety and tension in *The Wild One* (1953).[31] As with Prendergast, he does not explain why these jazz styles should be effective for such themes.

Brown's study of film music encompasses a far wider range of styles and composers than Prendergast. Nevertheless, his discussion of the jazz score is, although much more extensive than Prendergast's, still relatively brief. The bulk of his references to jazz as film music occur in his chapter, on "New Styles, New Genres, New Interactions," which details developments in film music beyond the traditional Hollywood symphonic score. Brown notes that:

> Jazz made inroads into film music in the 1950s, although these roads have never become major highways . . . the entire jazz genre tended to attach itself in the cinema to the "-icity" of "lower-class" people involved in sleazy dramas of sex, drugs and/or crime.[32]

Brown's openness to music beyond the Hollywood tradition is important as far as the jazz score is concerned. It was in Europe, and France in particular, that the first fully fledged jazz scores were utilized, as opposed to the jazz-inflected scores of Elmer Bernstein, Alex North and David Raksin in Hollywood. The most significant of these scores is probably the music provided by Miles Davis for Louis Malle's claustrophobic thriller, *Ascenseur pour l'echafaud* (1957). Davis' score, improvised after he and the rest of his quintet (comprised of Barney Wilen, René Urtreger, Pierre Michelot and Kenny Clarke) had watched scenes from the film, was a pure jazz score, significantly in the modern style of bop, when such an experiment had yet to be attempted by an American film. Although Davis' music was for a French film that was not strictly a film noir, in that it did not exist within the established American series of films, this score has often been cited as an example of the relationship between the idioms of jazz and film noir. One of the most significant pieces of evidence, therefore, for the extent of jazz's involvement with film noir is seriously flawed because it was not actually present at the scene of the crime.

Russell Lack's *Twenty Four Frames Under: A Buried History of Film Music* (1997) provides a more detailed discussion of the use of jazz in film. Lack devotes a chapter to the subject, as well as a brief and speculative section on the likelihood of jazz being used in the pre-sound era of film. By far the best of the film music texts to cover jazz, Lack's book does not specifically refer to any association between jazz and film noir. He notes that "jazz as lifestyle had long been a source of lurid fascination to American producers" and discusses the rise of the jazz-inflected score in the 1950s.[33] Unlike the majority of texts on the subject, Lack does not refer to the use of jazz as a signifier of immorality and malaise, although that impression can still be reached from the sources he cites (including comments by Elmer Bernstein and Leith Stevens that appear in other examples of the literature). Instead, he argues that jazz, "supposedly embodying freedom," has worked best in films as a "correlate of personal expression."[34] Lack extends this argument to suggest why jazz can interact effectively with the moving image; as opposed to the claim of Prendergast that improvisation renders jazz too imprecise to be of effective use. For Lack, the fluidity of jazz was perfectly suited to new filmmaking techniques and philosophies, such as the French new wave.[35]

Less detailed and grounded in theory and analysis, Tony Thomas' *Music for the Movies* (1977) does demonstrate an awareness of the conventional use of jazz in film scores in the extract Thomas includes from an interview with Elmer Bernstein. Thomas observes that it is odd how "jazz is used mostly in films with connotations of sleaziness, crime, juvenile delinquency, drug addiction, etc.," and Bernstein agrees:

> It doesn't speak well for jazz at all. . . . We're born into a society that has inherited all sorts of prejudices—racial, religious and even musical, and this one concerning jazz, like most prejudices, has its roots in truth or reality at some point. There's no question at the time of the origin of jazz it was something that grew up in a rather sleazy atmosphere. But that was a long time ago and the prejudice has no relevance in contemporary terms. However, it is a subtle prejudice and I find myself fighting it within myself. The times I've used jazz to color my music have been in films with sleazy atmospheres— *The Man with the Golden Arm* was about narcotics, *Sweet Smell of Success* dealt with some very unsavory characters in New York, and *Walk on the Wild Side* was largely set in a New Orleans house of ill repute. So I'm guilty, although I don't think it's necessary to use jazz in this way. It's simply something that is very difficult to avoid.[36]

Thomas does not explore the question of why it is difficult for composers to avoid using jazz as an underscore for sleazy themes, and the issue receives no further discussion. Bernstein's response offers a clue in his statement that it is the society we are born into that shapes the way we hear and understand music. There is nothing inherent in jazz that would lead every listener to interpret it as the sound of a "sleazy atmosphere." As Peter Martin (1995) has extensively demonstrated, "the meanings of music are neither inherent nor intuitively recognized, but emerge and become established (or changed or forgotten) as a consequence of the activities of groups of people in particular cultural contexts."[37] Martin observes that "taken-for-granted notions" about music, such as jazz being the sound of crime and sleaze, become so established in their specific cultural context that ultimately we can "find it hard to accept that they are not natural and inevitable."[38] This certainly seems to be the case with the perception of jazz as the sound of crime and immorality.

The last ten years have seen the publication of a number of film music texts that discuss why certain music has been repeatedly used in films for particular themes and situations. The work of such theorists as Claudia Gorbman, Caryl Flinn and Kathryn Kalinak has sought to move beyond the "visual orientation" in film studies and consider the ideological implications of the musical score. Gorbman, Flinn and Kalinak all note how the musical score has tended to reinforce the dominant ideological values of Hollywood films—namely, white, heterosexual patriarchy. In this sense, the musical score has often functioned in partnership with the classical Hollywood narrative to ensure a sense of closure and the maintenance of the established ideological framework.

The term, the "classical Hollywood score" should be clarified, since it does not necessarily mean the use of classical music. It is classical music, particularly the romantic tradition of the mid-to-late nineteenth century, however, that Hollywood film music has privileged. Gorbman defines the "classical Hollywood model" of film scoring as being typified by the compositional style of Max Steiner. This model does not exclude nonclassical music, but if such music is included in a score, then the film, as Gorbman argues, "always motivates it in conventional ways."[39] Therefore, the jazz or jazz-inflected scores that first began to appear in Hollywood films of the 1950s were not radical breaks from traditional scoring practices:

> There is little that's progressive or subversive about jazz in the milieu of drug addiction in *The Man with the Golden Arm*, the electronic sounds that waft over the strange *Forbidden Planet*, or the electronically generated music complicit with the alcoholic dementia of Ray Milland in *The Lost Weekend*. David Bordwell in fact cites *Hangover Square's* score to argue for Hollywood's capacity for "non-disruptive differentiation," as the film's discordant music is narratively motivated by its connection to a deranged character.[40]

Both Flinn and Kalinak expand on Gorbman's discussion of the classical Hollywood score. Kalinak argues that the classical Hollywood score has been equally guilty of marginalizing women and perpetuates the visually expressed dominant ideology "which punished women for their sexuality."[41] To achieve this negative image of women, Kalinak notes how jazz was utilized because of its "implications of indecency and promiscuity."[42] This use of jazz to suggest the threat of female sexuality, observes Kalinak, was bound up with the issue of race:

The classical score frequently encoded otherness through the common denominator of jazz. For white audiences of the era, jazz represented the urban, the sexual, and the decadent in a musical idiom perceived in the culture at large as an indigenous black form. Playing upon these culturally empowered stereotypes, the classical score used jazz as a musical trope for otherness, whether sexual or racial.[43]

As with Lack, Kalinak does not explicitly mention film noir in her discussion of the use of jazz in film, but the suggestion is present as she focuses on the music for the classic noir *Laura* (1944). Flinn, however, has specifically examined the music of film noir. In her article "Male Nostalgia and Hollywood Film Music: The Terror of the Feminine," later developed in the book *Strains of Utopia* (1992), Flinn analyzes the use of music in the film noir *Detour* (1945). Flinn draws upon the work of Theodor Adorno, Roland Barthes and Julia Kristeva, which "upholds the connection between women and music."[44] It is Flinn's argument that the music for the film "chides film scholars who . . . buy into the belief that music in movies can do nothing but point backwards and seductively pine away."[45] Flinn discusses how music is often used to signal the male protagonist's yearning for a golden past and utopian future, but that, in film noir, this past threatens to return as a "nostalgia gone bad." Noting that the central character, pianist Al Roberts, turns to the music of Chopin as a means of "raiding history for utopian models of the future," Flinn observes that jazz is used as a musical threat to this concept of "better times." Jazz signifies the "decadent culture" in which Roberts is trapped.[46]

The potential for music to function as signifier is also identified by Simon Frith in his discussion of the semiotic aspects of the film score and its reference to the cultural code. Frith notes how film music often has to quickly establish a specific mood or situation by employing a "musical shorthand" through the use of "generic conventions," such as bagpipes to imply that a film is set in Scotland or a theremin to suggest that a character is actually an alien invader intent on stealing the American president's brain (or something like that).[47]

The inference to be drawn from these theorists is that the increased presence of jazz in scores of the 1950s was not due to any growing appreciation of the music and its validity; rather, it provided a convenient way to impart specific meanings to the audience. Such meanings gradually become "taken for granted" and difficult to avoid. The composer David Burnand has demonstrated how a certain style of jazz brings noir associations to its use in film.[48] In an example of the potential for music to represent characters and their particular psychology, Burnand, speaking at the 1998 "School of Sound" symposium in London, twice screened a scene from Pasolini's *Accattone* (1961) with different accompanying music and no other sound. Accattone is a small-time Italian thief, pimp and wife-beater. In Burnand's chosen extract, Accattone is seen walking back to his house after a heavy drinking session. For his hypothetical scores, Burnand made use of his two "joint-favorite" musicians: Johann Sebastian Bach and Miles Davis. The Davis piece selected by Burnand was a bluesy, small-group performance of cool jazz. When Burnand screened the extract again, he used a piece of orchestral Bach.

In fact, revealed Burnand, Pasolini does use Bach's "St. Matthews's Passion." The use of Bach, suggested Burnand, is ambiguous, posing questions to the audience that the Davis piece does not. Why use sacred music, full of glory, for the image of a washed-out villain? Is Accattone searching for redemption? Yet the Davis music, Burnand claimed, supports what the audience already knows about Accattone: that he is a seedy criminal. This is not to say that jazz cannot express the sacred or the spiritual. John Coltrane, Jan Garbarek, John Surman and Duke Ellington in some of his later works are only some of the jazz musicians who have sought, at various times in their careers, to make spiritual expressions through music. Nor is Burnand claiming that the Miles Davis music *is* the perfect soundtrack to capture the essence of a shot of an Italian criminal walking drunkenly home (in effect, that Davis had this image in his mind when performing the piece). Rather, it is that such a piece of music is likely to generate inevitable associations in an audience's perception of the film. These associations, a product of socialization and not inherent in the music, have proven remarkably durable. As the next section demonstrates, the connection between jazz, crime and immorality has not gone unnoticed by jazz writers.

JAZZ IN FILM

Much of the early literature that specifically considered the use of jazz in films came in the form of journal and newspaper articles. Throughout the 1950s, the jazz journal *Down Beat* carried a brief review column titled "Filmland Upbeat" that offered particular comment on those instances when jazz appeared in film. In January 1950, the journal's film correspondent, Charles Emge, posed the question, "Will Hollywood ever turn out a good jazz picture?" to Les Koenig, an associate producer at Paramount who also operated a jazz record label.[49] Koenig's response acknowledged that a good film about jazz had yet to be made, but that it was not simply enough to put jazz musicians on screen. Koenig was certain that a successful jazz film would be made, but that it would require a good story.[50]

Yet for *Down Beat*, Koenig's prediction of a good jazz picture did not materialize in the 1950s. Three years later, *Down Beat* ran an article under the headline "Little of Jazz Interest in 25 Years of Sound Films," which concluded that the best film to feature jazz was the 1944 short *Jammin' the Blues*.[51] Although Koenig would claim that it was not enough for a film to bring in a "big name band" for a jazz sequence, that remained the standard Hollywood practice. By 1957, the situation for the representation of jazz musicians had, according to *Down Beat,* still not improved:

> Jazz musicians on camera in Hollywood pix have generally found themselves somewhat in the position of domestics in a mansion: quickly perform better than well; that done, get out of sight.[52]

The majority of the literature to comment on the portrayal of jazz musicians has been, at best, unimpressed by Hollywood's approach and echoes the opinions of *Down Beat* in the 1950s. In 1980, an entire volume of *Jazz Forschung* (Jazz Research) was given over to papers addressing the relationship between jazz and the media. Willis Conover's paper, "Jazz in the Media: A Personal View," is sweepingly dismissive of the use of jazz in films:

> To approach the word "media" a bit more closely, let's look at the cinema. Or, better, let's not look at the cinema. With few exceptions, especially the 10-minute "short-subject" films that big bands used to make . . . the cinema has presented jazz ridiculously and misleadingly.[53]

As Conover surmises, films presented jazz musicians either as entertainers or "dangerous drug-users or other kinds of criminals."[54] Conover does not propose an alternative to the standard presentations of jazz that he describes, and his discussion promptly moves onto the press, radio and television.

Kenneth Spence's 1988 article is a more extensive critique of the history of jazz in Hollywood film. Spence notes and expands upon the cinematic stereotypes referred to in *Jazz Forschung.* Like Conover, Spence is unable to suggest how Hollywood should have represented jazz and, ultimately, reaches the conclusion that it possibly shouldn't have approached it at all. Spence argues that Hollywood has seldom been interested in presenting the "reality" of jazz and the jazz life. Instead, it has "worked hard at expressing *its* need to explain how jazz is 'created' and how ultimately successful one can be in that creation providing it is the 'right' kind of jazz."[55] Discussing the emergence of modern jazz in the 1940s, through the styles of bebop, cool and progressive jazz, Spence confirms the association of jazz with film noir, noting that the "startling quality of the new music seemed fit for *film noir,* characterized by its brooding, somber, anxious nature."[56] Notably, none of the films noir with a modern jazz content that Spence refers to stem from the 1940s, and I will argue in Chapter 3 that 1940s film noir was unable to feature modern styles of jazz. Spence's claim that it was the modern forms of jazz that were used in a "plethora of films" of the 1950s is not reflected in *Down Beat*'s "Filmland Upbeat" columns of the time. These columns mainly reserved comment for the on-screen involvement of jazz musicians with film, but in the early 1950s an increased presence of jazz began to take place in the nondiegetic score. *Down Beat* covered the more high-profile and obvious instances of these scores, particularly *The Man with the Golden Arm* (1955), *Sweet Smell of Success* (1957), and *I Want To Live!* (1958).

The jazz-inflected scores for these 1950s films did not receive close attention until the composer and theorist Fred Steiner, in the first of two articles published in 1976, discussed Leith Stevens' use of jazz for *The Wild One* (1953). Steiner notes that "the blues aspect of jazz, rather than its rhythmic pulse," had been incorporated in film scores as early as the 1930s, but that this use could not be considered "truly creative" until the "composition of original jazz-style pieces and jazz-derived dramatic music."[57] Steiner suggests that the use of jazz as source music enabled filmmakers to "express malaise in a scene depicting the seamier side of contemporary American life, or it might underscore a tense scene by playing against it."[58] For Steiner, the use of jazz as source music underwent a "noticeable change" around the beginning of the 1950s by taking on a psychological dimension that was no longer incidental and "sometimes had a subtle yet palpable relationship to personages or situations on the screen."[59] The premise is sound, but Steiner's placing of this change during the early 1950s is somewhat belated. He does refer to *Citizen Kane* (1941) as offering an early example of the use of jazz as a means of expression, but neglects much more famous instances that predate his suggestion. The sexual metaphor that is the jam session in *Phantom Lady* (1944) is notably ignored. This sequence will be discussed in detail in Chapter 3.

Steiner asserts that jazz-oriented scores began to flourish in the late 1950s and early 1960s. Again, his section on the nature of the jazz-oriented score is brief, but interesting. Instead of providing "musicological criteria," Steiner seeks to determine what styles of jazz these scores implied. The conclusion he reaches is that it is the modern jazz of the 1940s, with its advanced harmonies and rhythmic possibilities, that formed the basis of the jazz-oriented score, which was "unhampered by the formulaic restrictions of the schemata intrinsic to jazz of the old New Orleans and Chicago traditions."[60] Despite Steiner's earlier claim that it was not until the end of the 1950s that the "real move" in jazz-inflected scores began, he also argues that the presence of modern jazz in film scores started in the early 1950s. He closes his discussion of the jazz-oriented score by citing the observations of the French jazz writer Henri Gautier:

> One thing is certain: the cinema, when it decided to confide important roles to jazz, considering it as an actor, turned by preference to the representatives of the modern styles. It is necessary . . . to understand the reason for this choice in the fact that these styles, the "Bop," the "Cool" and even the older-style orchestras, such as, for example, that of Ellington, are more qualified

than the old New Orleans to express the modern man, his personality, his anxiety, and the world in which he lives.[61]

Steiner does not elaborate upon this statement and, again, there is no explanation of why bebop and cool jazz are more qualified to express the anxiety of "modern man." Gautier and Steiner's claim that the cinema would turn by preference to representatives of modern styles of jazz is not reflected in the films of the 1940s and 1950s, as Chapters 3 and 5 will argue. They neglect a host of jazz sequences, such as those featuring Louis Armstrong and his All Stars in the film noir *The Strip* (1951), that are performed by exponents of older forms of jazz.

The first important publication to extensively consider the use of jazz in film was David Meeker's *Jazz in the Movies* (1981).[62] Meeker's book is an encyclopedia of appearances by jazz musicians in films, either on-screen or in the soundtrack. It is a fascinating work and has done much to expose the racism that was particularly active in Hollywood films of the 1930s, 1940s and 1950s. As Meeker's study has revealed, jazz musicians, especially black musicians, have seldom been credited for their film work. A black musician on the soundtrack would typically be represented on-screen by a white actor miming to their music. As Meeker notes, black composers were allowed to provide jazz band arrangements. It was not until Quincy Jones' score for *The Pawn Broker* (1965), however, that certain racist practices had relaxed enough for a black composer to be permitted to work with a string section, the instrumentation previously considered the preserve of the white European symphony orchestra.[63] Despite the last edition of his book being published in 1981, Meeker has continued his research to the present day and maintains a constantly updated version of *Jazz in the Movies* that takes into account the films of the 1980s and 1990s.[64]

It was not until 1995 that two works appeared, edited by Krin Gabbard, that critically discussed the implications of representations of jazz. *Jazz Among the Discourses* and *Representing Jazz* are landmark works for jazz studies. Of the two, it is *Representing Jazz* that specifically looks at the jazz-film collaboration. Gabbard collects a wide range of essays discussing representations of jazz in various media. Literature, photography, dance, paintings and sculpture are all discussed, but the greatest coverage is given to jazz and film. Gabbard writes that it is his intention to (begin to) document the "other history" of jazz, arguing that film and other media representations of jazz, although often inaccurate, justify serious study because they reveal the way that American culture has sought to make sense of jazz.[65] Yet, surprisingly, none of the essays about representations of jazz on film make reference to film noir.

Gabbard's later book, *Jammin' at the Margins* (1996), continues his interest in the use and representation of jazz in film. Gabbard's book is a landmark text, devoted to jazz in American cinema. His basic premise is that "most jazz films aren't really about jazz," reflecting instead ideological concerns, and he argues that Hollywood has represented jazz most success-fully when the music has not been central to a film's narrative. The deter-mining factor of race is central to Gabbard's discussion of how films have incorporated jazz. Gabbard's discussion of the jazz soundtrack is compara-tively brief, however, although it is easily the most extensive of any pub-lished before or since. Gabbard does acknowledge that *The Strip* is a film noir that contains "the kind of generic jazz score that was becoming typi-cal for the genre," but he does not offer any study of the use of jazz in film noir.[66] This is not a criticism of the book, and Gabbard himself makes it clear in his preface that it would be possible to write another book on jazz and film that concentrates on different areas and films.[67] It would be churl-ish and quite wrong to criticize Gabbard over his choice of films to dis-cuss in his book. *Jammin' at the Margins* has ensured its status as the fountainhead for future literature that studies the partnership of jazz and film.

JAZZ AND FILM NOIR

The New Grove Dictionary of Jazz (1995) contains a substantial sec-tion concerned with the collaboration between jazz and film. Identifying recurring themes in feature films that jazz has been associated with, the dictionary's entry notes that:

> Jazz has been identified from the silent era with film crime, murder, and mayhem. It was also used to suggest a close, mutual relationship with vari-ous forms of aberrant behavior, and associated with the mad, the deranged, the psychopathic, and the just plain eccentric. There was some truth in at least part of this screen image, since gangsters had played a dominant role in establishing the nightclubs, gambling rooms, and dance halls in which jazz had flourished. Most gangster films set in the Prohibition or Depression era contained scenes that employed jazz bands for atmosphere.[68]

This statement is followed by a list of films that confirm the association of jazz with crime, providing brief plot summaries and details of the music used. The dictionary's entry concludes with a review of original jazz scores and suggests that the music did indeed feature strongly in film noir:

> During the 1950s and 1960s the Hollywood studios tended to concentrate more and more on themes that had to do with crime, violence, loneliness, alienation, drug addiction, racial and generational conflict, juvenile delin-quency, and the brittle antagonisms that were the result of a crowded and stressed existence. At the same time jazz-flavored scores and soundtracks became synonymous with these themes and with *film noir* productions, and

a cadre of film composers, arrangers and orchestrators emerged to provide many of the original compositions and jazz-influenced music.[69]

Referring to this "cadre" (comprising Benny Carter, Leith Stevens, Alex North, Elmer Bernstein, David Raksin, Ray Heindorf, Buddy Bregman, Pete Rugolo, Duke Ellington and Shorty Rogers), the entry claims that, in the early 1950s, "jazz-textured scores became dominant."[70] This is a bold assertion to make and directly contradicts Orr's comment that jazz was "conspicuously missing" from film noir soundtracks or, for that matter, Brown's statement that although jazz made a greater number of appearances in the film scores of the 1950s, these appearances have "never become major highways," which can hardly be translated into them being "dominant." There are obviously vastly differing opinions as to when and how the jazz score was used in the 1950s.

The true nature and extent of the association between jazz and film noir is not easily determined from the literature discussed in this chapter. By cross-referencing Alain Silver and Elizabeth Ward's 1980 directory of films noir[71] with Meeker's directory of films that feature jazz musicians, it is possible to arrive at a more accurate indication of the consistency with which jazz has been used in film noir. Meeker refers to 30 of the 302 films noir identified by Silver and Ward as featuring jazz on-screen or in the nondiegetic score. Only eight films are referred to by both studies: *Phantom Lady* (1944), *D.O.A.* (1950), *The Strip* (1951), *Nightmare* (1956), *The Beat Generation* (1959), *Odds Against Tomorrow* (1959), *Farewell, My Lovely* (1975) and *Taxi Driver* (1976). In this group, the latter two films were both made after the classic period of film noir had ended, and *The Beat Generation* is something of a marginal selection—a film not automatically considered to be genuine noir. It would be difficult to assert that jazz has been a dominant musical idiom in film noir from these figures. Yet, as we have seen, the perception of an extensive association between jazz and film noir is widely held. It may be that we have convinced ourselves that jazz and film noir are inseparable, when the truth is somewhat different. Barry Keith Grant has discussed the tendency for music to be associated with the historical context in which it occurs.[72] This point provides a potential explanation for the perceived symbiosis between jazz and film noir. David Reid and Jayne Walker comment that "apart from *film noir* and bebop, the postwar forties enjoy remarkably little purchase on what passes for popular memory."[73] The suggestion is that jazz, specifically bebop, is associated with film noir because they share the same historical context.

A number of film theorists make reference to jazz being an effective and staple feature of film noir. Pfeil, as I noted earlier, includes "lurid jazzy bars" in his list of noir iconography. Jon Tuska goes even further, arguing in the case of *Street of Chance* (1942) and *Phantom Lady* (1944) that their status as film noir is increased through their incorporation of jazz. For Tuska, both films are "notable for the effective use they make of jazz music on the sound track and jazz musicians as a grotesque and even threatening manifestation of big city life."[74] In selecting *I Want To Live!* (1958) as one of the "most brilliantly conceived and executed *film noirs* ever made," Tuska again includes the presence of a jazz band as one of the "traditional characteristics of visual *noir*."[75] James Ursini's discussion of television noir, "Angst at Sixty Fields per Second," refers to jazz and blues as being "traditional signifiers in *noir*."[76] Ursini does not provide any examples of these uses of jazz, other than the series *Johnny Staccato* (1959–1960) and the episode of *Peter Gunn* (1958–1961) that he analyzes in the essay. For Ursini, it is alienation, despair, edginess and volatility that are signified by jazz, and bebop in particular.

The Alain Silver and Elizabeth Ward edited guide to film noir contains short critiques for over three hundred films. The vast majority of these summaries make no reference to jazz, even when the music plays a significant part, as in *The Sweet Smell of Success* (1957). Yet, there are some notable exceptions that suggest an established relationship between jazz and film noir. In discussing the early film noir *Among the Living* (1941), Robert Porfirio comments that "the jazz sequence in a bar and the shot of Paul killing the B-girl in the alley . . . are particularly important and set a stylistic precedent for expressing confusion and violence."[77] Porfirio is the most "jazz conscious" of the book's contributors, and he has done much to draw attention to the music's function in films such as *Nightmare* (1956) and *When Strangers Marry* (1944). For Porfirio, the latter film displays a typical use of jazz in film noir:

> William Castle (the director) creates an oppressive New York atmosphere in studio sets. This artificial setting is laced with those undertones of fear and hysteria that constitute some of the definitive motifs of the noir studio film. Millie Baxter is alone and frightened in a hotel room with jazz blaring next door, while the neon "dancing" sign alternately fills the room with light then leaves it in darkness.[78]

Porfirio (1999) argues that jazz flourished in film noir because of its "unfortunate association with brothels, speak-easies and dope" that in turn "reinforced its association with sex, violence and death."[79] Porfirio's article does not explore the ideological perspectives that ensured jazz remained attached to these associations, however. The emphasis in Porfirio's article is on film noir of the 1940s. Yet, as I noted earlier, it is important to consider the use of jazz throughout the development of film noir. Do Porfirio's observations, which I readily agree with for films noir of the 1940s, hold true for the use of jazz in 1950s film noir or the neo-noirs of the last twenty-five years? Equally, do all styles of jazz carry the same associations?

Elsewhere, claims about the use of jazz in film noir have been made that are quite simply untrue and misleading. In their study of the films noir developed from the writing of Cornell Woolrich, Reid and Walker assert that the famed jazz sequence in *Phantom Lady* (1944) is "all bebop, gin and marijuana."[80] The style of jazz in the sequence is clearly not bebop, but stems from an earlier tradition. Bebop had only just begun to emerge in 1944 and was certainly not in existence when Woolrich wrote the novel in 1942. I discuss in Chapter 3 how bebop was unable to be featured in films noir of the 1940s, but that it still became associated with noir themes. In Chapter 5 I demonstrate how these associations have resulted in modern jazz, such as bebop, being perceived as the sound of the original noir period, when the reality was different. Reid and Walker fall prey to this perception as well as contributing to it.

Nicholas Christopher suggests that the modern jazz that was contemporaneous to the original films noir was indeed noir music even if it did not feature extensively in the films themselves. Arguing that film noir has traveled beyond its screen confines and can now be "seen in virtually every artistic medium," Christopher states that noir found its musical expression in, among other idioms, bebop:

> As noir progresses into the 1950s, in films and in popular culture in general, elements of pop eccentricity and high funk—as well as unabashed surrealism—color it more powerfully. The nocturnal bebop jazz of Charlie Parker and John Coltrane, the explosion of rock and roll—Elvis Presley and Little Richard—with its sexual electricity and Bacchic ritual, and the newly emergent blues . . . provide the background roar as postwar melts into Cold War and the full after effects of the war hit America and her cities.[81]

Again, the music of Charlie Parker and John Coltrane was not used in films noir of the 1950s. Yet it is noticeable that the musicians Christopher cites as best representing jazz's noir sensibility are both black, underlining Orr's assertion that black jazz was conspicuously absent from the original film noir soundtracks.

Clearly, this is not an area in which there is a great deal of critical writing. The fact that new, relevant literature, for example, the Gabbard books, is being produced, however, confirms that this current dearth of texts should not be interpreted as meaning that the subject is irrelevant or unworthy of serious study. The literature reviewed can be split into two strands of opinion. Generally, those writing from a film studies perspective do not consider the role jazz has played in film noir. Jazz writers, however, tend to be in no doubt as to the involvement of jazz. These differing viewpoints are possibly due to the vested interests of both camps. For the film studies writer, taking into consideration the large amount of films noir that have been made, the number of jazz scores and scenes with jazz musicians may well be insignificant. Yet, given the lack of representation that jazz has received from film, the perspective of the jazz writer is inclined to be different. From this point of view, a handful of films noir that include jazz musicians or jazz scenes as part of their narrative could result in jazz being considered to have made a significant contribution to film noir.

There is considerable confusion as to when and to what extent jazz has appeared in film noir. Equally unclear is which styles of jazz have been most extensively used and whether all styles of jazz have functioned as signifiers of the same things. What is required is a closer study of those films noir that have made use of jazz and a greater body of appropriate literature to discuss them. A consistent failing of much of the literature that refers to jazz and film noir is the lack of attention given to why jazz and film noir should be associated. The standard explanation is that jazz was connected to sex and crime through the venues in which it was often heard. In the next chapter I suggest that this connection goes far deeper than that.

NOTES

1. These postings can be found at the following Web address: http://www.jazzjukebox.com/EmazeForums/program/readForum.cfm?confID=11&forumID=854.

2. Pfeil, F. 1993. Home Fires Burning: Family *Noir* in *Blue Velvet* and *Terminator 2*. In J. Copjec, ed. *Shades of Noir*. London: Verso. p. 229.

3. Meeker, D. 1981. *Jazz in the Movies*. New York: Da Capo Press. Meeker makes this comment in the Introduction to the book. There is no page number included.

4. Young, A. 1993. We Jazz June/We Die Soon: Jazz Film Thoughts. *Antaeus*. no. 71-72, p. 124. Hugh Masekela, quoted by Al Young.

5. Lees, G. 1975. Adventures of a Black Composer in Hollywood. *New York Times*. March 16. Quincy Jones, interviewed by Gene Lees.

6. Frith, S. 1996. *Performing Rites: Evaluating Popular Music*. Oxford: Oxford University Press. pp. 108–9.

7. Fordham, J. 1997. "The Printed Media" presented at the conference "Jazz in the Media," held in Leeds, May 8.

8. Undated flier for the February 11, 1994 concert by Bobby Previte's Empty Suits at the Royal Northern College of Music, Manchester. Published by the Contemporary Music Network through the Arts Council of Great Britain.

9. Nicholson, S. 1990. *Jazz: The Modern Resurgence*. London: Simon & Schuster. p. 234.

10. Program notes by Stuart Nicholson for the February 1994 tour of England by Bobby Previte's Empty Suits. Published by the Contemporary Music Network through the Arts Council of Great Britain.

11. Orr, J. 1993. *Cinema and Modernity*. Cambridge: Polity Press. p. 179.

12. Ibid., pp. 179–80.

13. Ibid., p. 179.

14. Pfeil, F. 1993. In J. Copjec, ed. *Shades of Noir*. London: Verso. p. 227.

15. Silver, A., and Ursini, J., eds. 1996. *Film Noir Reader*. New York: Limelight Editions. p. 11. Although the parameters of film noir, and the films to be included within them, have been debated, Silver asserts that: "If observers of film noir agree on anything, it is on the boundaries of the classic period, which begins

in 1941 with *The Maltese Falcon* and ends less than a score of years later with *Touch of Evil.*"

16. Cowie, E. 1993. *Film Noir* and Women. In J. Copjec, ed. *Shades of Noir*. London: Verso. p. 121.

17. Silver, A., and Ursini, J., eds. 1996. *Film Noir Reader*. New York: Limelight Editions. p. 10.

18. Borde, R., and Chaumeton, É. 1996. Towards a Definition of *Film Noir*. In A. Silver and J. Ursini, eds. *Film Noir Reader*. New York: Limelight Editions. p. 25. Originally published in 1955.

19. Place, J., and Peterson, L. 1996. Some Visual Motifs of *Film Noir*. In A. Silver and J. Ursini, eds. *Film Noir Reader*. New York: Limelight Editions. p. 65. Originally published in 1974.

20. Pfeil, R. 1993. In J. Copjec, ed. *Shades of Noir*. London: Verso. p. 230.

21. Flinn, C. 1992. *Strains of Utopia: Gender, Nostalgia, and Hollywood Film Music*. Princeton: Princeton University Press. pp. 5–6.

22. Tilton, R. 1956. Jazz Dance. *Film Music*. vol. 15, no. 4, p. 19.

23. Ibid.

24. Ibid.

25. Ahnert, S. 1995. Klang der Dunkelheit: Der Film noir und seine Musik. Translated by Susie Hird, *Neue Zeitschrift fur Musik*. vol. 156, no. 4, p. 40.

26. Ibid., p. 41.

27. Ibid.

28. Prendergast, R. 1992. *Film Music: A Neglected Art*. New York: W.W. Norton and Company. p. 117.

29. Ibid.

30. Ibid.

31. Burt, G. 1994. *The Art of Film Music*. Boston: Northeastern University Press. p. 30.

32. Brown, R.S. 1994. *Overtones and Undertones: Reading Film Music*. Berkeley and Los Angeles: University of California Press. p. 183.

33. Lack, R. 1997. *Twenty Four Frames Under: A Buried History of Film Music*. London: Quartet Books. p. 198.

34. Ibid., p. 201.

35. Ibid., p. 197.

36. Thomas, T. 1977. *Music for the Movies*. South Brunswick and New York: A. S. Barnes and Company. pp. 190–191. Elmer Bernstein interviewed.

37. Martin, P. 1995. *Sounds & Society: Themes in the Sociology of Music*. Manchester: University of Manchester Press. p. 57.

38. Ibid., p. 60.

39. Gorbman, C. 1987. *Unheard Melodies: Narrative Film Music*. London: BFI. p. 153.

40. Ibid., p. 153.

41. Kalinak, K. 1992. *Settling the Score: Music and the Classical Hollywood Film*. Madison, Wisconsin: University of Wisconsin Press. p. 120.

42. Ibid.

43. Ibid., p. 167.

44. Flinn, C. 1990. Male Nostalgia and Hollywood Film Music: The Terror of the Feminine. *Canadian University Music Review*. vol. 10, no. 2, p. 20.

45. Ibid., p. 26.

46. Ibid., pp. 22–23.

47. Frith S. 1996. *Performing Rites: Evaluating Popular Music.* Oxford: Oxford University Press. p. 20.

48. Burnard, D. 1998. School of Sound. Symposium held in London, April 18.

49. *Down Beat.* 1950. vol. 17, no. 2, p. 8.

50. Ibid.

51. *Down Beat.* 1953. vol. 20, no. 17, p. 3.

52. *Down Beat.* 1957. vol. 24, no. 11, p. 30.

53. Conover, W. 1980. Jazz in the Media: A Personal View. *Jazz Forschung.* vol. 12, p. 36.

54. Ibid.

55. Spence, K. 1988. Jazz Digest: From Big Band to Be-Bop. *Film Comment.* vol. 24, no. 6, p. 38.

56. Ibid., p. 42.

57. Steiner, F. 1976. An Examination of Leith Stevens' Use of Jazz in *The Wild One. Film Music Notebook.* vol. 2, no. 2, pp. 29–30.

58. Ibid., p. 29.

59. Ibid.

60. Ibid., p. 30.

61. Ibid., p. 31.

62. Meeker, D. 1981. *Jazz in the Movies.* New York: Da Capo Press.

63. David, M. 1999. Interview by the author, October 27.

64. Ibid.

65. Gabbard, K., ed. 1995. *Representing Jazz.* Durham and London: Duke University Press. pp. 2–3.

66. Gabbard, K. 1996. *Jammin' at the Margins: Jazz and the American Cinema.* Chicago: University of Chicago Press. p. 223.

67. Ibid., pp. ix–x.

68. Kernfeld, B., ed. 1995. *The New Grove Dictionary of Jazz.* London: MacMillan. pp. 379–80.

69. Ibid., p. 385.

70. Ibid.

71. Silver, A., and Ward, E., eds. 1980. *Film Noir.* London: Secker and Warburg.

72. Keith Grant, B. 1995. Purple Passages or Fiestas in Blue? Notes Toward an Aesthetic of Vocalese. In K. Gabbard, ed. *Representing Jazz.* Durham and London: Duke University Press. p. 291.

73. Reid, D., and Walker, J. 1993. Strange Pursuit: Cornell Woolrich and the Abandoned City of the Forties. In J. Copjec, ed. *Shades of Noir.* London: Verso. p. 88.

74. Tuska, J. 1984. *Dark Cinema: American Film Noir in Cultural Perspective.* Westport, Conn.: Greenwood Press. p. 195.

75. Ibid., p. 214.

76. Ursini, J. 1996. Angst at Sixty Fields per Second. In A. Silver and J. Ursini, eds. *Film Noir Reader.* New York: Limelight Editions. p. 281.

77. Porfirio, R. 1980. Among the Living. In A. Silver and E. Ward, eds. *Film Noir.* London: Secker and Warburg. p. 11.

78. Porfirio, R. 1980. When Strangers Marry. In A. Silver and E. Ward, eds. *Film Noir*. London: Secker and Warburg. p. 307.

79. Porfirio, R. 1999. Dark jazz: Music in the film noir. In A. Silver and J. Ursini, eds. *Film Noir Reader 2*. New York: Limelight Editions. p. 177. I am extremely grateful to Robert Porfirio and Alain Silver for forwarding me an advance copy of "Dark Jazz: Music in the Film Noir" ahead of the publication of *Film Noir Reader 2*.

80. Reid, D., and Walker, J.L. 1993. In J. Copjec, ed. *Shades of Noir*. London: Verso. p. 83.

81. Christopher, N. 1997. *Somewhere in the Night: Film Noir and the American City*. New York: The Free Press. p. 48.

2

All God's Chillun' Got Rhythm

*The Influence of Racial Myths,
Dualisms and Ideology on Early
Representations of Jazz*

In this chapter I discuss the racial myths and ideologies that have influenced the use of jazz in Hollywood films of the first half of the twentieth
century. These influences were not exclusive to Hollywood and reflected
instead the dominant Eurocentrism that informed representations and dis-
cussions of jazz in other forums. It is my intention to demonstrate here how
certain dualisms that have flourished in Hollywood films—from the binary
opposites of the Western genre, such as civilization versus wilderness, to
the more universal pairings of good versus evil and black versus white—
attempted to accommodate jazz. The crucial dualism for jazz was that of
mind versus body. I will feature examples of the application of this dualism
to representations of jazz in a number of films, ranging from those of the
pre-sound era to the 1950s, before concentrating on film noir in the
remaining chapters.

THE SPIRIT AND THE FLESH

Fundamental to an understanding of the way that jazz has been used and
represented in film is the dualism of mind and body. The implications of
this dualism, however, go far beyond jazz and film and have affected the
construction of notions of whiteness and non-whiteness that privilege the
former while encouraging the oppression and denigration of the latter. In
this opening section I outline the origin of this dualism and its function in
white imperialist ideologies of the nineteenth century.

In his groundbreaking study, *White* (1997), which destabilizes the assumption of whiteness as representing the "normality" of the human race, Richard Dyer argues that the Christian conflict between the spirit and the flesh, or mind and body, has provided the basis for racial myths and Eurocentric ideologies.[1] This conflict, Dyer observes, is most clearly manifested in the figures of Christ and Mary. Both represent an unattainable ideal of transcendence from the earthly body into pure spirit. Yet it is an ideal that must still be sought through "suffering, self-denial and self-control," qualities that, Dyer notes, provide a "thumbnail sketch of the white ideal."[2] As I later discuss, the loss of self-control that jazz was perceived to encourage contributed to its representation as an inferior or immoral music.

Dyer is quick to point out that he is not suggesting that Christianity is a white or European religion. Its imagery has been whitened, however, and it has served as justification for European expansion in such movements as the Crusades, the voyages of "discovery" or *conquista* and colonialist domination by imperial forces. As Lola Young notes, Christian tradition helped to provide the "fabric of racist ideologies" that resulted in the "brutal exploitation of African and other peoples":

> Images of the "good/white" overcoming the "evil/black" were a recurring theme in Biblical art and images of blacks as lascivious, childlike and demonic, were derived, in part from the Bible itself. Indeed, one of the standard biblical "explanations" for people having black skins originated from the story of the curse of Ham whom God made black-skinned for looking at his naked father lying drunk in a tent.[3]

The rulings of the Christian church have also shaped the interpretation of certain musical styles. In a chapter on the social construction of musical meaning, Peter Martin notes the medieval church's opposition to the spread of modern tonality. Referring to the work of Deryck Cooke, Martin indicates how the perceived "joy" of a musical structure such as the major third was considered a threat to the church:

> The major scales conveyed feelings of joy and earthly well-being, in contrast to the severe and spiritual messages of the modes, and so what was ultimately at stake was the authority of the church itself.[4]

Here again, we find the dualism of mind and body at work. The perception of particular musical qualities as expressing higher values, of being worthier than other musical forms, has since moved beyond the church and is expressed by other institutions or, as Louis Althusser termed them, Ideological State Appartuses.[5] As Martin acknowledges, one suggested result has been a "hierarchy of styles and traditions" in which formal edu-

cation encourages the "distinction between 'serious' and 'popular' music
. . . to the general detriment of the latter."[6] The uneasy position of jazz in
such a hierarchy is explored later in this chapter.

The mind/body dualism remained in force throughout the scientific and
philosophical developments of the Enlightenment and the years of imperialist conquest that followed. Young demonstrates how the desire for
taxonomies and "hierarchical ordering" was extended, via empirical observation, to an understanding of racial difference on the basis of skin color
and that black skin was "correlated with what was characterized as an in-
capacity for rational thought."[7] As Young notes, scientific developments
such as eugenics and Darwinism, which encouraged the consideration of
non-whites as being primitive, contributed the rationale for the imperialist
"Christian" mission:

> Ideologically, nineteenth century British colonialism was justified as a moral
> duty, a benevolent effort to spread Christianity and civilization across the
> continents of Africa, Asia and America. . . . Much literary production dur-
> ing the late nineteenth century is replete with examples of "knowledge" about
> the character of Africans based on white supremacist attitudes towards
> "race." In particular the notion of atavism—the belief that the "primitive"
> people of Africa constituted an earlier stage of human development—often
> recurs: all the references to primeval swamps, to primitive rituals, the colo-
> nial subjects' perceived deficiency of language, intellect and culture attest to
> this belief.[8]

The conflict of mind and body, inextricably linked to sexual reproduc-
tion, is particularly visible in the imperial adventure film, as explored by
Shohat, Stam and Young.[9] These films reflect white anxiety about the
reproductive capacity of non-whites in their depiction of a handful of
resourceful white protagonists pitted against undifferentiated non-white
hordes. Shohat and Stam discuss how imperialist films such as *Sanders
of the River* (1935) portrayed "exotic" traditions under the cover of
ethnography for the "unleashing of pornographic impulses":

> Formulaic scenes of dark frenzied bodies entranced by accelerating drum
> rhythms relayed a fetishized image of indigenous religions. Ceremonial pos-
> session (portrayed as a kind of mass hysteria) evoked the uncontrollable id
> of libidinous beings.[10]

White imperialist ideology could only consider black culture as being an
expression of black hypersexuality and irrational thought. Inevitably, as in
black music, the same associations were applied to jazz when it first flourished in the 1920s.

SEXUAL RHYTHM?

In his study of the meaning and value of popular music, Simon Frith devotes two chapters to the commonly held association between rhythm and sex. As Frith notes, the rhythm that has most frequently been related to sex is that of black musical genres or genres derived from them. He challenges this simple equation as being a "product of European high cultural ideology rather than of African popular musical practice."[11] That is to say, there is nothing inherently sexual about black music, but Eurocentric ideologies have emphasized its perceived sexual connotations in order to provide a method of interpreting it.

Although Frith's central interest is in rock and pop music, he discusses how the connotations of sex perceived in those genres were previously applied to jazz and are rooted in the dualism of mind and body. This binary opposition is only one of a series of such oppositions that constitute the framework of Eurocentric thinking. Margery Hourihan's study of the dualisms inherent in literature featuring the dominant Western hero figure can also be applied to Hollywood films. Hourihan notes that a dualism is "more than a dichotomy" because:

> In a dualism one of the two contrasting terms is constructed as superior and the other as inherently inferior in relation to it. The inferiorized "other" is treated in a variety of ways: It may be backgrounded, that is simply regarded as not worthy of notice. . . . It may be defined as radically different . . . thus underlining its inferiority. . . . The inferiorized group tends to be treated as homogenous in order to emphasize its distinctness from the dominant norm. . . . Further, the inferior group is defined only in relation to the superior; its members' lack of the superior qualities is presented as the essence of their identity. No attempt is made to elucidate their own qualities from their own perspective, or to show them as significant in their own right.[12]

In the mind/body dualism, it is the former aspect that has been privileged in dominant European ideology, while the body has been assigned inferior qualities. Frith locates the establishment of the mind/body dualism in the Industrial Revolution and the distinction between mental and manual labor:

> In the mid-nineteenth century this was mapped onto the original Romantic dichotomy between feeling and reason: feelings were now taken . . . to be best expressed spiritually and mentally, in silent contemplation of great art or great music. Bodily responses became, by definition, mind-less.[13]

As David Meltzer's anthology of jazz writing demonstrates, much of the early writing that was critical of jazz cited the music's effect on its audience as evidence of its inferiority rather than offering a musicological critique. The bodily response provoked by jazz was often referred to as being base and primitive and thus justified the condemnation of the music. Anne Shaw Faulkner, for example, posed the question, "Does jazz put the sin in syncopation?" and suggested that:

> We have all been taught to believe that "music soothes the savage beast," but we have never stopped to consider that an entirely different type of music might invoke savage instincts. Never in the history of our land have there been such immoral conditions, and in surveys made by many organizations, the blame is laid on jazz and its evil influence on the young. Never before have such outrageous dances been permitted in private as well as public ballrooms, and never has there been such a strange combination of tone and rhythm as that produced by the dance orchestras of to-day.[14]

Maxim Gorky, writing in *Pravda*, provided a vivid account of the negative effects of jazz. Again, Gorky's piece refers to the audience's response and contains much sexual and animalistic imagery in its account of the "music of the degenerate":

> This insulting chaos of insanity pulses to a throbbing rhythm. Listening for a few minutes to these wails, one involuntarily imagines an orchestra of sexually driven madmen conducted by a man-stallion brandishing a huge genital member. The monstrous bass belches out English words; a wild horn wails piercingly, calling to mind the cries of a raving camel; a drum pounds monotonously; a nasty little pipe tears at one's ears; a saxophone emits its quacking nasal sound. Fleshy hips sway, and thousands of heavy feet tread and shuffle.[15]

As both these examples demonstrate, the rhythmic qualities of jazz and the emphasis given to the beat or pulse of the bass and drums were particularly referred to as being representative of jazz's primitivism and sexual element. The "outrageous" dancing encouraged by the "monotonous" drums was interpreted as orgiastic. Frith notes that this view of rhythm is founded on a misunderstanding of its function in popular music, which has "nothing to do with going wild," but requires instead a sense of discipline and is "always about bodily control."[16] These claims about bodily responses were not exclusive to jazz and would later be applied to other music, such as rock 'n' roll, which encouraged dancing. The argument that jazz, and black music in general, are primitive and offer "jungle rhythms" is founded on a racist perception. As Frith summarizes:

> Because "the African" is more primitive, more "natural" than the European, then African music must be more directly in touch with the body, with unsymbolized and unmediated sensual states and expectations. And given that African musics are most obviously different from European musics in their uses of rhythm, then rhythm must be how the primitive, the sexual, is expressed.[17]

In his discussion of the oral culture that is essential to black American music, Ben Sidran notes that rhythm in particular has offered a "cultural catharsis" from the daily pressures of life in a racist society to the black community. Sidran refers to Raymond Williams and his discussion of the communicative potential of rhythm, which enables an experience to be transmitted from one person to another and re-created, or "lived," by the recipient as not just an abstract concept but a "physical effect on the organism—on the blood, on the breathing, on the physical patterns of the brain."[18]

Sidran, like Frith, does not deny that rhythm can be compared to sex, and observes that through its potential to create and resolve physical tension, rhythm has been frequently linked to the sexual act.[19] Sidran asserts, however, that this equation is often a Eurocentric one, and that it is to "Western man" that "Afro-American rhythms have often been particularly associated with this (sexual) act."[20] The misunderstanding of what African, or African-derived, rhythms "mean" frequently results in a basic onomatopoeic link between the pounding of a drum and the pounding of the body.

Although the perceived sexual connotations applied to jazz would also be applied to other musics as they emerged, the association of jazz with sex has persisted. Michael Bywater has claimed that jazz, unlike the rock 'n' roll of Elvis Presley, should be considered the real "music of sex."

> *Jazz* is the music of sex: subtle, ardent, the drumbeat marking the boundaries of a space in which the instruments and voices slide, coil and intertwine: question and answer, solo and chorus, advance and retreat. But *Elvis*? . . . . The stolid, trailer-park beat imposed upon and drowning out everything else; the nonsensical, histrionic, unconvincing climax: Elvis is the perfect musical analogue of a lousy lover, and the preferred three-minute duration of his little efforts could hardly be more appropriate.[21]

Bywater's analogy between Elvis' brand of rock 'n' roll and mindless sex is remarkably similar to the descriptions provided by critics, such as Gorky, of early styles of jazz. For Bywater, it is, again, the rhythmic qualities of the respective musics that are analogous to "good" or "bad" sex. Notably, Bywater emphasizes the drums and "stolid, trailer-park beat." Bywater interprets jazz as being "subtle" and "ardent," however, a balance between mind and body, unlike Elvis' music, which, he claims, suggests unthinking sex. In making a connection between rhythm, sex and thought, Bywater's analogies parallel Frith's argument that the "sexiness" of rhythm is derived from the promise of "ideal time" and its bringing together of spheres that are traditionally separated:

> The individual and the social, the mind and the body, change and stillness, the different and the same, the already past and the still to come, desire and fulfillment. Music *is* in this respect like sex, and rhythm is crucial to this—

rhythm not as "releasing" physical urges but as expanding the time in which we can, as it were, *live in the present tense.*[22]

It is not my intention, therefore, to deny any parallels between jazz and sex or attempt to purify jazz of its sexual connotations. Indeed, such efforts would contradict many of the statements by jazz's leading practitioners and risk the flaws of positive/negative image analysis. Krin Gabbard has discussed at length the phallic qualities of the jazz trumpet, particularly in relationship to Louis Armstrong, and notes that "members of his band are said to have referred to their accompanying figures on Armstrong's 1931 recording of 'Star Dust' as 'the fucking rhythm.'"[23] Similarly, Scott DeVeaux, in his study of the saxophonist Coleman Hawkins, refers to the comparison Hawkins made between his solos and the sexual act. Advising the vocalist Thelma Carpenter of his short-lived 1940 big band on the best way to approach a song, Hawkins recommended:

> "First, you have to tell them the story," he told her. "Then it's like making love. Suppose you get in bed with a woman. You jump on her—and that's it. No! You must romance her." On another occasion, he clarified, "You greet the song, then you slowly get closer to it, caressing it, kissing it, and finally making love to it." Hawkins used his recording of "Body and Soul" as a point of reference. Of the climax, he said: "that's when you're having the orgasm"; of the unaccompanied coda—"well, now that's the satisfaction."[24]

Hawkins remains one of the most important musicians in jazz, redefining the role of the tenor saxophone during the 1920s and 1930s. He maintained an interest in "progress" through his support for the younger generation of musicians that formed the emerging idiom of bebop in the early 1940s. Hawkins' fellow musicians particularly respected him for the breadth of his musical knowledge, and he gained the nickname "Bean" because "he was so intelligent about music."[25] The contrast between Hawkins' musical knowledge, especially his understanding of harmony, and his sexual metaphor for the process of his soloing demonstrates a balance between the binary opposites of mind and body. As we have seen, the dominant understanding of jazz, during the first decades of Hawkins' career, did not perceive this balance, but cast the music instead in the "inferiorized group" belonging to the mind/body dualism. This understanding informed the representation of jazz in Hollywood films from the pre-sound era onward.

THE LAND OF JAZZ: SEX AND VOODOO IN THE "JAZZ AGE"

It is difficult to determine to what extent jazz was incorporated into the musical accompaniments of pre-sound films, and it is beyond the reach of this book to do so. It is likely that a number of jazz musicians would have found employment as accompanists in the exhibiting theaters. The pre-sound era was also the pre-swing era in jazz, and the demand for big bands, and thus the musicians needed to fill them, had yet to arise. Many jazz musicians, particularly black musicians, would find themselves struggling to make a decent living without a band to provide a home for them. Jazz musicians have long worked in whatever situation is available to them. The theme of the jazz musician striving to play the music he loves but forced to apply his skills to those jobs where he can earn money (weddings, bar mitzvahs, "sweet" dance bands and so on) even became the subject of a Hollywood film, *Young Man with a Horn* (1950).

Benny Goodman's biographer Ross Firestone notes how, prior to his spectacular success as the "King of Swing," Goodman found much work in the early 1930s as a session musician for Paramount's Astoria studios in New York. This work helped to sustain Goodman through the initial years of the Depression. According to Firestone:

> A good part of Benny's income now, as much as eighty dollars a day, came from recording movie sound track music. . . . Benny remembered doing "a lot of tunes for the movies" . . . [and] also worked for the animated cartoon studios, which were still centered in Manhattan, and played on some of the music tracks that were being dubbed onto the old silent comedies.[26]

It is reasonable to assume, therefore, that some early jazz styles would have been incorporated into the music for a number of pre-sound films. Although much of the music of the Jazz Age does not correspond to our understanding of jazz today, it seems inevitable that the popularity of "jazz" would be reflected in the content of some of the films of the 1920s. Lack identifies the presence of jazz in a variety of silent films—*The Girl with a Jazz Heart* (1921), *The House that Jazz Built* (1921), *Children of Jazz* (1923) and *His Jazz Bride* (1926), for example—although he acknowledges that it is not possible to determine to what extent jazz would have been employed in their musical accompaniment.[27]

A study of the screenplay for the 1920 film *The Land of Jazz* provides a fascinating early example of the aspects of jazz that Hollywood films would repeatedly refer to throughout the sound era. Written, produced and directed by Jules Furthman, *The Land of Jazz* is a bizarre tale. It begins in Santa Barbarello, which is described as one of the "most exclusive million-aire colonies on the Pacific coast," thus linking jazz from the start with a rich and decadent lifestyle. The central figure in the film is Nina Dumbarton, who makes her way, with her companions Nancy Lee and Captain Felix de Dordain, to the mysterious island home of Dr. Vane Carruthers. Dr. Carruthers is a grim and emotionally repressed man who studies insanity and other mental diseases, believing love to be such an affliction.

It transpires that Nancy is engaged to Dr. Carruthers but loves Captain de Dordain. She enlists the aid of Nina to resolve the situation. Nina, it turns out, is in love with Dr. Carruthers. She has no way of breaking through his icy exterior, however, until he is transformed after being exposed to the delights of dancing to jazz. Jazz is used as a "cure" for the doctor's emotional difficulties; it is through experiencing the jazz dance (which is referred to as the "shimmy") that he is able to loosen up as a person and acknowledge love. As Dr. Carruthers dances (scene 167), he laughs and asserts that although he has heard considerable negative criticism of the shimmy and its vulgar movements, it nevertheless generates a pleasurable sensation in the neck and shoulder muscles, as well as exhilarating the nerves.[28]

Although *The Land of Jazz* appears to be enthusiastic about jazz and its "healing" properties, it presents jazz in such a way that calls into question the merits of the music. Thomas Wesley Chapman, the character that introduces jazz to the island, is insane. He is also referred to as the "shimmy fiend." Formerly a publisher of hymn books, he now performs violent shimmy dancing in front of a Victrola record player. The screenplay appears to suggest that in his obsession with jazz and the shimmy, he has suffered a fall from grace. Jazz is cast as the opposite of hymns or sacred music, and the implication seems to be that it is the "devil's music."

Chapman is first introduced in the screenplay (scene 156) with his back to the camera and appearing to possess a youthful figure. On turning to face the camera, however, he is revealed as an old man with mutton chop whiskers. Entering Nina's room, he yells in delight, "at last I have a dance partner! No longer will I have to shimmy alone!" Constantly shimmying, Chapman forces himself on Nina who "struggles violently," but is unable to break free from his grip. This sequence can be read as a coded rape scene. As the sequence continues, the sexual connotations of the jazz dance are made even clearer by the screenplay. Chapman is described (scene 159) as dancing with the struggling Nina in great ecstasy while the Victrola plays a record titled "Land of Shimmy and Jazz." Soon Nina becomes totally enthralled by the "spell of the shimmy fiend" and ceases to struggle, shimmying with "great abandon" in a dance that is described (scene 161) as becoming wilder and wilder until both dancers part and work alone while still facing each other.[29]

The dance does not end there. The icy Dr. Carruthers walks into the room and finds he is also unable to resist the urge to shimmy. Presently everybody on the island is dancing to the jazz record—patients, tax inspectors and the butler's frosty wife. One character, a giant, holds the Victrola machine aloft and shimmies down to the beach leading the rest of the dancers along as if he were the Pied Piper of Hamelin. When the dance finally finishes, all the characters collapse exhausted and fall asleep on the beach. It is at this point that Nina confesses her love for Dr. Carruthers (even though he is sleeping and does not hear her). Effectively, what has just taken place is an orgy. The characters lose control of their senses and are driven by an uncontrollable desire to dance "violently," with "ecstasy" and "great abandon." Jazz is presented as music founded on impulse and devoid of reason, an interpretation of jazz that Hollywood would maintain for years, as we shall see in the rest of this chapter. There are also racist connotations in *The Land of Jazz*'s use of jazz. The setting of an exotic island and the bewitching effect of the jazz music are clearly suggestive of voodoo and the notion of jazz as music derived from "primitive savages." This casting of jazz as a forbidden and mysterious pleasure was a feature of the way the music, particularly the jazz of the black bands, was promoted in the early decades of its development. As David Meltzer describes it, jazz was (and Meltzer argues that to some extent still is) viewed as "slave music" pursued by white "hunters." The cornered music would not submit readily, however, and Meltzer suggests that the hunter would often become the victim who is "hurled back into a primal state of being," simultaneously "'out of control' yet controlled by thrombotic drums, spine-loosening wails, and horn-shrieks, the untying genital sounds of slurred squealing saxophones."[30]

The allusions to voodoo in *The Land of Jazz* are representative of the dominant Eurocentric understanding of black music during the 1920s and 1930s. Anne Shaw Faulkner asserted a direct link between jazz and voodoo:

> Jazz originally was the accompaniment of the voodoo dancer, stimulating the half-crazed barbarian to the vilest deeds. The weird chant, accompanied by the syncopated rhythm, also has been employed by other barbaric people to stimulate brutality and sensuality.[31]

These examples reflect the atavism that Lola Young observes was a feature of white beliefs about non-white peoples. As Young notes, white texts tended to embody this belief in the figure of the witch doctor.[32] Sidran has attributed the fascination of the white middle class with voodoo to the "get rich quick" sensibility and affluence of the Jazz Age, suggesting that the emotional honesty of black music offered an antidote to the "spiritual vacuity" of post-war America and its growing emphasis on materialism.[33] Yet the spiritual qualities of black music were misinterpreted, and the focus of white interest centered instead on the perceived "hedonism" of jazz permitted by its emotional honesty. In this respect, Sidran argues that white society was merely seeking in jazz a validation of its own intentions, incorrectly perceiving in black culture the hedonistic freedom whites sought for themselves.[34]

The Land of Jazz supports Sidran's claims. Dr. Carruthers is healed of his emotional repression and cold intellectualism by the power of jazz and the shimmy. J.A. Rogers, a white jazz critic of the 1920s, noted this perceived effect of jazz:

The true spirit of jazz is a joyous revolt from convention, custom, authority, boredom, even sorrow—from everything that would confine the soul of man and hinder its riding free on the air . . . . And that is why it has become such a balm for modern ennui, and has become a safety valve for modern machine-ridden and convention-bound society. It is the revolt of the emotions against repression.[35]

Yet the restorative qualities of jazz ultimately result in an orgiastic sequence in which the film's characters lose control of their senses. The bodily abandon of the jazz dance in *The Land of Jazz* reflects the Eurocentric misunderstanding of the function of rhythm as being expressive of sex and cultural primitivism, as discussed by Frith.

Again, this perception of black music was not the construct of Hollywood films alone. The connection of jazz with such themes as voodoo and primitivism could also be found in literature and those white variants of jazz, such as Paul Whiteman's band, which claimed to "improve" the music. A striking literary example can be found in a 1935 Cornell Woolrich short story, "Dark Melody of Madness," also known as "Papa Benjamin." Woolrich is an important figure in terms of the later emergence of film noir. Although the writers of the "hard-boiled" school, such as Raymond Chandler, Dashiell Hammett and James M. Cain, are readily associated with film noir, it is Woolrich's output that has been most extensively adapted into film noir. Born in New York, in 1903, Woolrich's first novels reflected, as Francis M. Nevins has observed, the influence of F. Scott Fitzgerald and the "heightened materialism" of the Jazz Age.[36] *Cover Charge* (1926) and *Children of the Ritz* (1927) contained only hints of the mood of doom and despair that typified his later work and made it so adaptable to film noir. A marked shift in Woolrich's writing took place with the sale of ten crime stories in 1935, one of which was "Dark Melody of Madness." This story concerns a white jazz bandleader, Eddie Bloch, who is in search of a fresh and authentic sound for his music. Eddie attends a ritual in a New Orleans voodoo cult and effectively sells his soul, participating in the ritual in exchange for the music of the cultists. Incorporating the "voodoo" music into his band, he is ultimately hunted down and destroyed by the unnatural forces whose musical secrets he has used. The punishment of the white bandleader is interesting in that it reflects the resentment that many black musicians felt at seeing their musical innovations being stolen by whites and turned to a financial gain unavailable to themselves. The figure who attracted much of this resentment was the white bandleader, Paul Whiteman. Whiteman achieved great success with his approach to "symphonic jazz" and collaborated with George Gershwin. Whiteman's success was frustrating for many black musicians, however, who were unimpressed at his claim that he sought to make a "lady" out of "discordant early jazz" and thus to all intents and purposes was "presenting an appropriated music in heavily diluted form and was successfully selling it as the real thing."[37]

Although "Dark Melody of Madness" punishes the white bandleader for his theft of black music, it is still framed by the Eurocentric reading of jazz as expressing primitivism, sex and immorality. The passage in which Eddie attends the voodoo ritual is particularly worth noting:

> It's a roomful of devils lifted bodily up out of hell. . . . Eddie quickly slips down among them on his haunches and gets busy. He too starts rocking back and forth and pounding the flooring beside him with his knuckles, but he's not in any trance, he's getting a swell new number for his repertoire at Maxim's . . . *Boom-putta-putta-boom!* Young and old, black and tawny, fat and thin, naked and clothed, they pass from right to left, from left to right, in two concentric circles, while the candle flames dance crazily and the shadows leap up and down on the walls. The hub of it all, within the innermost circle of dancers, is an old, old man, black skin and bones . . . . An animal pelt is banded about his middle; he wears a horrible juju mask over his face— a death's head. On one side of him, a squatting woman clacks two gourds together endlessly, that's the "putta" of Eddie's rhythm; on the other, another beats a drum, that's the "boom."[38]

This passage anticipates a later Woolrich novel, which would provide the basis for one of the most striking uses of jazz in a film. The jam session sequence from *Phantom Lady* (1944), adapted from Woolrich's novel with the same name, is discussed at much greater length in the next chapter. Both sequences describe the setting of the music as being "hellish." In *Phantom Lady*, Woolrich establishes the jam session as a "sort of Dante-esque Inferno."[39] Notably, the musical element that Eddie deems worth stealing for his band is the "*boom-putta-putta-boom*" of the drums in the voodoo ritual, thus conforming with the cultural primitivism attached to the rhythms of black music. The stereotype of jazz as "jungle" music was most famously applied to the early Duke Ellington Orchestra for their residency at the Cotton Club, which provided "exotic" black entertainment for an exclusive white clientele in New York during the late 1920s. It was more awkward for the white bands to be described as playing "jungle" music; as such, the label would imply their primitivism, and thus their connection with images of blackness. Instead, the promotion of white orchestras, such as that of Paul Whiteman, often emphasized the fact that they played a "purer" and more "refined" sound, suggesting that their music was more acceptable to the European concert hall.

EARLY JAZZ AND THE BLACK COMMUNITY

We can only guess with what kind of jazz the characters in *The Land of Jazz* would have shimmied themselves into exhaustion. It is highly likely that the music playing on the Victrola machine would not have been "pure" jazz but a watered down, commercial variety. The perception of jazz by those white socialites who typified the Jazz Age was a misguided one, and the word jazz was used instead to describe the spirit of the age, as opposed to an accurate label for its music. Meltzer comments on the irony that the "Flappers of the Jazz Age moved to ersatz jazz; the authentic jazz remained unknown to them," while also acknowledging that the term jazz was appropriated by a middle-class white culture as a "negative moral epithet."[40] In his study of the black activists and organizations that enabled jazz to flourish in the early 1920s, Ted Vincent (1995) observes that there were many in the black community who were keen for jazz to lose its negative connotations. Vincent acknowledges two approaches to jazz by the black community. For some sections, jazz was an embarrassment that undermined their efforts to be accepted by white society.[41] This attitude tended to be strongest among the black upper and middle classes, a view supported by the white jazz writer, James Lincoln Collier. Collier has argued that jazz should not really be considered a black music per se and cautions that it is "important for us to keep in mind that large numbers of blacks were hostile to ragtime, jazz and the blues" during their initial development.[42]

An example of the black middle classes' lukewarm response to early jazz is the brief existence of Black Swan Records, throughout 1921 and 1923, which aimed to promote black artists. Black Swan Records was significantly supported by the National Association for the Advancement of Colored People (NAACP), but its recorded output consisted of few jazz and blues performers:

> The company became a pet project of the prudish Black upper class. The board of directors was dominated by academicians, society matrons and other musical snobs who influenced the workers at the company's recording studios to favor polite-sounding soft blues and swing rather than "hot" jazz, and to emphasize the company's "high-class" concert-music offerings.[43]

The writer, entrepreneur and civil rights activist, Lester Walton, however, took a positive approach to the immoral connotations of black music. Walton opposed the "demeaning lyrics in ragtime songs and 'smut' in Black vaudeville shows," but did not connect the lyrics with the music.[44] In 1913, Walton interviewed the composer Scott Joplin, who had become disillusioned by the degrading of ragtime and noted the embarrassment it caused many in the black community:

> I have often sat in theatres and listened to beautiful ragtime melodies and to almost vulgar words as a song, and I have wondered why some composers will continue to make the public hate ragtime melodies because the melodies are set to such bad words. . . . If someone were to put vulgar words to a strain of one of Beethoven's beautiful symphonies, people would begin saying: "I don't like Beethoven's symphonies." So it is the unwholesome words, and not the ragtime melodies, that many people hate.[45]

The black ragtimers could not be entirely removed from the immoral associations of the music. Russell Davies has noted the high proportion of ragtime pianists who also had successful careers in pimping. Davies cites the observation of the black pianist, James P. Johnson, that "all the best early ragtimers in the South from Baltimore on down were pimps."[46] Walton's response was to clean up ragtime of its unsavory lyrics and promote black music as "dignified music" where he could. Walton later applied the same approach to jazz, writing in his column for *New York Age* that "Syncopation Charms Churchgoers," and enthusing, in a piece from May 1919, that "jazz music is now all *the* rage throughout the United States."[47]

Not all black political groups shared the NAACP's unease with jazz. Marcus Garvey's Universal Negro Improvement Association (UNIA) actively supported jazz and realized that it could form an integral part of their movement. More militant and radical than the NAACP, as expressed by Garvey's calling for the return to Africa, the UNIA made jazz a feature of its events, combining music and politics. Jazz and blues were often incorporated into UNIA marches and could be regularly heard at the UNIA's Liberty Halls, venues run by blacks with the intention of boosting the morale of the black community.

Sidran has also argued that jazz and blues performed a vital function in the black community. Initially, the career of professional musician was not considered reputable by the black middle class, but gradually grew in respectability. In his discussion of the decline of black Christian authority among the black working class at the end of the last century, Sidran suggests that the professional black musician adopted the "socioeconomic role" of the church and became endowed with a "religious spiritualism."[48] These aspects of jazz were not perceived by the majority of white critics at the time. Much of the climate of immorality associated with the Jazz Age stems from the iconography of gangsters, flappers and prohibition: aspects that, Vincent argues, resulted in the decline in fortune of authentic black jazz. Vincent proposes that the end of the Jazz Age, in the true sense of the term (that is, the period in which jazz flourished during the 1920s), can be dated as being "no later than 1926" if one considers the cut-off point to be "the time when the music lost touch with its community."[49] Black-owned performance venues increasingly changed to white ownership and control throughout the latter half of the 1920s. The presence of gangsters was widespread by 1925, and with them came a lasting association between jazz and crime that would not be neglected by Hollywood films:

> Jazz clubs were associated with enough violence to be stereotyped by Hollywood as locales where someone was always throwing someone else through the plate-glass mirror behind the bar, and the reminiscences of the musicians support this image. In his autobiography, Cab Calloway tells how he was

expecting his "big break" in New York when he arrived at the brand-new Plantation Club . . . at which he was the advertised star for the club opening. But rival gangsters, apparently from the Cotton Club, had got inside the Plantation Club and busted up the large mirrors, furniture, ornate bars, etc., making the place useless for a pleasant musical evening.[50]

This negativity surrounding jazz would shape its use and representation in films throughout the sound era. Jazz became a useful means of suggesting a number of sordid and immoral themes that the censorship laws prevented from being explicitly depicted. In *Baby Face* (1933), Barbara Stanwyck plays Lily Powers, a woman who escapes from a life as a prostitute to rise up through the business world by immoral means (as the tag line for the film put it, "She climbed the ladder of success—wrong by wrong!"). In order to secure her advancement in a firm, the film suggests that she offers sexual favors to her employers. Although the Hays Code of censorship regulations would not be introduced until July 1, 1934, the film does not portray Lily's sexual encounters explicitly on-screen. Instead, sex is suggested through a combination of acting and the use of a famous jazz/blues standard on the soundtrack that leaves the audience in little doubt as to what is taking place off-screen.

Trying to secure her employment, Lily flirts with one of the senior workers who is clearly physically attracted to her. Lily persuades the man to take some time off from behind his desk, and the camera cuts to a shot of the front of the office-block building while the W. C. Handy composition "St. Louis Blues" is heard on the soundtrack. The song was well known and remains a popular standard in the jazz repertoire today. Its lyrics ("St. Louis woman, without a care"), although not sung in this scene, would have been familiar to audiences of the day. The association of jazz with sex and immorality would have confirmed for many exactly how Lily was advancing through the business. As if to emphasize the connotations that the film wanted the song to convey, the same technique is reused soon after this scene. Lily is now moving further up the business' chain of command, and the camera cuts to another shot of the office-block, again with "St. Louis Blues" on the soundtrack, before tracking up to a higher floor, suggesting Lily's next promotion.

The association of jazz with immorality ensured its establishment in films as a recognizable code for the seedy and the deviant. In this fashion, the use of jazz did not contradict the values of the classical Hollywood score, as outlined by Claudia Gorbman (1987). Because jazz was a black music, and by implication an inferior music, it would be acceptable for it to be used as the sound of an unfilmed sex scene. This approach to the use of jazz as a sexual metaphor is rooted in racism, but Hollywood films would find other uses for jazz that also maintained its inferiority. It is these uses that I discuss next.

REPRESENTING JAZZ IN THE SWING ERA

As with the Jazz Age, the origins and nature of the Swing Era, an expansive title for a period that flourished between the mid-1930s and mid-1940s, have become mythologized. Part of the myth of the Swing Era is that it burst into existence after a performance by the white Benny Goodman orchestra at the Palomar Ballroom in Los Angeles in 1935. However, as Scott DeVeaux has demonstrated, the socioeconomic and musical changes that enabled swing to become a national craze had been in motion for some time.[51] The majority of the musical changes, principally rhythmic, that became the trademark of the big bands of the Swing Era, stemmed from black bands and musicians. Yet, again, it was the white bands that reaped most of the rewards. The difference with the Jazz Age was that it was less easy for the black elements and influences in the music of the white bands to go unacknowledged. Toward the end of the film *King of Jazz* (1930), a vehicle for Paul Whiteman, Whiteman is seen stirring together the various nationalities and ethnic groups that have contributed to the development of jazz. There are no representatives of black musicians. This total erasure of the vital black presence in jazz became less permissible during the Swing Era.

It was the arrangements of a black musician that would provide the dominant white account of the Swing Era with its "creation myth." The enthusiastic response to a "hot" arrangement of "King Porter Stomp" by the black musician and bandleader Fletcher Henderson was alleged to have given Goodman his breakthrough in 1935. Indeed, the core of the music played by the Goodman orchestra at this time was comprised of Henderson arrangements. Yet it was Goodman, and not the black bands of musicians such as Count Basie and Jimmie Lunceford, who became established as the "King of Swing," a title conferred on him by the white entertainment industry. For DeVeaux, the implications of this use of black arrangements were extensive and far-reaching, helping to break down the unacknowledged racial barriers in the musical repertory:

> White musicians brought the rhythmic sensibility that had for several years been the stock-in-trade of the black dance orchestras to a vast new audience, one at the center of all subsequent dance crazes in the twentieth century: the white adolescent market.[52]

Swing became a national craze and Goodman its iconic figurehead. Additionally, swing was now a burgeoning business. As DeVeaux outlines, within a few years the swing bands were generating close to $100 million dollars a year and employed something like forty thousand musicians in addition to several thousand managers, promoters and others. The upshot was that swing, through the music business, now stretched right across the entertainment industry and thus necessitated a band seeking financial success "to be versatile, responding to widely divergent performing situations."[53] These performing situations included films. Hollywood acknowledged the mass popularity of swing and the possibilities for its exploitation. Many of the leading bands found themselves being incorporated into a film for no other purpose than providing swing fans a reason to see it. The Goodman orchestra, for example, would make a number of appearances in such films as *The Big Broadcast of 1937* (1936) and *Hollywood Hotel* (1937). Goodman was unconsciously creating problems for Hollywood in his decision to work with black musicians, however.

Although there had already been mixed-race bands in America, none of them commanded the coverage of Benny Goodman's. Goodman was on the bandstand, the radio, in films and, most significantly, the classical concert stage when his band appeared at Carnegie Hall in 1938. In his decision to bring the black musicians Teddy Wilson and Lionel Hampton into his small units and on rare occasions the big band as well, Goodman presented Hollywood with a problem as to how these groups could be filmed. Even after the mixed-race Goodman trio and quartet of the mid-to-late '30s, Hollywood refrained from presenting mixed-race bands whenever possible. The 1944 short film *Jammin' the Blues,* a conscious attempt to present jazz simply as it was without any of the traditional Hollywood justifications for it, could not break away from the issue of musicians of different color appearing on screen at the same time. *Jammin' the Blues* featured a predominantly black band (with musicians of the caliber of Lester Young, Jo Jones, Illinois Jacquet and Harry "Sweets" Edison), but it did include one white musician in the form of guitarist Barney Kessel. That was one too many for the studio, however. The film's producer, jazz impresario Norman Granz, had to argue with studio head Jack Warner for Kessel's inclusion in the film, and a solution was reached whereby Kessel was either framed in the shadows or through distorting camera effects so that his whiteness would not be noticeable. Such was the concern over Kessel's appearance alongside the black musicians that when he was filmed in close-up, the studio insisted that his hands be stained with berry juice.[54]

Similarly, *Young Man with a Horn* (1950) faced restrictions from the studio over its representation of a mixed-race band. In one sense, the film could be considered progressive in that the white protagonist, trumpeter Rick Martin (played by Kirk Douglas), is taught to play jazz by a black musician, Art Hazzard (played by Juano Hernandez). Yet pressure from the studio toned down the extent of the film's mixed-race relationships. An interoffice communication from Warner Brothers' employee Steve Trilling to the film's producer, Jerry Wald, outlined the studio's concern at the pre-production stage over the way black and white musicians would be filmed together in the Galba's nightclub sequence:

Stage the interior of GALBA'S on page 55 so that Rick does not sit in and
play with the colored musicians. He might play from the floor or the colored
boys can leave the stand and he play solo on the stand. You understand the
reason for this and we must make the change now so it does not creep into
the script.[55]

In fact, quite significant changes were made to *Young Man with a Horn*.
Originally a novel of the same name by Dorothy Baker, the film departs
from its source in terms of the number of mixed-race relationships. In the
novel, Rick's teacher is black, as is his girlfriend and his closest friend,
Smoke. The teacher-pupil relationship is maintained, but Rick is seen to
surpass his black mentor and become the better trumpeter. In the film, Rick's
close friend, still called Smoke, is changed to a white character played by
the pianist Hoagy Carmichael. More controversial was the suggestion of
miscegenation, which was expressly forbidden by the Hays Production
Code, in Rick's relationship with a black singer. Not surprisingly, this part
was also recast as a white character and was played by Doris Day. The
Production Code's ruling on miscegenation would remain in force until the
1960s, and the slightest suggestion of infraction was subject to scrutiny. The
1955 film noir, *Kiss Me Deadly*, for example, originally featured a scene
in which the white protagonist, Mike Hammer, visits a bar where an "extremely attractive young colored woman" is singing a blues number with
a black jazz band. In the original script, the scene ends with the singer appearing keen to meet with Hammer. She anxiously reminds Hammer that
he had asked her to wait for him, and he touches her cheek as he leaves
the bar.[56] This brief exchange is not included in the finished film, so any
possibility of a romantic or sexual encounter between Hammer and the
black singer is avoided.

When black musicians were allowed to feature in a mainstream Hollywood film, their music was still constructed to be inferior to that of whites.
Sometimes this distinction was subtly inferred in a scene that appeared to
be celebrating black performers. The song and dance sequence "All God's
Chillun' Got Rhythm" from the 1937 Marx Brothers film *A Day at the
Races* provides an interesting example of the tensions at work in the on-
screen representation of black music and performers. This musical sequence,
nearing ten minutes in duration, is an unusually lengthy showcase for black
performers within a mainstream Hollywood film. The sequence takes place
as the Marx Brothers and their love-interest colleagues, on the run from
the authorities, take refuge in the black ghetto. Harpo begins to play a
whistle, a drum starts to beat, and the black community forgets its sorrows
and burst into joyous song. Ivie Anderson, then the vocalist with the Duke
Ellington orchestra, sings the title song, "All God's Chillun' Got Rhythm,"
and the brilliant dance group Whitey's Lindy Hoppers takes center stage
for over a minute.

Despite this apparent celebration of black talent, which Robert Crease notes was acknowledged by the black press—*Amsterdam News* renamed the film "A Day at the (Negro) Races"—a number of racial stereotypes remain in force.[57] In his discussion of the Lindy Hop, and Whitey's Lindy Hoppers in particular, Crease observes that the representation of one of the dancers, Leon James, is "especially troubling."

> James . . . is shown grinning antically and rolling his eyes skyward, Sambo-style. This disturbs because it recalls a stereotype that the Lindy Hoppers precisely were in the process of surpassing. Their dance involved the genuine recovery and celebration of African rhythms and body movements.[58]

As soon as the white authorities arrive, the black performers quickly disappear from the screen. Crease notes that the interaction of black and white performers takes place in a controlled environment. The white actors merely "happen across" the "hot and exciting, but nonthreatening" black performers and can easily leave the ghetto without any consideration. The scene, nevertheless, manages to maintain "a margin of independence and integrity."[59]

Yet, the lyrics of "All God's Chillun' Got Rhythm" prevent the black performers from totally achieving independence from their surroundings. "All God's Chillun' Got Rhythm" perfectly expresses Eurocentric attempts to "explain" the abilities of black musicians and performers. In doing so, it also allows a space for white musicians to have their superiority asserted. The lyrics of the song assert the myth of the innate musical ability of blacks and, as DeVeaux observes, the association of "hot rhythm" with black music. DeVeaux notes the origin of this myth in the Sambo figure, which was further developed through the minstrel era and transformed into the belief that blacks naturally possessed greater sexual prowess and athletic ability. This assumption had an impact on the responses of white audiences to early jazz, which were "more inclined to believe that black bands could authentically deliver the 'hot stuff,' and perhaps were ultimately more comfortable seeing blacks rather than whites engaged in such a subversive activity."[60]

The discomfort of white audiences watching their own race engaged in "subversive" and "hot" dances is still apparent, however, in the film *A Song Is Born* (1948), released when the Swing Era was effectively at an end. In this film, Professor Frisbee, a white musicologist, finally discovers jazz and researches several of its styles by visiting a series of clubs and theatres. Frisbee's field research is presented as a sequence in which he attends performances by the white Tommy Dorsey orchestra, a black spirituals group, the Golden Gate Quartet, the white Charlie Barnet orchestra and a small combo led by the black musicians Louis Armstrong and Lionel Hampton. A comparison of the mise-en-scène in the respective clubs reveals prevailing white concerns about black music. Dorsey's orchestra performs for an all-white audience in a brightly lit, sophisticated ballroom. The clientele wear expensive suits and gowns, and the dancing couples are restrained in their movements. The scene reflects Dorsey's personal ethos for swing, which, he felt, should be relaxed, easy listening for the "most conservative dancer," with no opportunities for "'out-of-the-world'" solo improvisations.[61]

Frisbee then goes to hear the Golden Gate Quartet of black vocalists. The group performs in front of an entirely white audience. The scenes are shot in such a way that Frisbee and the white audience are distanced from the black performers, however. The white audience sits at tables, separated from the black musicians on stage. Frisbee is shown in one shot with the black musicians, but significantly they do not share the same physical space—the black musicians are visible in the shot only through their reflection in a mirror behind Frisbee. Additionally, the Golden Gate Quartet are less threatening as black performers for a white audience through their repertoire of Christian spirituals. The white audience in the club featuring Charlie Barnet's big band is also not seen dancing or particularly approving of the music. The final club Frisbee visits, where Armstrong and Hampton are playing, hosts a predominantly black audience (there are some white females visible, but attention is not drawn to their presence). The club is darkly lit and crowded, and the audience is much more expressive in their enjoyment of the music. As Frisbee enters the club, with a look of astonishment, a section of the audience yells their approval as they move to the music. At one point, Armstrong has a brief exchange with a woman in the audience, where he appears to be flirting with her through his trumpet playing. There is a greater sense of interaction between musicians and audience, unlike the preceding scenes with Dorsey, Barnet and the Golden Gate Quartet. The whole atmosphere feels less repressed than the scenes with the Dorsey orchestra, but clearly conforms to the "natural rhythm" stereotype. This sequence also reflects the unease, referred to by DeVeaux, for a white audience in watching its own race physically moved by black, or black-derived, music.

The myth of innate black musical ability serves to maintain the authority of white culture and society. As Janey Place observes, in her study of women in film noir, "popular culture functions as myth for our society: it both expresses and reproduces the ideologies necessary to the existence of the social structure."[62] Effectively, the "natural rhythm" stereotype, as expressed in *A Day at the Races*, argues that if all God's (black) children possess rhythm simply as a birthright, then the ability of a black musician becomes less challenging for a white audience. Black musical skill is presented as not being achieved through practice, study, individual talent and mental application, but acquired simply by virtue of being born black. It would be for whites to take "raw" and "uneducated" black music and "advance" it to a point that the "simple" and "innocent" black musician could not hope to achieve. Such a view contradicted the efforts of black musicians like Coleman Hawkins. The claim that "all God's chillun' got rhythm" depersonalizes the black performers. The individual voice and unique talents of different black musicians are not acknowledged. Yet, as Richard Dyer suggests in his discussion of the privileging of the white performer by movie lighting, white achievement and talent has been represented and considered to be a result of our individual efforts:

> It is at the least arguable that white society has found it hard to see non-white people as individuals; the very notion of the individual, of the freely developing, autonomous human person, is only applicable to those who are seen to be free and autonomous, who are not slaves or subject peoples.[63]

Similarly, in her analysis of imperialist adventure films, Lola Young refers to Albert Memmi's observation that, "the colonized is never characterized in an individual manner; he is entitled only to drown in an anonymous collectivity. ('They are this.' 'They are all the same.')"[64] This "strategy of depersonalization" is frequently at work in representations of black music through the natural rhythm myth and typifies the Eurocentric ideological framework present in much of Hollywood's output. The song and dance routine in *A Day at the Races* presents a number of dualisms that have become features of Western culture. Drawing on the work of the eco-feminist writer Val Plumwood, Hourihan lists the following set of dualisms:

reason-emotion	mind (soul)-body
civilization-wilderness	male-female
reason-nature	human-nonhuman
order-chaos	master-slave[65]

The "All God's Chillun' Got Rhythm" sequence asserts the physical abilities of the black performers, their emotional and natural expression, and—coupled with the anarchic comedy of the Marx brothers—introduces chaos before the white authorities intervene to bring back a state of order. All of these aspects are, if momentarily celebrated, ultimately cast as being inferior.

Yet ongoing developments in jazz would further complicate its on-screen representation. As jazz continued to gain respectability from musicologists and classical composers, such as Stravinsky and Milhaud, the question of whether it could be considered an art was increasingly debated. Jazz would find itself caught up in another set of binary opposites—art versus entertainment. Put more bluntly, this dualism would set jazz against classical music, an opposition I next discuss.

JAZZ AND CLASSICAL MUSIC GO TO WAR

The swing style of jazz entered the 1940s as a genuinely popular music. By the end of the decade, the Swing Era was over and the big bands had lost their mass audience.[66] Duke Ellington could only maintain his orchestra through the royalties he received from his popular compositions of the 1920s, '30s and '40s. The other leading big bands perished or performed infrequently.[67] Even Goodman, the "King of Swing," had to accept the grim reality of falling ticket sales. Increasingly, many in jazz, such as Stan Kenton, sought the status of art. Krin Gabbard has discussed at length the transition of jazz from being considered popular or folk music to art, and Hollywood's response to this shift.[68] It is beyond the scope of this book to enter into a discussion of jazz's artistic status and whether acquiring it has been wholly beneficial. Roger Taylor has suggested that the desire to classify jazz as an art "proffered misunderstandings of jazz, and has led to the death of jazz as popular experience and to its decline as any kind of developing social process."[69] During the 1930s and 1940s, however, jazz formed a convenient opposition to "serious," classical music, and was often cast as the antithesis of art music. This dualism became a frequent theme of films featuring jazz.

Appearances by jazz musicians in Hollywood films of the 1930s and 1940s tended to be brief and were seldom woven carefully into the narrative. At best they might provide a brief, naturalistic interlude in a scene set in a nightclub. But styles of jazz were also known to make more bizarre and illogical appearances, and this trend was something that the critic and pianist Leonard Feather elicited in his July 1944, "Jazz Symposium" column in *Esquire*. Feather asked a selection of jazz musicians and fans, "If you had a million dollars to spend on jazz, how would you use it?" One response, by Sam Donahue, the leader of a band in the U.S. Navy, demonstrated an all too dissatisfied perception of Hollywood's treatment of jazz per se. Donahue proposed making an educational film, preferably with a black band such as Duke Ellington's:

> I'd tear down the studios' haphazard method of sloughing off good music. Instead of having some chick bursting into song somewhere in the middle of a forest, accompanied by an invisible fifty-piece band from out of space, I'd work the music in logically and give the musicians a break.[70]

Feather bleakly summed up Hollywood's attitude toward jazz, observing that:

> In the movies you find (jazz) all too seldom. The bands that get the biggest film breaks generally aren't jazz outfits and even when they are, their presentation is usually inadequate. As for small groups, Hollywood has virtually ignored them.[71]

For black musicians, this disconnection of jazz from a film's narrative was due in large part to racism. Black performers were divorced from the narrative so that their scenes could simply be cut from a film when it was screened in regions where racism was prevalent. The sequence from *A Day at the Races* is additionally remarkable for the fact that a certain amount of narrative development takes place during the course of the moment of spectacle provided by the black performers. As Crease notes, to cut the entire sequence of the black characters would be to disrupt the film's narrative logic (it is during this sequence that the Marx Brothers discover that their horse is a champion jumper, thus giving them the means by which they can save a threatened hospital).[72] A brief burst of largely irrelevant but good-natured syncopation was thus the extent of most jazz musicians' involvement in the majority of films in which they appeared throughout the 1930s and early 1940s.

The conflict between jazz and classical music was, perhaps, most explicitly portrayed in an earlier film. *Murder at the Vanities* (1934) featured Duke Ellington and his orchestra incurring the murderous wrath of the classical establishment in a production number titled "The Rape of a Rhapsody." Ellington and his musicians invade a symphony orchestra's performance of Liszt's *Second Hungarian Rhapsody*. As the classical piece progresses, the Ellington orchestra begins to add its own version, ultimately taking over the stage as the white symphony musicians leave infuriated. Ellington's band is accompanied by a singer, while a chorus line of black female dancers performs a routine. Ellington's triumph is short-lived, however. The enraged symphony conductor returns with a machine gun and mows down Ellington, his orchestra, his singer and his dancers in a hail of bullets. Ellington is punished for attempting to usurp classical music's throne at the top of the musical hierarchy.

Later Hollywood films of the 1940s would not represent the "rift" between jazz and classical music so graphically. Yet, although he notes Jane Feuer's suggestion that Hollywood often showed how classical music could be improved if it was "jazzed up," Gabbard argues that the motivation for these efforts to portray jazz as art was to suggest the superiority of white swing and not to "redeem" black jazz:

Hollywood has opportunistically appropriated the new idea that jazz is serious art in order to promote the white swing bands with which the movie industry had established a symbiotic relationship. . . . When jazz and swing ceased to be popular in the 1950s, Hollywood no longer had any need to make the claim that Armstrong or any other jazz musician was creating "art."[73]

It is worth noting James Lincoln Collier's reminder that "during the swing period itself, the jazz critics tended to be scornful of the swing bands," acknowledging the occasional "hot solo" as being jazz, but also a "rare gem" in a "vast dross of commerce."[74] In *The Glenn Miller Story* (1954), Miller (played by James Stewart) clearly expresses the distinction between his swing music and Armstrong's jazz. Participating in a jam session with Armstrong and his All Stars band, Miller admits afterward that he cannot compete with Armstrong "when it comes to playing jazz." Armstrong's musical talent is acknowledged, but the music of Glenn Miller's white orchestra, which achieved great popularity with white audiences, is also subtly distanced from its black connections.

In the 1940s, however, the notion of an art discourse for jazz was desirable for a number of Hollywood films. The entry of America into the Second World War saw an effort by Hollywood to make the "serious" arts more accessible to the masses, and jazz was one of the methods employed to achieve this effect:

> One of the most extraordinary things about the Second World War was that it actually made culture patriotic. The arts, by some mysterious process, suddenly became a vitally important part of what we were supposed to be fighting for . . . of course, in order to be accepted in this way, they had to be democratized and humanized—a process that usually found its way to the screen in the form of embarrassingly coy disputes on Bach versus Boogie.[75]

The need for Hollywood to present a united front during the Second World War also meant that many black performers were granted significantly more coverage than they had previously been accorded, as Donald Bogle asserts:

> USO troupes were entertaining the boys overseas while at home the black entertainers stated through their song and dance that America was indeed a good and decent country full of joy and unity, a place well worth fighting for.[76]

If jazz was used to make America appear "good and decent," then jazz had to appear to be good and decent as well. But rather than allowing jazz to be represented on its own terms, Hollywood films tended to discuss the merits of jazz by comparing them with those of a completely different aesthetic. In this comparison, the values of the white European tradition would consistently be favored over those of black American music.

Arguably the most successful and least embarrassing film to humanize classical music was Disney's *Fantasia* (1940). *Fantasia* contained a series of animations that were underscored by a symphony orchestra, conducted by Leopold Stokowski, playing famous classical pieces. Thus, Stravinsky's *The Rite of Spring* underscores an animation depicting the rise and fall of the dinosaurs, and, perhaps most famously, Dukas' *The Sorcerer's Apprentice* turns out to be none other than Mickey Mouse. The animation pieces are linked by a kindly, academic voice-over offering us information on what we are about to hear over images of the orchestra as silhouetted figures. The musicians remain faceless shadows to us. The audience has no idea as to the identity of the players or how they look in concert.

The only sense of "character" they are given is in a brief moment when jazz, once again, sneaks into the concert hall. As the musicians pause and tune their instruments between performances, one of the clarinets impishly starts to play the tune "Bach Goes to Town," an early example of "jazzing the classics," and a tune made famous by, among others, Benny Goodman. The other musicians laugh as the clarinetist plays, and soon a double bass joins him, followed by a vibraphonist and strings. This infectious "jam session" soon peters out, but its brief message is significant. It demonstrates to the audience that these musicians aren't serious *all* the time. They can have fun as well! The implication for jazz is that it is seen as an antidote to serious music. It is also merely a momentary aberration. The conductor's baton brings it to an end, and the announcer's voice-over laughs, embarrassed, as if to say, "ahem, well, that's enough playing around. Let's get back to the serious stuff."

Later, films that gave jazz musicians a greater focus also maintained the notion that jazz was not as serious as classical music. *A Song Is Born* (1948) concerns the efforts of a group of serious musicologists, led by Professor Frisbee (Danny Kaye), to come to terms with jazz and popular music. Frisbee's field of interest is folk music, and he suddenly realizes that, while he and his colleagues have been shut inside the Totten Institute for Musicology, music has changed. Frisbee leaves the institute to conduct field research in nightclubs, bars and theaters, a sequence discussed earlier in this chapter. Frisbee organizes a jam session and seminar on the "history of jazz" at the institute between the various musicians he has encountered and his colleague, Professor Magenbruch. The other musical academics are not allowed to attend. Frisbee is concerned that it may prove "too much" for them. As they are left in their study, one of the musicologists mutters, "Oh I wish we could go too," and the academics sound like children who have not been invited to a party.

The jam session develops with jazz musicians Mel Powell and Lionel Hampton informing Professor Magenbruch that they don't use any music and haven't got anything written down. Magenbruch protests—how can they play without music? Hampton calmly reassures him that that is the way Benny Goodman plays, but Magenbruch has never heard of the jazz clarinetist. The joke here is that Professor Magenbruch *is* Benny Goodman. Goodman's bespectacled, bookish looks and his renown as a musician who practiced obsessively made him the perfect choice for the "restrained" professor. Joining in with Powell and Hampton, Goodman/Magenbruch unleashes a full-blooded clarinet solo that makes the other musicians, Armstrong included, sit up and listen. As Magenbruch plays, the emotionally introspective academic disappears and is replaced by a grinning, foot-stomping musician. Jazz is clearly connected here to loss of constraint and control. It is, however joyously, impulsive and subversive and a relinquishment of the intellect. Magenbruch has had no training in jazz, and his sudden ability to improvise perpetuates the myth of the jazz performer as being a natural musician. Jazz cannot be taught—it is an instinctive gift.

The film has already made the same point in a more patronizing manner. Two black window cleaners, played by the dance duo Buck and Bubbles, enter the institute to ask the professors' help with a competition in which they are trying to identify the title of a number of classical pieces. One of the window cleaners is able to reproduce on the piano, in boogie-woogie style, everything the musicologists play to him. Both cleaners are portrayed as being devoid of musical theory or training, and the spectator is led to believe that their exceptional playing and improvising must come from some mysterious, innate source.

The characters of the window cleaners are based on racist perceptions. An earlier version of the screenplay for *A Song Is Born*, dated May 23, 1947, is significantly different in its characterization of the window washers. In this earlier draft there is only one window washer and there is nothing in the script to suggest that he is black. As in the finished film, the window washer plays several styles of jazz piano and amazes the professors with this music that they have never heard. After the window washer has completed his recital, the professors enthuse to each other about its musical merits. The scene as filmed and the draft of the script differ in the window washer's musical knowledge, however. In the May 23 draft, the window washer is a more vociferous character, able to express his opinion on the various forms of jazz. Most notably, the window washer as originally scripted leaves the professors having had the last laugh at their expense. Frisbee and his colleagues discuss the window washer's piano playing and are put in their place. Frisbee suggests that the contrapuntal style of the boogie-woogie piano is akin to that of a Bach fugue, but the window washer corrects him. Informing Frisbee that he has made a common error, the window washer goes on to comment in musicological terms that his music is actually founded on a simple harmonic structure and not the "highly intellectual" form of the canon or fugue. With that, the window washer bids the professors goodbye, leaving them astonished at his playing and knowledge of musical language.[77]

By the time this scene came to be filmed, however, the window washer character had transformed into two cleaners played by Buck and Bubbles. The characters are not allowed to demonstrate any musical knowledge at all or "put one over" the musicologists, unlike the window washer in the earlier draft of the scene. When the musicologists rave over Buck and Bubbles' music, the two washers don't understand what they are talking about. ("I didn't play all that, did I?" asks one. "He's just playing boogie-woogie," says the other.) Later, when the jazz musicians attend the institute, the white musicologist, Frisbee, provides a history of the development of jazz. Unlike *King of Jazz* (1930), which denied the role of black musicians in jazz, this history acknowledges black efforts while still suggesting that it is the white swing musicians who have advanced the music. Two aspects are important here. The first is the tendency, noted by Shohat and Stam, for Hollywood films to "explain" jazz through a white spokesperson. This practice, Shohat and Stam argue, clearly reproduces the "colonialist discourse by which Europe serves as global impresario or stage manager, while non-European cultures remain the raw material for the entertainment industry."[78] Also evident is the notion, identified by Young in her analysis of *The Song of Freedom* (1936), that black culture requires the "refinement of European training" to become "fully cultured and thus acceptable."[79] Although the window washer scene reveals the brilliant playing of a black musician, he is not granted an awareness or understanding of what he is doing. He just does it. Even if the scene had been filmed as it was originally scripted, it would still have asserted that jazz was built on a "very simple harmonic framework" and was not "highly intellectual." In this meeting of jazz and classical music, jazz may be more fun, but it is still inferior.

Peter Martin has discussed how improvisation, which is crucial to jazz, has acquired its mythic status and argues an alternative sociological model of its production. Martin notes that, viewed from a classical perspective, improvisation in jazz has tended to be seen as:

> . . . a gift given only to a few individuals, a "somewhat mystical art," as Tirro puts it, but not one who could or should be incorporated into either established performance conventions or aesthetic theories. Indeed, Bailey suggests that the term 'improvisation' has acquired largely negative connotations among orthodox musicians: ". . . something without preparation and without consideration, a completely ad hoc activity, frivolous and inconsequential, lacking in design and method."[80]

A Song Is Born celebrates jazz, but also confirms for the audience that it is a music with no claims to seriousness and therefore artistic legitimacy. The film refers to several jazz styles, but favors swing, even though swing was losing its status as the leading style of jazz when the film was made. The emerging idiom of bebop is referred to briefly, in name only, by the window washers, and none of its exponents are featured in the "history of jazz" seminar scene. The possible reasons for the lack of attention given to bebop by Hollywood films are discussed in Chapter 3.

In *Mildred Pierce* (1945), jazz is used as a means of showing the depths to which a character has sunk from her refined, classical training. Michael Curtiz directed *Mildred Pierce* as a powerful combination of film noir and domestic melodrama. The film is essentially concerned with attitudes toward working women. Mildred (an Oscar-winning performance by Joan Crawford) is a housewife who spoils her eldest daughter Veda. Veda grows up expecting to get whatever she wants and is full of snobbish attitudes. She uses her smattering of French and classical piano as a means of patronizing her mother and asserting her superiority over her. When Mildred leaves her husband, she is forced to take a job as a waitress in order to support herself and her family and Veda's excessive material demands. Veda is disgusted and ashamed to discover that her mother has turned to waitress work. Later in the film, her ex-husband, Bert, takes Mildred to a dingy nightclub so that she can see Veda, now singing to the "syncopated rhythm" of a small jazz combo. Veda is dressed in a Latin/Hawaiian outfit and moves saucily across the stage. She is obviously there as a source of titillation for the predominantly male audience and not for any great musical virtue. She is also working as a vocalist. The irony is clear: Veda disowned her mother for becoming a working woman, and now she herself is working for a living. Not only that but she is a singer in a jazz group, a clear "fall" given her classical piano background. Veda's music, jazz, is work; it therefore is not art, unlike the classical music she once played. This reflects the claims of Theodor Adorno and his assertion that jazz, in the 1920s and 1930s, was a functional music and not an autonomous or absolute music of the mind.[81] Curtiz is careful not to have Veda fronting a pure jazz group, but there is nevertheless an association of cheapness and sex with jazz. Disgusted at what she has seen and heard, Mildred tries to lure Veda back with the offer of a new piano so that she can return to her "acceptable" classical music.

Mildred Pierce was an early film noir that utilized jazz in a nightclub setting.[82] As one of the principal locations of film noir, the nightclub offered an excellent opportunity for jazz to appear sensibly and naturalistically in a Hollywood film, instead of the "haphazard method" described in Leonard Feather's *Esquire* article. The kind of jazz that would be heard in the nightclubs of the films noir was still a matter for consideration, however, and one in which the myths and ideological concerns discussed in this chapter would be involved. The style chosen, particularly in early and mid-era film noir, tended to emphasize "hot jazz." This style focused on the rhythmic qualities of jazz and thus, stereotypically, its sexual element. It is on this development that I concentrate in the next chapter.

NOTES

1. Dyer, R. 1997. *White*. London: Routledge. pp. 14–18.
2. Ibid., p. 17.
3. Young, L. 1996. *Fear of the Dark: 'Race,' Gender and Sexuality in the Cinema*. London: Routledge. p. 41.
4. Martin, P. 1995. *Sounds & Society: Themes in the Sociology of Music*. Manchester: Manchester University Press. p. 36.

5. Althusser, L. 1992. Ideology and ideological state apparatuses. In A. Easthope and K. McGowan, eds. *A Critical and Cultural Theory Reader*. Buckingham: Open University Press. pp. 50–58. (Originally published in 1970.)

6. Martin, P. 1995. *Sounds & Society: Themes in the Sociology of Music*. Manchester: Manchester University Press. pp. 67–68.

7. Young, L. 1996. *Fear of the Dark: 'Race,' Gender and Sexuality in the Cinema*. London: Routledge. p. 41.

8. Ibid., pp. 56–57.

9. Shohat, E. and Stam R. 1994. *Unthinking Eurocentrism: Multiculturalism and the Media*. London: Routledge. pp. 100–136. Also, Young, L. 1996. *Fear of the Dark: 'Race,' Gender and Sexuality in the Cinema*. pp. 55–83.

10. Ibid., pp. 108–9.

11. Frith, S. 1996. *Performing Rites: Evaluating Popular Music*. Oxford: Oxford University Press. p. 141.

12. Hourihan, M. 1997. *Deconstructing the Hero: Literary Theory and Children's Literature*. London: Routledge. pp. 16–17.

13. Frith, S. 1996. *Performing Rites: Evaluating Popular Music*. Oxford: Oxford University Press. p. 125.

14. Meltzer, D., ed. 1993. *Reading Jazz*. San Francisco: Mercury House. pp. 121–23. Faulkner's article was originally included in *The Journal of the Century*, an undated work from the 1920s, compiled by Bryan Holme and the editors of The Viking Press and the *Ladies' Home Journal*. It is reprinted in *Reading Jazz*.

15. Ibid., pp. 111–2. Gorky's article, "O Musyke Tolstykh," comes from an undated issue of *Pravda*. It is included in Meltzer's collection of writing from the Jazz Age of the 1920s.

16. Frith, S. 1996. *Performing Rites: Evaluating Popular Music*. Oxford: Oxford University Press. p. 143.

17. Ibid., p. 127.

18. Sidran, B. 1995. *Black Talk: How the Music of Black America Created a Radical Alternative to the Values of Western Literary Tradition*. Edinburgh: Payback Press. p. 8.

19. Ibid., p. 9.

20. Ibid.

21. Bywater, M. 1997. If Only the King Were Dead, *The Independent on Sunday*, August 17.

22. Frith, S. 1996. *Performing Rites: Evaluating Popular Music*. Oxford: Oxford University Press. p. 157.

23. Gabbard, K. 1996. *Jammin' at the Margins: Jazz and the American Cinema*. Chicago: University of Chicago Press. p. 143.

24. DeVeaux, S. 1997. *The Birth of Bebop: A Social and Musical History*. Berkeley and Los Angeles: University of California Press. p. 103.

25. Ibid., p. 65. Tenor saxophonist Budd Johnson, quoted by DeVeaux.

26. Firestone, R. 1993. *The Life and Times of Benny Goodman*. London: Hodder & Stoughton. p. 70.

27. Lack, R. 1997. *Twenty Four Frames Under: A Buried History of Film Music*. London: Quartet Books. pp. 44–5.

28. Undated screenplay for *The Land of Jazz*. Scene 167. Arts Special Collections, UCLA.

29. Undated screenplay for *The Land of Jazz*. Scene 159–61. Arts Special Collections, UCLA.

30. Meltzer, D., ed. 1993. *Reading Jazz*. San Francisco: Mercury House. pp. 22–3.

31. Ibid, pp. 121–23.

32. Young, L. 1996. *Fear of the Dark: 'Race,' Gender and Sexuality in the Cinema*. p. 80.

33. Sidran, B. 1995. *Black Talk: How the Music of Black America Created a Radical Alternative to the Values of Western Literary Tradition*. Edinburgh: Payback Press. p. 55.

34. Ibid., p. 54.

35. Ibid., pp. 53–54. This comment was made in Rogers' article "Jazz at Home," *Survey,* March 1, 1925.

36. Nevins Jr., F.M. 1981. The Poet of the Shadows: Cornell Woolrich. In C. Waugh and M. Greenberg, eds. *The Fantastic Stories of Cornell Woolrich*. Carbondale and Edwardsville: Southern Illinois University Press. pp. vii–xxvi.

37. Sidran, B. 1995. *Black Talk: How the Music of Black America Created a Radical Alternative to the Values of Western Literary Tradition*. Edinburgh: Payback Press. p. 69.

38. Woolrich, C. 1935. Dark melody of madness. In Waugh and Greenberg (1981: 44). (Originally published in 1935.)

39. Woolrich, C. (writing as William Irish). 1982. *Phantom Lady*. New York: Ballantine Books. p. 135. (Originally published in 1942.)

40. Meltzer, D., ed. 1993. *Reading Jazz*. San Francisco: Mercury House. p. 74.

41. Vincent, T. 1995. *Keep Cool: The Black Activists Who Built the Jazz Age*. London: Pluto Press.

42. Collier, J.L. 1993. *Jazz: The American Theme Song*. New York: Oxford University Press. p. 203.

43. Vincent, T. 1995. *Keep Cool: The Black Activists Who Built the Jazz Age*. London: Pluto Press. p. 93.

44. Ibid., p. 38.

45. Ibid., p. 39.

46. Davies cites Johnson's comment in episode three of his radio series, *Jazz Century,* broadcast January 16, 1999 at 18:00, BBC Radio 3.

47. Vincent, T. 1995. *Keep Cool: The Black Activists Who Built the Jazz Age*. London: Pluto Press. p. 42.

48. Sidran, B. 1995. *Black Talk: How the Music of Black America Created a Radical Alternative to the Values of Western Literary Tradition*. Edinburgh: Payback Press. p. 38.

49. Vincent, T. 1995. *Keep Cool: The Black Activists Who Built the Jazz Age*. London: Pluto Press. p. 174.

50. Ibid., pp. 176–77.

51. DeVeaux, S. 1997. *The Birth of Bebop: A Social and Musical History*. Berkeley and Los Angeles: University of California Press. pp. 116–20. An excellent overview of the origins of the Swing Era.

52. Ibid., p. 123–4.

53. Ibid., p. 127.

54. Kington, M. 1993. *The Jazz Anthology*. London: Harper Collins. pp. 200–1. Barney Kessel's account of his experiences on *Jammin' the Blues* are quoted by

Kington. Alternatively, see Arthur Knight's excellent essay "Jammin' the Blues, or the Sight of Jazz, 1944," in Gabbard, K. ed. 1995. *Representing Jazz*. Durham and London: Duke University Press. pp. 11–53.

55. Interoffice communication from Steve Trilling to Jerry Wald, March 11, 1947. Box 29: *Young Man with a Horn*, Jack L. Warner Collection, Special Collections, USC Cinema and Television Library.

56. Original, undated, screenplay for *Kiss Me Deadly* by A.I. Bezzerides. p. 96. Arts Special Collections, UCLA.

57. Crease, R. 1995. Divine frivolity: Hollywood representations of the lindy hop, 1937–1942. In K. Gabbard, ed. *Representing Jazz*. Durham and London: Duke University Press. p. 215.

58. Ibid.

59. Ibid., p. 216.

60. DeVeaux, S. 1997. *The Birth of Bebop: A Social and Musical History*. Berkeley and Los Angeles: University of California Press. p. 124.

61. DeVeaux, S. 1997. *The Birth of Bebop: A Social and Musical History*. Berkeley and Los Angeles: University of California Press. p. 150.

62. Place, J. 1978. "Women in Film Noir," in E. Ann Kaplan, ed. *Women in Film Noir*. London: BFI. p. 35.

63. Dyer, R. 1997. *White*. London: Routledge. p. 102.

64. Young, L. 1996. *Fear of the Dark: 'Race,' Gender and Sexuality in the Cinema*. London: Routledge. p. 80.

65. Hourihan, M. 1997. *Deconstructing the Hero: Literary Theory and Children's Literature*. London: Routledge. p. 17.

66. For a good account of the decline of the big bands see Stowe, D. 1994. *Swing Changes: Big Band Jazz in New Deal America*. Cambridge, Mass.: Harvard University Press. pp. 180–220.

67. Count Basie's orchestra briefly disbanded in 1950. Benny Goodman also stopped touring that year, only to reform his orchestra for specific projects.

68. Gabbard, K., ed. 1996: *Jammin' at the Margins: Jazz and the American Cinema*. Chicago: The University of Chicago Press. pp. 101–37.

69. Taylor, R. 1993. Art an enemy of the people, in Meltzer, D., ed. *Reading Jazz*. San Francisco: Mercury House. pp. 122–37. (Originally published in 1978.)

70. Knight, A. 1995. "Jammin' the Blues, or the Sight of Jazz," 1944. In K. Gabbard, ed. *Representing Jazz*. Durham and London: Duke University Press. pp. 11–12.

71. Ibid., p. 27.

72. Crease, R. 1995. Divine frivolity: Hollywood representations of the lindy hop. In K. Gabbard, ed. *Representing Jazz*. Durham and London: Duke University Press. pp. 214–15.

73. Gabbard, K., ed. 1996: *Jammin' at the Margins: Jazz and the American Cinema*. Chicago: The University of Chicago Press. p. 122.

74. Collier, J.L. 1993. *Jazz: The American Theme Song*. New York: Oxford University Press. p. 174.

75. Taylor, J.R. 1983. *Strangers in Paradise*. London: Faber & Faber Ltd. p. 208.

76. Bogle, D. 1994. *Toms, Coons, Mulattoes, Mammies and Bucks: An Interpretive History of Blacks in American Film*. Oxford: Roundhouse. p. 121.

77. Revised screenplay for *A Song is Born*, May 23, 1947, pp. 12–14. Arts Special Collections, UCLA.

78. Shohat, E., and Stam, R. 1994. *Unthinking Eurocentrism: Multiculturism and the Media.* London: Routledge. p. 227.

79. Young, L. 1996. *Fear of the Dark: 'Race,' Gender and Sexuality in the Cinema.* London: Routledge, p. 76.

80. Martin, P. 1996. *Improvisation in Jazz: Towards a Sociological Model.* Manchester: Manchester Sociology Occasional Paper no. 45, p. 2.

81. Adorno's discussion of the jazz of this period is seriously flawed. In his study of the sociology of music, Peter Martin notes that it is clear that by "jazz" Adorno "did not mean the improvised music which emerged from the African-American tradition but rather the 'essentially commercialised mass music' of the 1920s and 1930s." Martin suggests that in writing his 1936 essay on jazz (written in England) it is doubtful whether Adorno "had paid much attention to the work of the early soloists." Martin, P. 1995. *Sounds & Society: Themes in the Sociology of Music.* Manchester: Manchester University Press. p. 97.

82. Tuska, J. 1984. *Dark Cinema: American Film Noir in Cultural Perspective.* Westport, Conn.: Greenwood Press. p. 195. One of the first noirs to make a significant use of jazz was *Street of Chance* (1942) directed by Jack Hively and based on a Cornell Woolrich story. Tuska notes that the use of jazz in this film and *Phantom Lady* heightens their sense of noir: "both films are notable for the effective use they make of jazz music on the soundtrack and jazz musicians as a grotesque and even threatening manifestation of big city life."

3

Absolutely Functional?

Jazz in 1940s Film Noir

The early part of the 1940s saw jazz musicians still typecast as popular entertainers and a convenient "other" to "serious" musicians. Yet not all jazz musicians were content with being seen as entertainers, and many were keen to promote their music as legitimate art instead of light entertainment. When those films that would eventually be termed films noir began to emerge in the early 1940s, however, Hollywood found a darker use for jazz that offered to free its musicians from the entertainer syndrome. With particular reference to *Phantom Lady* (1944), *The Asphalt Jungle* (1950), *D.O.A.* (1950) and *Young Man with a Horn* (1950), I argue that, although jazz and the "jazz life" made for a potentially strong noir theme, the conventions of '40s film noir still prevented jazz from being portrayed positively. The development of the modernist jazz style bebop in the early and mid-1940s contributed to a growing intellectualization of jazz, but, as I discuss, Hollywood was slow to reflect this change, and bebop would be absent from film soundtracks until the 1950s.

JAZZ AS SEXUAL METAPHOR IN *PHANTOM LADY*

As I noted at the end of the previous chapter, the nightclub setting, which was a consistent feature of film noir, enabled jazz to be included in a film in such a way that made narrative sense. The nightclub often functioned as a location of potential sexual transgression. On a number of occasions, jazz was used to further the suggestion of sexual immorality in a site of desire and temptation. The jazz cellar scene in *Phantom Lady* (1944), from Cornell Woolrich's 1942 novel of the same name, is probably the most extreme example of jazz as sexual metaphor in film noir. Robert Siodmak, the director, intercuts shots of the drummer's masturbatory playing with the silent desire of the film's heroine to create a sequence that is, critic Tom Flinn argues, not simply the most striking scene in the film alone:

> [the jazz scene in *Phantom Lady*] ranks as one of the most effective bits of cinema produced in the 1940s. Siodmak gives full reign to his expressionistic propensities in a rhythmically cut riot of angles that "climaxes" in a drum solo that melds sex and music into a viable metaphor of tension and release.[1]

Phantom Lady makes little use of music, and that which is employed is mostly diegetic. The film's opening and closing orchestral title music, credited to Hans Salter, is upbeat and jaunty, certainly not noirish or even thrilling, and suggests nothing of the tale of murder and psychosis to come. The lack of music in the film was a deliberate strategy by Siodmak, who had decided to "tell the story in large part through implication and mood, rather than by action and dialogue alone."[2] This tactic gives the unbridled appearance of the jam session even greater impact and a heightened sense of release for the audience after the tension that Siodmak has tautly constructed through silence or sound effects. Indeed, the film's official press book noted that more than half of *Phantom Lady* was completely devoid of sound effects or dialogue.[3] *Variety* gave the film a positive review and drew attention to Siodmak's unusual approach to sound and music as contributing to the film's overall success.[4] The *New York Times*, however, was not impressed by the film, commenting that:

> some aptly sensational settings background the whole affair. But sensation is specious without reason. And reason is what this picture lacks.[5]

Without doubt, the jazz cellar is the film's most "sensational" setting. The sudden burst of jazz is vividly at variance with the film's silence and its characters that frequently repress their true feelings for each other.

The sequence occurs as Kansas (Ella Raines), a secretary for an engineer, is tracking down the witnesses who will be able to free her employer from jail and the charge of murder. Kansas is allowed an unusually proactive role for a female character and even, as Tony Williams notes, usurps "that prerogative which Mulvey associates with male-dominated cinema—the sadistic power of the gaze," as she hunts one witness to his death.[6] Less sadistic, but just as domineering, is Kansas' pursuit of a second witness, a trap drummer called Cliff (played with characteristic seediness by Elisha Cook Jr.). Kansas adopts the manners and appearance of a "loose woman" in order to pick him up and gain the information that she and her employer desperately need. Meeting Kansas after the show in which he performs, Cliff asks her, "D'you like jive?" to which Kansas responds, "You bet. I'm a hep kit!" The change in Kansas is dramatic, and it is clear that it is a role that is completely alien to her serious and sophisticated persona that the film has hitherto established. Leading her downstairs, Cliff opens the door to a cellar revealing a world with which Kansas is obviously uncomfortable: a quintet of musicians (string bass, piano, trumpet, trombone and clarinet) in the midst of a full-blooded jam session on a driving blues theme. The sequence begins by outlining the intensity and abandon with which the musicians play and Kansas' distaste and disorientation. Nevertheless, she is also aware of her role as Cliff's "girl" and forces herself to appear as if she is enjoying the proceedings.

The sequence reflects the atmosphere of the relevant passage in Woolrich's novel:

> The next two hours were a sort of Dante-esque Inferno. She knew as soon as it was over she wouldn't believe it had actually been real at all. It wasn't the music, the music was good. It was the phantasmagoria of their shadows, looming black, wavering ceiling-high on the walls. It was the actuality of their faces, possessed, demonic, peering out here and there on sudden notes, then seeming to recede again. It was the gin and marihuana cigarettes, filling the air with haze and flux.[7]

As in his short story "Dark Melody of Madness," discussed in the previous chapter, Woolrich's protagonist is both fascinated and repelled by jazz. Although the music itself is described as being "good," its setting and effect is "demonic" and the suggestion of the occult, very much a feature of "Dark Melody of Madness," is present.

Kansas looks shocked upon first entering the cellar, and disgusted when Cliff kisses her, but remembers her "act" and smiles when Cliff touches her neck and encourages her into the room. She looks further misplaced when a clarinet nearly pokes her in the face.

After kissing Cliff, she applies some lipstick and looks into a mirror, where she appears shocked and shakes her head in surprise at the person she sees reflected there. In her "loose woman" guise, surrounded by the insistent music, which features stomping piano bass lines, Raines suggests her character's difficulty in recognizing herself and her disbelief at what she seems to have become. It is after this mirror scene that the most dramatic and overtly sexual part of the sequence begins.

The suggestion of sexual desire has been present from the outset of the sequence. When Cliff begins a drum solo, Kansas is instrumental in encouraging him, driving his arms faster and faster. Although it is Cliff's drum solo, it is Kansas who is in control, goading him, standing dominant over him as he sweats and struggles at the drum kit, desperate to keep up with her. Siodmak cuts between shots of Cliff's drumming as it grows in intensity and shots of Kansas, filmed from a low angle so that she appears to be towering above Cliff, as she laughs silently and mimes tugging Cliff toward her. Cliff is completely in her power, compelled to drum, and it is only when Kansas nods her head to the door and narrows her eyes that she gives him the release to leave the drums. It is a powerful sequence, with its sexual undertones barely hidden, and it remains one of the most striking metaphors for sexual desire in film. It is possible that, although jazz would seldom be featured so graphically in this way again, our contemporary perception of jazz's involvement with film noir stems from here.

The film received mixed reviews. There was widespread praise for Ella Raines' portrayal of Kansas, but the jazz sequence was also singled out as one of the film's most notable aspects. *Motion Picture Daily* described the use of jazz as "unique," and *The Hollywood Reporter* remarked that "that short sequence of a hide-out jam session is unforgettably new to films."[8] The jam session was not identified as being a particularly fertile source of exploitation for marketing the film. Instead, the press book suggested that the focus should be on the *Phantom Lady* "fashion," especially the film's plot device of the "hat of horror" that identifies the woman who can clear the name of Kansas' employer.[9] In terms of the music, it was the song "Chick-Ee-Chee" (referred to as "Chick-Ee-Chick" in the official press book) that was considered to have the most commercial potential:

> Ghost Dances Tune to Jive
> Although *Phantom Lady* . . . is a foreboding and moody mystery drama, it introduces an exciting jive tune. The "you-send-me" piece, titled "Chick-Ee-Chick," is sung by Aurora, Brazilian newcomer to Hollywood films. Music is by Jacques Press, lyrics by Eddie Cherkose.[10]

The music in the jam session is not similarly identified, and it is noticeable that the music heard there is not promoted as music in itself, but rather, in terms of its tone and connotations. The film's publicists appear to have been fully aware of the originality of the jazz sequence, and the official press book refers to the "'jive' sequence" as "one of the wildest scenes recently put on the screen."[11] Given the level of attention that it received, it is perhaps not surprising that the sexual connotations of the jazz sequence were identified by the board of censors as meriting their attention.

The jazz cellar scenes were subjected to close scrutiny by the Production Code Administration (PCA) and were perceived as being potentially controversial at the script stage before filming began. There was a significant amount of correspondence between Maurice Pivar of Universal Pictures and Joseph Breen, then Director of the PCA. The song "Chick-ee-Chee" had to have its lyrics vetted, and there was some concern over the sexual nature of much of the dialogue and the amount of drinking referred to in the script.[12] The most specific warnings from Breen and the PCA concerned the jazz sequence.

In a memo dated September 3, 1943, Breen commented to Pivar that the sequence in the jazz cellar (which was described on pages 64 to 67 of the screenplay) should be "handled with the greatest care" so that it was clear that Cliff and his fellow musicians were not drug addicts.[13] The depiction of drug use was expressly forbidden by the PCA. It was still ten years before Otto Preminger's *The Man with the Golden Arm* (1955) would challenge the PCA with its graphic (for the time) portrayal of a heroin addict and be denied a PCA seal of approval for doing so. Woolrich's novel is quite open in its account of the presence of narcotics at the jam session, and Cliff is "already doped with marihuana" before his drumming is complete:

There was a battered wooden table in the middle, and they put bottles of gin on it, nearly one to a man. One of them spread a piece of brown wrapping-paper out and dumped quantities of cigarettes onto it, for anyone to help themselves at will. Not the kind the world upstairs smoked; black-filled things; reefers, she heard them call them.[14]

In the film, however, the final realization of the jazz sequence avoids any on-screen suggestion of drug use by the musicians, although Siodmak's riotous direction and cutting could be interpreted as suggestion enough. Yet, the inference that Cliff is a drug addict seems to be one that the film was determined to make. When Cliff takes Kansas to his tawdry room in the scene immediately following the jam session, Kansas expresses her disgust at his living quarters. Cliff responds that "it's just a room." When Kansas counters that she is surprised at the state of the room because of "all the money" that he makes, Cliff darkly says, "my money goes on other things." The audience is given no clues as to what these "other things" might be, except for the fact that Cliff is a jazz musician with a liking for liquor and loose women. This information is clearly felt by Siodmak and his scriptwriter to be enough to imply that the "other things" are drugs, a reflection of the already common association of jazz with drug use.

Breen also stressed the need to be cautious with the representation of Cliff and Carol's (the original name of the character in Woolrich's novel who would become Kansas) relationship. Particular attention was to be given to Carol's dancing during the jam session "to avoid any offensive sex suggestiveness."[15] The sexual undertones of this scene and their potential appearance on screen were clearly evident in the screenplay, and Breen again, in a later memo of September 16, 1943, referred Pivar to the jam session and Carol/Kansas' dancing, noting that there should be "no offensive movements of her body at any time."[16] Pivar, Siodmak and the rest of the *Phantom Lady* cast and crew honored the wishes of Breen and the PCA, but only up to a point. The final cut of the jazz sequence contains no dancing by Kansas, and it is made clear that she finds Cliff and his surroundings distasteful and is only pretending to enjoy herself in order to get the information that she seeks. Siodmak found other ways of investing the sequence with a sexual element, however; namely, through the drum solo. It is quite possible that the focus of the PCA on the movement of the female body and the request that her dancing be eradicated forced Siodmak to turn his attention to the potential of the drums. Had the sequence developed as the screenplay intended, with Kansas dancing provocatively, its emphasis would have been on the effect of Cliff's music on *her*. Shot as it was, the scene became far more subversive: it is Kansas who dictates the flow of the music and at what point Cliff can cease to drum. The scene is about her effect on Cliff, and she maintains her control.

As Tony Williams acknowledges, Kansas is arguably recuperated at the end of the film by the patriarchal order, when her previously passive employer takes her as his wife as well as his secretary and she is rescued from the killer by the male authority figure, Inspector Burgess. Yet, Williams suggests that Kansas' role of avenging female as she tracks down those men complicit in her employer's arrest cannot be easily forgotten:

> It is hard to believe that she will ever successfully settle down into the passive role of wife/secretary. The needle [on the dictaphone playing her employer's marriage proposal, "You're having dinner with me tonight, and tomorrow night, and every night"] sticks on the words "every night," the time in which Carol was at her most powerful. Carol's triumphant look may assert the latent presence of the "masochistic aesthetic" still awaiting another re-emergence in opposition to patriarchal power.[17]

Williams notes Woolrich's subversion of traditional gender roles in his writing, a trait possibly attributable to his homosexuality, and his alternative to the "'hard-boiled' school of Hammett, Cain and Chandler, with their emphasis on phallic pleasures of control and mastery."[18] The filmed jazz sequence perfectly realizes this aspect of Woolrich's ethos and, in rejecting the dance that Kansas/Carol is required to perform in the original novel and screenplay, arguably improves upon it. In the novel, Kansas/Carol is more passive than on-screen and protests her unease in the situation:

> "Come on, get up on the barrel and dance!"
> "I can't! I don't know how!"
> "It don't have to be your feet. Do it with what else you've got, that's what it's for. Never mind your dress, we're all friends."
> "Darling," she thought, sidling away from a rabid saxophone-player until he gave up following her any more with a final ceilingward blat of unutterable woe, "Oh darling, you're costing me dear."[19]

Similarly, in the novel, Carol has to urge Cliff to leave the cellar and "take me out of here. I can't stand it! I can't stand any more of it, I tell you! I'm going to keel over in another minute."[20] The filmed version, however, culminates with Kansas giving Cliff permission to stop drumming and leave by slyly nodding her head to the exit. To summarize, Kansas' possession of the phallic privileges of control and mastery are more evident in the film's interpretation of the jam session than Woolrich's original account.

That so much of Woolrich's predilection for the reconfiguration of accepted gender roles survived the transition from novel to film is possibly due to the presence of a woman, Joan Harrison, as the film's producer. *Phantom Lady* was promoted as unique in offering a female perspective on what had, hitherto, been considered a male genre. According to the film's press book, the studio chose the story for "a singular reason."

> It was a mystery story from the woman's point of view, a formula which never before had been translated for the screen. Love stories, yes, thousands of them, and musicals with matinee idols especially designed for feminine filmgoers, and lots of family dramas with women as the dominant characters. But not a single mystery film based on feminine psychology for its essential appeal. So Miss Joan Harrison . . . was engaged to produce.[21]

As has so often happened, the demands and restraints of the censors resulted in the filmmakers turning to subtler, more creative means of suggesting their taboo themes. These means would ultimately prove far more memorable than a more literal representation could have hoped to achieve. Yet, although the jazz sequence in *Phantom Lady*, as filmed and cut, managed to get through the PCA without further censor and the film earned its seal of approval, the sexual subtext to Cliff's drum solo was not lost on all those judging it for official approval. The local censor board of Pennsylvania reported to Breen that they required the elimination of all close-up shots of Cliff "in frenzy while beating drums."[22] Breen went further, outlining that the scenes for elimination were (in double reel 3, section A) numbers 22, 25, 27, 29, 31 and part of scene 32, of Carol [sic], which would continue to the moment when Cliff stops drumming and leaves the cellar.[23] These cuts, had they been enforced on the film by the PCA in general instead of being limited to screenings in Pennsylvania alone, would have resulted in the jazz sequence losing virtually all of its dramatic tension and energy.

Phantom Lady uses jazz to create a sense of confusion and to imply sexual desire, drug use and a general loss of morality. Although it is possible to interpret the film's equation of jazz with sex and immorality as being typical of the Eurocentric belief that jazz expressed African primitivism, Robert Porfirio has argued that it can also be considered representative of Siodmak's origins in Weimar culture and its opinion that:

> The improvisational nature and affective qualities of jazz were quite compatible with the expressionistic quest for deeper meanings that focused upon heightened states and the unconscious in order to probe the secrets of the soul.[24]

Porfirio notes that Siodmak makes a similar use of jazz in two of his later films noir, *The Killers* (1946) and *Criss Cross* (1949), neither of which contain anything as extreme as the jam session of *Phantom Lady*. Although Porfirio's argument may be true for Siodmak, it cannot be fully extended to Woolrich, who provided the source material for the jazz sequence, the majority of which was faithfully translated to the screen and had no background in Weimar culture. After an initial stage of his career writing novels that reflected the sensibilities of the Jazz Age, Woolrich's later suspense fiction is full of the psychology of terror and despair, while his writing about jazz also reflects the Eurocentrism and association of jazz with primitivism discussed in the previous chapter. Whatever Siodmak's perspective of the jazz sequence in *Phantom Lady*, its realization on screen still made it compatible with the dominant understanding of jazz at the time.

THE BEAT GOES ON: *THE ASPHALT JUNGLE* AND *D.O.A.*

Phantom Lady, however, is not unique in its use of jazz; other films noir incorporated the music into their narrative, although seldom with the same verve and visceral quality. John Huston's *The Asphalt Jungle* (1950) employs a spartan musical soundtrack that creates a similar effect to *Phantom Lady* in its sudden instances of music. Miklós Rózsa's score barely runs six minutes in length, being comprised of just two cues: the main title and a closing theme that underscores the central character's death ("Dix's Demise").[25] A striking diegetic use of jazz, however, is made toward the end of the film. The film's plot centers on a group of criminals who undertake a diamond robbery masterminded by the precise genius of Doc Riedenschneider (Sam Jaffe). Riedenschneider's scheme goes awry and, one by one, the criminals are undone by their respective flaws. Riedenschneider flees with his share of the spoils and has all but escaped the police when his particular weakness for voyeurism and young women brings about his capture. Stopping briefly at a diner, Riedenschneider is distracted by a girl dancing with a boy to a piece of big band jazz emanating from a jukebox. After their money runs out, Riedenschneider gives the girl more money so that he can watch her dance again. By the time the record has finished, the police have caught up with the Doc, and he is placed under arrest. The film's script does not specify the jukebox music as being jazz or any other genre, noting instead the erotic effect that the girl's dancing holds for Riedenschneider, brushing past his knees as he gazes on.[26]

The two "jitterbugs," as the music copyright department listed them, used for this sequence are brash, contemporary big band compositions by André Previn, titled "Don't Leave Your Guns" and "What About the Dame," both of which had been used in a number of other films.[27] The dramatic irony of the sequence is clear as Riedenschneider, the cool and calculating intellectual genius behind the robbery, is undone by his voyeurism and sexual desire. The suggestion, again, is that of the dualism of mind and body and that reason is drowned out by emotionalism, signified by the loud jazz that prevents Doc from hearing or observing the arrival of his pursuers.

Released in the same year as *The Asphalt Jungle, D.O.A.* (1950) does come close to matching *Phantom Lady* with a lengthy jazz sequence that, as Porfirio has discussed, also serves as a metaphor for sexual immorality and the confusion of the central character, heralding the slow fall to his doom.[28] While visiting The Fisherman, a San Francisco nightclub, during a business trip, Frank Bigelow (Edmund O'Brien) is poisoned with a drink laced with luminous toxin. His attention is diverted by a "jive crazy" woman long enough for his drink to be spiked. Bigelow is punished for contemplating an encounter with a woman other than his fiancée Paula. This sequence features a group of black musicians playing an intense number. The band plays exuberantly, and the camera emphasizes their sweating and grinning. Although the style of jazz is not bebop, the drummer, in black shades and sporting a crew cut, is clearly fashioned after the popular image of the bop musician (suit and tie, dark glasses, goatee beard and beret), associated with the likes of Dizzy Gillespie and Thelonious Monk. The film spends a considerable amount of time establishing the mood of the club and its white clientele, and there is a lot of inter-cutting between shots, with frequent close-ups of the musicians and individuals in the audience. A woman yells, "cool, cool, really cool!" "Man, am I hip!" says someone else while a young man with a goatee beard clicks his fingers and enthuses, "Blowin' up a storm!" Again, there is a representation of the perceived affectations of a (white) bop audience. As in *Phantom Lady,* the sequence reaches its height of emotional expression and the associated connotations with sex through the drum solo. As the solo mounts in intensity, the camera cuts between the drummer and the audience, focusing in particular on a white couple sitting and shaking ecstatically. "Stay with the beat!" yells the man, while the blonde woman looks on eagerly at the black drummer.

What makes the drum solo in *D.O.A.* particularly interesting is the ecstatic connection that is established between black and white characters. Segregation was still enforced in America. Miscegenation was expressly forbidden by the PCA, and the film is careful not to show black and white characters in the same shot. Yet the cutting between shots of the black musician's face as he drums vigorously and the white woman watching him intently, coupled with the overwhelming atmosphere of emotional abandon, creates a potent suggestion of desire. Over ten years later, the opening sequence of *Paris Blues* (1961), quite radically for the time, presented a vibrant jazz club where the clientele comprised mixed-race couples, as well as same-sex couples, and the band itself was mixed. *Paris Blues* could not maintain its initial promise, however. Later scenes in the club removed the mixed-race couples and reduced the number of black characters in the audience. Most significantly, the film's proposed storyline for a mixed-race romance between the lead stars was dropped due to pressure from the studio.[29] Given this reluctance to portray blacks and whites enjoying themselves in the same social venue in 1961 and the concern of contemporary films to avoid such relationships that I discussed in the previous chapter, the jazz sequence in *D.O.A.* becomes quite striking in its escape from the censors. That being said, the cutting of the film, with no black and white characters visible in the same shot, would have made it possible for the black musicians to be removed in order to meet the demands of certain exhibitors.

It is important to note that the use of jazz in the 1940s as a sexual metaphor and aural threat is not exclusive to film noir. Yet instances of jazz being used in other kinds of films consistently carried noir associations. *It's a Wonderful Life* (1946) uses jazz to help suggest the depths to which the town of Bedford Falls would sink should the film's hero, George Bailey (James Stewart), never have been born. In a nightmare sequence, George's guardian angel transports him to a parallel universe in which the warmth and homeliness of Bedford Falls has become a "dark den of sin, crime and corruption."[30] A black pianist now plays loud boogie-woogie jazz in what was George's local bar. The streets are now full of seedy bars, burlesque clubs and pawn shops. The sounds of the various establishments fill the soundtrack, and jazz is prominent in the mix. It is during this sequence that the film takes on the ethos of film noir as George's desperation at being trapped in a hometown that is completely unaware of him, his alienation total, becomes unbearable. These are the central themes of film noir, as initially identified by Raymond Borde and Étienne Chaumeton, and it is noticeable that *It's a Wonderful Life*, in its brief noir passage, uses diegetic jazz to increase George's isolation.

The jazz sequence in *D.O.A.* is another example of the representation of jazz as being a music that forsakes the intellect and musical thought for cheap thrills and instinctive responses, on the part of both performer and audience. But the tendency of film noir, and Hollywood in general, in the 1940s to portray the sexual, rhythmic, impulsive aspects of jazz (the very aspects upon which the white culture industry mythologized jazz as dark, exotic, forbidden music) would not find favor with what was happening in the jazz underground. In the early 1940s, a new generation of black musicians developed a complex style of jazz that advanced its harmonic and rhythmic horizons. The new music became known as bebop, but its importance was not simply musical. Show business principles were often scorned and seen as damaging to the musician's artistic integrity. As Ben Sidran writes, the boppers literally turned their back on the "non-serious" listeners who they felt had become attached to swing:

> Many bop musicians were quoted at various times as saying, "I don't care if you listen to my music or not," a far cry from the entertainers' posture de-

veloped by Armstrong and his contemporaries during the twenties. As Stearns indicated, the Negro . . . "then proceeded to play the most revolutionary jazz with an appearance of utter boredom, rejecting his audience entirely."[31]

Additionally, if bop was to be considered serious art, then traditional connotations of jazz with sex and seediness had to be rejected as well. Yet, the predominant understanding of jazz ensured that Hollywood was still unable to portray it as art.

CASE STUDY: *YOUNG MAN WITH A HORN*

As I discussed in the previous chapter, *Mildred Pierce* was no exception to typical uses of jazz in Hollywood film. A later Michael Curtiz film would look more closely at jazz, however, and specifically raise the issue of the musician's dilemma in choosing between art and commerce. *Young Man with a Horn* (1950) was based on Dorothy Baker's novel of the same name, which was in turn inspired by the lyrical white trumpeter Bix Beiderbecke. Beiderbecke died in 1931 at age twenty-eight, from pneumonia and the effects of alcoholism. In the years after his death, however, his playing acquired legendary status among jazz fans. Beiderbecke is now generally considered to be the first important white jazz musician, and his less fiery approach to the trumpet a significant alternative to that of Armstrong.

The Beiderbecke figure in *Young Man with a Horn* is trumpeter Rick Martin, played by Kirk Douglas. Douglas was not the first choice for the role, and a host of other actors was proposed and given screen tests. The producer's initial hope had been to cast James Stewart in the part, but he was unable to secure his involvement. There then followed a period of debate in which the producer, Jerry Wald, sought an actor who could portray Rick effectively, a part that Wald felt called for "a shy young man."[32] The names of Mel Ferrer, Duane Clark, Ronald Reagan and bandleader Bobby Sherwood were all considered and rejected before Douglas was selected.

Rick's character would have presented a number of concerns for Hollywood's typical image of masculinity. A shy, sensitive musician who was more interested in music than women, with this description Rick's heterosexuality could have been called into question, and the film employs a number of tactics that serve to disavow any such doubts. Rick's relationship with Smoke, his best friend and musical partner, is an intimate one, as they share Rick's truest love, jazz—a love that Rick is unable to share with any of the women in his life. Rick and Smoke set out on a period of playing jazz wherever they are able to, and Smoke describes the time as the three best years of his life and Rick as "an exciting guy to be around. We had a lot of fun for a while." A scripted montage sequence was to show some of the venues in which they find work, including a striptease bar.[33] As they play, women's underwear is tossed onto their grinning heads. The scene acts as reassurance to the audience that although Rick and Smoke may be creative artists without girlfriends, they are nevertheless heterosexual, and sex is still a part of their lives. It is also a scene that confirms the association of jazz with sex and seediness.

Much later, Rick marries Amy (Lauren Bacall), a "restless, intellectual and nervous girl."[34] The marriage is a disaster, presented as a psychological experiment carried out by Amy. Faced with the need to offer an explanation for the failed marriage that does not call Rick's sexuality into question, the film opts to suggest that it is Amy's sexuality that is at fault. When Rick returns home from the funeral of his trumpet teacher, he encounters Amy leaving their apartment with another woman. Both the scripted scene and its realization on screen are coded for lesbianism:

Amy and a young, exotically pretty but rather poorly dressed girl comes through the door way. Amy, her hand on the girl's elbow possessively, is very vital and charming, and the girl is obviously impressed with her.

AMY: See you at seven then, Bobbie.[35]

The girl's ambiguously gendered name, Bobbie, and the interaction between the two actresses imply a lesbian relationship that helps to draw attention away from the male musician's masculinity and his responsibility for the broken marriage.

The casting of Douglas provided the film with a lead that corresponded with Hollywood's concept of masculinity, and he acquits himself well in the role of Rick. Keen to learn how to handle a trumpet and develop a correct embouchure, Douglas offered to study the instrument on his own time in order to appear convincing in the trumpet-playing sequences.[36] The film itself charts Rick's career as a musician. Rick falls in love with jazz as a boy and is taught to play the trumpet by a black jazz musician, Art Hazzard (Juano Hernandez). Initially, he plays in regimental, "sweet" dance bands, and Rick quickly becomes frustrated at the repetitive playing demanded by the commercial music industry. Rick's frustration is very real. At the same time that the film was being made, the sociologist and musician Howard Becker was conducting research on fellow Chicago-based musicians and their struggle in choosing between personal integrity or financial security, conformist or outsider:

The most distressing problem in the career of the average musician . . . is the necessity of choosing between conventional success and his artistic standards. In order to achieve success he finds it necessary to "go commercial," that is, to play in accord with the wishes of the nonmusicians for whom he works; in doing so he sacrifices the respect of other musicians and thus, in most cases, his self-respect. If he remains true to his standards, he is usually doomed to failure in the larger society. Musicians classify themselves according to the degree to which they give in to outsiders; the continuum ranges from the extreme "jazz" musician to the "commercial" musician.[37]

Becker's research was compiled in his collection of essays titled *Outsiders: Studies in the Sociology of Deviance*. The jazz musician's (and in *Young Man with a Horn*'s case, Rick Martin's) status as outsider makes him an excellent potential noir character. For black musicians, and the beboppers in particular, the sense of being outsiders was exacerbated by racism. The frustration at being unable to both play a personally satisfying form of music and earn enough money to exist, compounded by the indignities of racism, resulted in many black bop musicians turning to drugs, notably heroin, the "endemic curse of the jazz profession," as a means of escape.[38] This link between jazz and drugs has been acknowledged in many Hollywood films to feature the music, but, as in *Phantom Lady*, seldom as a symptom of the social difficulties faced by jazz musicians. Many of these pressures remain in force for contemporary jazz musicians. Wills and Cooper's research into the effect of work pressure on musicians in different fields found that neuroses and anxiety were common among jazz musicians:

> Those who perform in the jazz idiom most closely exhibited the kind of temperament found in the "sensitive, dedicated artist," in other words, possibly those working in the field of orchestral playing. Performers of jazz appear to identify more strongly with their work and receive enjoyment and fulfillment from it. Perhaps because of its importance to them, the work is especially stressful for them, and they appear to suffer from anxiety more than other musicians in the popular field do.[39]

These characteristics are present in Rick and contribute to his alienation. When he is not able to play the music that brings him pleasure and satisfaction, either stylistically or technically, he goes into a rapid decline and drinks heavily.

Typically, noir's characters are outsiders or social outcasts, ranging from Humphrey Bogart's existentialist Philip Marlowe to the assorted criminals in John Huston's heist-noir *The Asphalt Jungle* (1950). In defining film noir, Fred Pfeil argues that the protagonist is forced to make an "absurd existential choice of moral behavior according to one's own individual ethical code, in a hopelessly dark universe."[40] For Rick, the absurd choice is that between artistic integrity and financial and personal stability. He cannot be a successful jazz musician *and* maintain steady personal relationships. As Jo, the female vocalist (Doris Day), tells him, he's married to his horn. His obsession with his music nearly drives him to ruin, however. It is this dilemma and obsession, and its resolution, which I believe elevates *Young Man with a Horn* to the ambiguous canon of film noir, a canon from which it has traditionally been excluded.

As he did for *Mildred Pierce*, Curtiz creates in *Young Man with a Horn* a film that combines domestic melodrama with elements of noir. Pfeil notes Vivian Sobchak's observation that domestic situations in film noir must ultimately come to nothing, arguing that "the noir chronotope has no room for children or for rituals of family continuity: no weddings, no births, no natural deaths, no family intimacy and connection can be eventful here."[41] Rick's marriage in the film is disastrous and devoid of any intimacy. It also triggers his decline as a trumpeter. Becker's study confirms that the life of the jazz musician places unusual and often severe demands on the musician's family and marriage.[42]

Both *Mildred Pierce* and *Young Man with a Horn* are filled with the cynicism that is typical not only of film noir but also of the cinema of Michael Curtiz. Curtiz biographers James C. Robertson and Kingsley Canham both comment on the director's personal cynicism and how this was reflected in his films.[43] *Young Man with a Horn* contains some acidic lines about jazz and the public's perception of it. Rick Martin and his colleagues are only too aware that the audiences do not want to hear jazz. They want to dance and buy the records so that "they can learn the words." This dialogue refers to the then-current shift in commercial jazz from the supremacy of the virtuoso soloist, such as Benny Goodman and Artie Shaw, to the growing dominance of the vocalist.

As film noir dictates, Rick is doomed. Desperate to achieve a note that has never been played before, Rick breaks down after a recording session in which he attempts but is unable to play a note in the trumpet's extreme high register. He succumbs to alcoholism and wanders the streets of New York. The first draft of the script, and the official synopsis that accompanied the film's PCA certificate of approval, actually begins with this passage of Rick's life before going into flashbacks of the events that led to his decline.[44] It is in this sequence, Rick's lowest point in the film, that Curtiz employs a cinematic style that is clearly in the noir tradition. Curtiz shoots Rick in an alcoholic haze on location in New York. The filmstock and pseudodocumentary style that Curtiz achieves is typical of that period of noir dubbed the "post-war realistic 1945–1949," by Paul Schrader.[45] This sequence of the film ends with Rick collapsing on the road; the dark, silhouetted city buildings surrounding him. As he lies helplessly, a taxicab drives by and crushes his trumpet. The image is as potent as any film noir has presented. The city/machine has destroyed art and music. The outsider who strove to be an individual and fought against the established order is reduced to a pathetic figure, drunk and alone.

Although Rick is rehabilitated and returns to the recording studio, the film's closing image is ambiguous. Hoagy Carmichael, who plays Smoke, tells us, in his narration-to-camera, that Rick:

> learned that you can't say everything through the end of a trumpet, and a man doesn't destroy himself just because he can't hit some high note that he

dreamed up. Maybe that's why Rick went on to be a success as a human being first—and an artist second. And what an artist.

But, although this sounds like a positive ending, what the spectator *sees* tells a different story. As Carmichael's narration ends, Rick rises up to play his trumpet *in support* of the female vocalist, Jo, singing "With a Song in My Heart." The mise-en-scène is identical to that of the earlier recording session when Rick broke down. Rick is trapped musically and has apparently sold out as a musician.

Baker's novel ends with Rick dying, as Beiderbecke did, by drinking himself into pneumonia, although "what really killed him was that he had the soul of an artist but he didn't have that ability to keep the body in check while the spirit goes on being what it must be."[46] This ending was considered too dark, and in scriptwriter Carl Foreman's first draft of the screenplay, delivered to Jack Warner in March 1947, the novel's ending was altered so that Rick was not seen to die. In this version, the film closes with Rick being driven away from the sanatorium in an ambulance, Jo and Smoke by his side; but he is allowed a final victory of sorts:

Rick opens his eyes and smiles weakly. He tries to talk again, and succeeds, his voice seeming a little stronger now. On the MUSIC TRACK, we hear the muted trumpet, but it suddenly lights into the number Jo and Rick recorded together.

RICK: But I'm not afraid any more . . . I'm not afraid of any trumpet ever made. What's a trumpet? Only brass. It's not alive until you make it live, and when you put it down it's dead. Only people are alive . . . (his hands fight their way out from under the covering blankets and his fingers begin to move as if they are pressing valves) I can play now, Jo. I can play pretty good . . .

The trumpet on the MUSIC TRACK is now hitting the same wild riffs as in the recording studio.

318. CLOSE SHOT RICK

His eyes are closed now, and it is as if he is listening to the unseen horn. It builds to the same staggering, brilliant finish, and then at the end it tries *and hits* that incredible, impossible note . . .

Rick smiles slightly in quiet triumph.

319. EXT. NEW YORK STREET DAY as the ambulance, its siren open wide, speeds away from the CAMERA. FADE OUT.

THE END [47]

Rick is able to achieve his obsession—to play something that nobody has ever played before, if only in his dreams. It is difficult to imagine how the film would have realized this impossible note, and that, at least, is a reasonable argument against Foreman's draft.

If Rick's "fantasy triumph" endows the film with something of a positive ending, however, the overall tone remains bleak. Unlike the film's eventual ending, Foreman's script does not allow Rick to be rehabilitated and seen returning to the recording studio. This draft of the script did not meet with the approval of head of studio Jack Warner. Warner requested that the film be rewritten in "the direction of a happy ending and a hefty reduction of the negro background material."[48] The original synopsis for the film concludes with the matter-of-fact statement: "that's practically the end of Rick Martin, except for the bowery haunts and the missions, and then the accident with the taxicab."[49] After Warner's request for a fresh ending, however, the official synopsis tags on an awkward addendum, which does not read like a satisfactory conclusion:

> That's practically the end of Kirk Douglas, except for the bowery haunts and the missions, and then the accident with the taxicab . . .
>   Carmichael takes Douglas from the alcoholic sanitarium to a hospital, and it is suggested that Douglas regains his health and returns to play his trumpet again.[50]

The resulting final scene—with Rick alive and well and seemingly content in his musical role as support to the pretty, female vocalist—did not convince everybody. The review in *Reporter* felt that "the conclusion will cause considerable comment, because it is simply a contrived happy ending," but did acknowledge that although they "couldn't accept the finale; others disagree."[51] The *New York Herald Tribune* also had mixed feelings:

> Under Michael Curtiz's direction it has moments of passion and moments of stock-arrangement corn. There is just enough of the first to make up for the second . . . [but] at the crucial moment the show takes refuge in romantic clichés instead of facing the real personal damnation of an inspired artist trying to sound notes that are in his head, but not on the trumpet.[52]

But even though Curtiz's ending appears to be the happy one Warner was looking for, it can be read as more of a compromise. Indeed, in noir terms, it arguably has the same conclusion as the original script. Carmichael's voice at the end of the film is a noir convention that does not bode well for Rick's future. Joan Copjec argues that:

> Nothing has seemed more obvious in the criticism of *film noir* than this association of death with speech, for the voice-over is regularly attached to a dead narrator, whether literally as in *Sunset Boulevard* and *Laura*, metaphorically as in *Detour*, or virtually as in *Double Indemnity*.[53]

Carmichael's speech, and the image it underscores, confirms that, in accepting the commercial route, both Rick and Carmichael's character (Smoke) are indeed dead! Artistically they have ceased to exist as jazz musicians.

YOUNG MAN WITH A HORN—UNABLE TO BOP!

Despite its cynicism, *Young Man with a Horn* is crucially flawed in the choice of music used to underscore it and, more specifically, the choice of trumpeter to dub in Rick's solos. Rick spends the film striving for a new sound, a new way of playing an "impossible" note. He is underscored throughout, however, by the sound of a white jazz musician who had clearly "gone commercial," Harry James, and a conventional Hollywood score with an emphasis on lush orchestration for strings. Rick is not underscored by his mentor, Art Hazzard, or the kind of music that he wants to play. Although Rick's character is inspired by Bix Beiderbecke, there is nothing remotely Bixian about Rick's trumpet playing. Rick's solos are dubbed in by James, an ebullient trumpeter in the more popular and influential tradition established by Louis Armstrong.[54] Beiderbecke's soft, poetic lyricism would have been better captured by a musician such as Bobby Hackett. But Rick is given a more aggressive, overtly masculine sound, and thus, by extension, a conformist sound (which is at odds with Rick's rebellious character). In his excellent study of cinematic representations of the jazz trumpet, Krin Gabbard differentiates between the phallic model for trumpeters, established by Armstrong, that emphasizes "pitch, speed, and emotional intensity," and the alternative paradigms of players such as Beiderbecke and Art Farmer.[55] For Gabbard, the qualities of Farmer's playing do not necessarily call into question his masculinity:

> His lyricism, soft tone, hesitant delivery and lack of stage mannerisms all represent a retreat from phallic bravado. Farmer's style might be called post-phallic rather than nonphallic because, on the one hand, it in no way suggests that Farmer has accepted castration, lost his subjecthood, or refused the sexuality of the idiom; on the other hand, there is no obvious hysterical edge to Farmer's self-presentation that spills over into showy displays of technique or extra-musical affectation.[56]

Rick's pursuit of an unheard note can certainly be termed hysterical, and his failure to reach it results in his symbolic castration, a feature that, Gabbard identifies, is common to many Hollywood films about jazz musicians.[57] Rick is recuperated by the end of the film when he learns to give up his single-minded obsession with music. The studio's concern over Rick's perceived masculinity is reflected in the lengthy deliberation over the choice of actor to portray him. The "shy, young man" that Jerry Wald perceived

Rick Martin to be does not come across, however, in the choice of Harry James to provide his solos. James' phallic style of playing the trumpet would possibly have been more reassuring for Hollywood and in line with accepted codes of masculinity, which was then attempting to portray musicians as "real" men.[58] As a result, the use of a principally non-jazz score and conformist approach to the trumpet means that the music does not underscore Rick, but serves instead to undermine him.

The choice of music in *Young Man with a Horn* also weakens the film's potential power. Although the film's production notes identified the period as being the late 1920s and early 1930s, the film does not really attempt to root itself in that particular time.[59] This is problematic when the film is dealing with a music, like jazz, that is constantly evolving. Because the audience is unsure as to when Rick is playing, it gets no sense of the traditional jazz that Rick is attempting to escape from with his new sound. If the film had sought to accurately re-create the 1920s jazz scene of Beiderbecke and Armstrong, then the style of jazz played by Rick could well have sounded new and innovative. As it is, his "subversive" jam sessions sound naive and innocent when contrasted with what was currently happening in jazz through the bebop, cool and progressive jazz movements. Indeed, the style of jazz that Rick plays is typical of the revivalist trend in jazz that developed in the late 1940s as a backlash to the then contemporary sounds and innovations.

Were Rick a "young man with a horn" in 1949 with the same thirst for new sounds and artistic integrity, it is unlikely that he would have become involved with the revivalist camp. Yet the official production notes for the film suggest that the makers of *Young Man with a Horn* were hoping to appeal to the revivalists instead of the modernists:

THE TIME IS NOW . . .

Young Man with a Horn, a musical drama of the late '20s and early '30s, breathes atomic-age life into the only-yesterday period when Jazz was Jazz, and be-bop and cyclotrons and existentialism were only flickering shadows of tomorrow. The Warner Bros. Production, which may well be a classic among musical films, doesn't seek to inspire a revival of the music of the period, because as everybody knows, like the weather and George Bernard Shaw, true American jazz will go on forever and ever; and it never died in the first place.[60]

Whatever "true American jazz" was felt to be, the film's producers did not seem to think that it included bebop. The claim that the film did not intend to instigate a revival of the older styles of New Orleans and Dixieland was superfluous because such a revival was already taking place. That bebop was not perceived by Hollywood to be "truly American" reflects an awareness of its advanced harmonies and rhythms (which some critics claimed had simply been borrowed from European classical music), its association with philosophy and the avant-garde (as evidenced in the reference to existentialism) and its status as a predominantly black music.

The amount of jazz in the film is small considering its story of a jazz musician and the involvement of Harry James. The production notes proudly announced that the musical director, Ray Heindorf, had hired "many of the great jazz musicians for the background bands," and that "the various bands are also spattered with musicians from such currently popular organizations as Phil Harris', Harry James', the Dorseys', Duke Ellington's, Charlie Barnet's, etc."[61] The overwhelming impression of the film's music, however, is not that of jazz, but, as the production notes acknowledged, "the abundant hit tunes of the last years."[62]

Established jazz musicians such as tenor saxophonist Bumps Meyers, trombonist George Washington, drummer Zutty Singleton and bassist Rocky Robinson were all listed as being present, but correspondence between the various people involved with the film's production suggests that the intention was not to have an emphasis on jazz at all. In April 1947, the film's producer, Jerry Wald, wrote to Jack Warner to reassure him about the film's jazz content:

> It is my opinion that in this property you have a ready-made audience of twenty-five million jazz enthusiasts. This picture is not to present high class music or low jazz, but actually popular musical numbers that the public will understand.[63]

Wald's comments affirm the film's jazz audience, but can also be read as questioning the music's quality and accessibility to the general public. Again, the reference to the public being able to understand the music suggests an awareness of the intellectualization of contemporary jazz and a concern that this development was not appropriate for a Hollywood film. But even though Wald felt that the public might not have understood jazz in its purest forms, presumably because it was too complex and intellectual, he still refers to it as being "low," as opposed to "high class music."

The jazz content in *Young Man with a Horn* could have been much more extensive had a number of suggestions at the pre-production stage been taken. The film was in development for a long time, and Dorothy Baker's novel had originally been assessed for its potential as a film as early as 1938. Meta Arenson read the novel for Warner Bros. story department and provided the following opinion:

> I think the idea of making a picture about swing at this time, symbolized by the rise of a great swing artist, would be an exciting one, both commercially and otherwise. I further believe that with a tighter story than this book has, but using the theme and characters, that this could be that picture. It goes so much farther, however, than most stories of its kind that unless someone

did it who had the sympathy for the characters and the music itself which this author has, it would miss completely.[64]

Notably, Arenson discusses the central character as being a player of swing rather than jazz, such was swing's dominance at the time. Despite Arenson's recommendation, the option to develop the book into a film was not pursued. There were mixed responses to the novel among Warner Bros. decision-makers. In an interoffice communication dated June 30, 1938, Irene Lee, although not personally considering *Young Man with a Horn* "particularly good for the screen," advised producer Sam Bischoff that he should read the book's synopsis on the basis of the "wide publicity" it had received.[65] Bischoff responded that he did not like the story at all.[66] Bischoff's was not the only opinion that Lee sought, and, although the general feeling was "can't see it for the screen," she did receive one response in favor of the book's development into a film:

> Excellent synopsis of what, apparently, is an excellent book. But the book's best points are its central characterization and its mood. Both *could* be used on the screen, but neither is typical "musical." Certainly there would be no point in purchasing this for transformation into a routine musical; the plot itself is too simple and too much a matter of emotion instead of formula action or comedy to justify it. From magazine reports it would seem to me that there are enough young people who take their swing *seriously* to justify consideration for this pretty much as it stands. It would be a director's picture. If someone sufficiently ingenious with the camera and soundtrack could capture the mood of the book, and if a careful exploitation campaign could be aimed at the jitterbug audience, the experiment might be worthwhile. Experiment it would be, however, and only an enthusiastic producer should tackle it.[67]

As it transpired, nobody would choose to tackle *Young Man with a Horn* until late in 1946, when Wald became its producer. There was still a considerable amount of uncertainty over the development of the project. According to Warner Bros. employee Steve Trilling, who was attached to the film, the studio had yet to decide by as late as mid-1949 whether the film would be a musical or a dramatic story with incidental music.[68] When the film was eventually completed and acquired its certificate of approval from the PCA, in September 1949, its official classification was that of "Drama— Psychological," suggesting a move away from the popular musical approach.[69]

The 1938 recommendations that the film would require a production team sympathetic to jazz and would be experimental in nature might have raised hopes of a major jazz artist being involved in the picture. Although Harry James had achieved great popularity and was an excellent trumpeter, he was not, certainly when *Young Man with a Horn* was being made, making consistently important jazz performances and recordings. Duke

Ellington's status as a composer and leading figure in jazz was undeniable, and he was briefly proposed as the film's composer. The reasons for Ellington not being employed are unclear and will be further discussed in the following chapter, but it is possible that Ellington's music and compositional style were perceived as being too jazzy, or "high class," and lacking the wide public appeal that Wald was looking for. Although the decision to combine a jazz soloist with a conventional symphonic Hollywood score was an original one, in terms of being an experiment, the score for *Young Man with a Horn* was a cautious one.

Other proposed collaborations that did not materialize included the involvement of Orson Welles as director and Louis Armstrong for the part of Art Hazzard, Rick's teacher, a character that is clearly modeled on Armstrong.[70] Welles would certainly have brought the sympathy for the characters and music that Arenson had advised were crucial to the film's success. Welles had a great love of jazz, and music in general, and part of the abandoned *It's All True* project that he worked on in 1941 was to have featured a history of jazz with the music being provided by Ellington. Armstrong's potential role in the film was under discussion for some time. Joe Glaser, Armstrong's manager, wrote to Steve Trilling, assuring him that Louis would "not only prove himself to be a valuable asset to the picture, but will do justice to any part given to him."[71] Yet just over a month later, Trilling replied to Glaser's business partner, Charlie Yates, with the news that Juano Hernandez had been signed to play the Art Hazzard character, and that James would be providing the trumpet solos. Trilling's explanation for the decision was that "the Hazzard part developed into more of an acting role with very little trumpet playing and no singing."[72] This argument seems to suggest that Armstrong was considered to be purely a musical entertainer and lacked the skills and seriousness to take on a dramatic role, an impression borne out by the vast majority of his film appearances, but one that Armstrong was also given little opportunity to redress.[73] With Armstrong rejected, the film lost the opportunity of having a genuine jazz master provide the solo's for the Art Hazzard character, an opportunity that would have greatly benefited the film's musical authenticity. Instead, Jimmy Zito played Hazzard's solos. According to the film's production notes, Zito was considered "one of the finest trumpet players of the day."[74] Zito's name, however, seldom features in jazz history books.

Ironically, the modernist jazz of bebop and its philosophy of anti-show-business values were mirrored by Rick's own frustrations with the culture industry. *Young Man with a Horn* would have been a totally different film if Rick Martin had been a young bop musician struggling to find an outlet for his music. And while it would have seemed appropriate for the time in which *Young Man with a Horn* was made and released, the "new sound" that Rick searched for could not have been bebop, or another modernist form of jazz, for a variety of reasons. First, bebop was a fundamentally black movement. Its pioneers (Charlie Parker, Dizzy Gillespie, Thelonious

Monk, Kenny Clarke, Charlie Christian) were all young, black musicians. Although white musicians did play bebop in its founding years—the Jewish trumpeter Red Rodney, who played with Parker's quintet, being a significant example—this was seen as whites playing in a black style. The white entertainment industry had colonized and commodified earlier forms of jazz, and this was one of the factors leading to the emergence of bebop:

> Young black musicians were, to some extent, reacting to the fact that their music had been accepted by whites partly because they themselves had been relegated to an inferior social position.[75]

Sidran notes that bebop was concerned with blackness and beating the white musician on his "own terms." For Sidran, bebop was not noticeably racist, but it did encourage the concept of "'blackness' as a cultural, rather than genetic, condition."[76] In effect, the black bop community could accept a white musician, such as Red Rodney, if he complied with their ethos as well as their music, while a black musician who corresponded to the older trope of the entertainer and its uncomfortable association with the Uncle Tom figure was not welcomed. Armstrong's musical achievements, therefore, were acknowledged, but his social persona was disdained. Sidran's interpretation of bebop is situated in a trope of revolution. As Scott DeVeaux has surmised, this position emphasizes the music as a "rebellion by black musicians against a white-controlled capitalist hegemony."[77] DeVeaux also acknowledges the reading of bebop as being a natural evolution of the "jazz tradition," more removed from social and political forces. Neither of these tropes are entirely rejected by DeVeaux, who seeks instead to move beyond their "limiting simplifications." In his social and musical history of bebop, DeVeaux describes the boppers as being professional musicians who acknowledged the need to work within the established commercial channels in order to earn a living while not necessarily approving of them. DeVeaux rejects the generalization of the bop musician as an alienated revolutionary in favor of overthrowing the music industry. Instead, he quotes Dizzy Gillespie, who clearly recognized the importance for black musicians to take bop beyond their somewhat clandestine community and use it to forge a career:

"Could the new style survive alone, commercially?" he asked rhetorically in his autobiography. "Could we all survive as modernists, without any further ties to the mother dance bands?"[78]

Despite the attempts of musicians such as Gillespie to make bop both a commercial prospect and artistically satisfying to play (a goal that Gillespie briefly achieved in the late 1940s with the formation of his big band), the style never flourished in mainstream entertainment as swing had a decade earlier. Bebop's status as a predominantly black music meant that it could not escape the racism that was rife in the entertainment industry. Even if the boppers were not aggressively distancing themselves from mainstream culture, that perception was still promoted by the media:

> In the mainstream press, the general public was given a less nuanced and informed view. Bebop, for many, was at best arrant foolishness, a farrago of nonsense syllables and noisy, incomprehensible music. At worst it was a musical practice that hinted darkly of an underground of drug users, anti-social deviants and racial militants. Both impressions, needless to say, were informed by racially grounded stereotypes.[79]

It is not surprising, therefore, that a Hollywood film did not attempt to focus on a style of music perceived to be so opposed to the values of the dominant culture and society.

At a more generic level, however, another reason bebop did not feature as Rick's style of jazz was film noir convention. Bebop was, in part, a conscious attempt to intellectualize jazz, and thus have it taken more seriously by unmoved critics and musical authorities. I have already discussed how the war years saw Hollywood try to make the "serious" arts accessible to all. Post-war film noir was also critical of cultural elitism and tended not to present art as cerebral pursuit in a positive light. The murderer in *Phantom Lady,* for example, is the sophisticated artist Jack Marlow (Franchot Tone). The *Phantom Lady* press book, discussing how the film's "mood is assured," claimed the fact "that the mysterious killer is a psychopathic intellectual also helps."[80] Robert Porfirio has observed, however, that Marlow, and his obsession with his artistic hands, is nothing more than a "throwback to the German classic, *The Hands of Orlac*," and that the "weaker part" of the film is the second half, in which Marlow's identity and motivation is revealed.[81] Even in an early film noir like *Phantom Lady*, the psychotic intellectual was already an established cliché. Similarly, Richard Dyer has observed the association between a "certain sort of good taste" and evil as being "central to film noir."[82] Jon Tuska goes further:

> Anti-intellectualism is a continuing theme throughout *film noir* and it is against the prescription for either a man or a woman to be interested in books or music. When a man is, he most often turns out, as Clifton Webb in *Laura* (1944), to be a savage murderer unloved and unwanted by beautiful women.[83]

The use of jazz also got caught up in this theme of anti-intellectualism. Jazz as visceral, rhythmic, sexual music was fine as an underscore to noir. Jazz as cerebral, harmonically complex music was not. Film noir, which could have offered a naturalistic haven for bop, could not harbor the music because of its desire for intellectual status.

Nowhere is film noir's abhorrence of "art" more explicit than in Robert Aldrich's *Kiss Me Deadly* (1955). The "hero," Mike Hammer (Ralph Meeker), does not think twice about destroying a man's collection of opera records in order to make him talk and give Hammer the information he requires to further his investigations, which are centered on the quest for a mysterious black box. As the film nears its climax, the guardian of the box, Dr. Soberin (Albert Dekker), warns the duplicitous femme fatale, Lily (Gaby Rodgers), not to open it. His warning is ineffectual and archaic, full of references to Greek mythology: "Cerberus barking with all his heads." And so it (that is, intellectualism) proves useless against desire. Lily opens the box and is consumed by a terrifying force of radioactive energy that shrieks relentlessly as the film ends.

Similarly, in *Young Man with a Horn* the character representing intellectualism, Lauren Bacall's trainee psychiatrist, is portrayed as decadent, bored, manipulative and incapable of love. Cast in the femme fatale mould, she introduces herself to Rick simply to satisfy her own intellectual curiosity. He is a diverting experiment for her. Later, she marries him for her own purposes, but quickly wearies of him. The audience does not feel that she will leave the marriage with any great sense of loss. Rather, we expect her to move on to another "experiment." Rick, however, is badly affected. He loses contact with his friends, his roots and eventually his trumpet playing.

Rick is never able to describe his playing, or his search for a note that nobody has ever played before, intellectually or in any musical detail. The audience has no idea of what Rick is trying to achieve on the trumpet. It is a magical note that the audience is left to guess at. This lack of explanation is typical of Hollywood's tendency, as I discussed in the previous chapter, to portray jazz musicians as having enormous natural talent, but no understanding of what it is they actually do. Hollywood jazz musicians still simply "play what they feel," and their musical gift continues to emanate from some mysterious source.

Young Man with a Horn does go some way to debunking this myth. It makes it clear that Rick gets to be as good a trumpeter as he is only after years of intense practice. Rick's commitment to his music is clear. The script describes him as possessing a "driving purpose" and "the face of a zealot, of a man who knows something few other people can know or understand," and Kirk Douglas effectively portrays this intensity.[84] Rick's mentor, the black trumpeter Art Hazzard, has taught Rick everything he knows. The implication is significant. Jazz can be taught and studied. A jazz musician is not simply born with the ability to improvise. The film also demonstrates that Rick has acquired a knowledge of his instrument—we see Art teaching him to adjust his embouchure in order to avoid getting a "roll" of notes. The jazz musician is shown to be a craftsman then, with an understanding of the workings of his trade. Rick is able to acknowledge that appreciation of jazz requires something other than a physical response. At an after-gig party, in another scripted scene that was not filmed, Rick discovers somebody playing his beloved New Orleans jazz recordings and dancing to them. Rick's response is short and sharp: "You don't dance to this kind of music—you listen to it. Go play yourself a comedy fox trot."[85] It is a condescending comment, typical of the jazz snob who deems all other music to be inferior, and does not help to make Rick's love of jazz admirable to the audience. Rick comes across instead as an obsessive and thwarted individual.

Yet, despite his assertion that jazz requires a thoughtful response, Rick is essentially presented as an instinctive, emotional player. As he says, he plays what he feels. The film, then, ultimately falls short of portraying jazz musicians as possessing an intellectual understanding of their music. In his search for this new sound, Rick sounds surprisingly similar to alto saxophonist Charlie Parker. Describing how he set about developing the musical innovations that would revolutionize jazz, Parker also mentions hearing an inner "sound." He knew there was *another way*. As he said, "I'd been getting bored with the stereotyped changes that were being used at the time, and I kept thinking there's bound to be something else. I could hear it sometimes but I couldn't play it."[86] However, unlike Rick, Parker is also able to go on and fully explain his music in a theoretical and intellectual fashion:

> Well, that night, I was working over *Cherokee*, and, as I did, I found that by using the higher intervals of a chord as a melody line and backing them with appropriately related changes, I could play the thing I'd been hearing.[87]

Film noir could never portray this positively, and so neither could *Young Man with a Horn*. Rick Martin's jazz is not intellectual, and the conventions of noir doom him for simply aspiring to play something other than popular, functional music.

RESPONSES TO *YOUNG MAN WITH A HORN*

Young Man with a Horn was a significant step forward for the use of jazz in film. At the time of its release, the majority of reviews were impressed by Harry James' work on the soundtrack, even if they remained unmoved by the film's actual dramatic content. The *New York Times* noted that James was the "unseen star of the picture" and his music fundamental to its chances of success:

> This is an instance where the soundtrack is more than a complementary force. It is the very soul of the picture because if it were less provocative and compelling the staleness of the drama could be stultifying.[88]

Despite being unconvinced by the film's ending, *Reporter* was more supportive of the overall film, deeming it "sincere and compelling," but, again, it was James who received the most glowing praise:

> It is James' magnificent trumpeting that carries most of the musical portion, and in itself it is worth the price of admission.[89]

Whether James' presence on the soundtrack ensured the film the support of its perceived "ready-made audience of twenty-five million jazz en-
thusiasts" is harder to determine. A jazz enthusiast in 1950 is likely to have
left the film feeling disappointed about its jazz content. As the reviewer in
Motion Picture Daily put it, the film is "full of popular music, played and
sung by experts," but not exactly full of jazz.[90] Three years after the film's
release, *Down Beat*, the leading jazz journal of the day, ran an article in
which the use of jazz in film was examined. The article's title was "Little
of Jazz Interest in 25 Years of Sound Films," and *Young Man with a Horn*
was specifically discussed as being a source of disappointment. Unlike those
initial reviews of the film, which tended to criticize the drama while prais-
ing the musical soundtrack, however, *Down Beat* was equally unimpressed
by the music and Harry James' involvement:

> In 1950 came the long-talked-of *Young Man with a Horn*, with jazz purists
> shuddering and bemoaning the selection of Harry James to record the trum-
> pet solos. . . . Screen writer Carl Foreman did his best to catch the spirit of
> the Dorothy Baker novel . . . but was forced to make changes that robbed the
> story of all significance and impact. The musical treatments were incoherent
> and uninspired.[91]

For its choice of best jazz film, *Down Beat* selected the 1944 short
Jammin' the Blues; such was the perceived lack of quality full-length films
to feature jazz. *Young Man with a Horn* was not even considered to be the
best full-length jazz film. That dubious honor went to *The Strip* (1951), a
film noir with Mickey Rooney in the lead role as an emotionally unstable
jazz drummer.[92] The on-screen jazz content in this film came from the Louis
Armstrong band (including Jack Teagarden, Earl Hines and Barney Bigard,
with Cozy Cole providing the drum soundtracks), while Pete Rugolo, a
composer with Stan Kenton's Progressive and Innovations in Modern Music orchestras, bands which will be discussed in greater detail in the following chapter, provided the somewhat jazz-inflected score. Charles Emge,
the film correspondent for *Down Beat*, was obviously relieved by *The Strip*'s
treatment of jazz:

> After years of sitting through the weird things that have resulted every time
> someone has tried to do a picture dealing with jazz music or a jazz musician,
> we take pleasure in reporting that in *The Strip* MGM has turned out a film
> that is not only adult entertainment but one that even the most uncompro-
> mising jazz authorities will be able to endure without unbearable mental
> anguish.[93]

Emge's "unbearable mental anguish" would not appear to have been
soothed by *Young Man with a Horn*. His hyperbole aside, Emge was realistic about the quality of *The Strip*, noting that although it was a "great

advance over previous attempts to catch the essence of jazz music and combine it as a factor in a screenplay," this advance alone was not enough to make it a great picture.[94] Emge praised the manner in which jazz was integrated with the story, a use of the music that avoided the "haphazard" incorporation of jazz that Feather observed was standard Hollywood practice in the 1940s.

Nevertheless, although *Young Man with a Horn* did not appear to find the approval of its contemporary jazz audience, James Robertson argues that, for its time, it was "one of the best films about jazz ever made."[95] But old conventions remained in force. The white pupil eventually surpasses his black teacher and neither are permitted to be intellectual instrumentalists. Rick may learn everything from Art, but it is still for him, the white musician, to improve upon the black musician's ability, as Foreman's script describes:

> Hearing him, we realize that he has developed the same power and drive that characterize Art Hazzard's playing, but that he has brought to it an easy, soulful, bell-like style.
>
> VOICE: It was the way he'd learned from those two genuine artists—Jeff Williams and Art Hazzard—and naturally he played their kind of music. But he brought something to it that was all his own. . . . [96]

Foreman's description of Art and Jeff Williams, a character who was ultimately dropped from the film with his dialogue being allocated to Art instead, as "genuine artists" is an unusual one for a Hollywood script to make given the almost exclusively negative black characterizations that filled films of the time. That racism affected the film is without doubt. As I discuss in Chapter 2, the film's production team was concerned about Kirk Douglas being seen playing alongside black musicians, and the central black characters of Rick's closest friend, Smoke, and his girlfriend were recast as white. Foreman's draft of the script, although endorsing these casting decisions, does demonstrate an awareness of how a Hollywood film of the time would likely portray black characters. Following Art's death in a road accident, Rick attends his mentor's funeral where he is the only white member of the congregation. Foreman's script is explicit as to how the black congregation should be represented:

> NOTE: Throughout this sequence, none of the people are played for comedy or in caricature. The church is small and old, but clean. The people are dressed for the occasion. They are human beings.[97]

Prior to this sequence, Foreman's script also suggests an understanding of jazz as being music of black origin. When Rick gets a job with the Jack Stuart band, a conventional dance band with no pretensions to playing jazz, he is criticized by his leader for attempting to introduce some jazz into the proceedings at the same time as having his musicianship acknowledged:

STUART: (raging) You play a pretty good horn, Martin, but I told you once and I'm telling you again! This is a white man's band, and that's the kind of music we play! Is that clear?[98]

Shortly after this outburst, Stuart confides in Rick that, "I happen to know you're the only real musician in the crew—you just forget that barrel house stuff and you can have anything I've got."[99] Rick, of course, doesn't forget that "barrel-house stuff," and it is during a later performance that he hosts an impromptu jam session. Once Stuart has returned and brought the jazz to a halt, Rick anticipates Stuart's anger with the comment, "I know—it's a white man's band."[100] The inference is that jazz is black music. Rick's obsession to play this music eventually leads to his downfall; jazz, the suggestion appears to be, is not a healthy pursuit. An oppositional reading of the film, and one that would follow a noir sensibility, however, can interpret *Young Man with a Horn* as being not so clear about the white musician's superiority. Ultimately, Rick is unable to "make it" as an out-and-out jazz musician; he is forced to admit defeat in his quest for the musical grail of a new sound. The white jazz musician fails. But, at the same time as the film's release, black musicians *were* pioneering new sounds and proving successful at playing them *and* leading stable lives. The obvious exception was Charlie Parker, the principal figure behind bebop, who died in 1955 at age thirty-five. Although it would be more than thirty years before a Hollywood film attempted to tackle Parker's extraordinary life, the myth of his life and music, particularly his capacity for substance abuse, would seep into images of jazz on film throughout the years following his death. Not surprisingly, many of those images were to be found in film noir.

NOTES

1. Tuska, J. 1984. *Dark Cinema: American Film Noir in Cultural Perspective.* Westport, Conn.: Greenwood Press. p. 195.

2. Official (undated) press book for *Phantom Lady* (Universal Pictures, 1944). Special Collections, USC, Cinema and Television Library.

3. Ibid.

4. *Variety,* January 26, 1944.

5. *New York Times,* February 18, 1944.

6. Williams, T. 1996. *Phantom Lady,* Cornell Woolrich, and the masochistic aesthetic. In A. Silver and J. Ursini, eds. *Film Noir Reader.* New York: Limelight Editions. p. 134.

7. Woolrich, C. (as William Irish) 1982. *Phantom Lady.* New York: Ballantine Books. p. 135.

8. *Motion Picture Daily,* January 21, 1944, and *The Hollywood Reporter,* January 21, 1944.

9. Official (undated) press book for *Phantom Lady* (Universal Pictures, 1944). Special Collections, USC Cinema and Television Library.

10. Ibid.

11. Ibid.

12. Letter from Joseph Breen to Maurice Pivar, September 16, 1943. MPAA files for *Phantom Lady*. Special Collections, Margaret Herrick Library.

13. Letter from Joseph Breen to Maurice Pivar, September 3, 1943. MPAA files for *Phantom Lady*. Special Collections, Margaret Herrick Library.

14. Woolrich, C. (as William Irish) 1982. *Phantom Lady*. New York: Ballantine Books. p. 134.

15. Letter from Joseph Breen to Maurice Pivar, September 3, 1943. MPAA files for *Phantom Lady*. Special Collections, Margaret Herrick Library.

16. Letter from Joseph Breen to Maurice Pivar, September 16, 1943. MPAA files for *Phantom Lady*. Special Collections, Margaret Herrick Library.

17. Williams, T. 1996. *Phantom Lady,* Cornell Woolrich, and the masochistic aesthetic. In A. Silver and J. Ursini, eds. *Film Noir Reader*. New York: Limelight Editions. p. 140.

18. Ibid., p. 130.

19. Woolrich, C. (as William Irish) 1982. *Phantom Lady*. New York: Ballantine Books. p. 135.

20. Ibid.

21. Official (undated) press book for *Phantom Lady* (Universal Pictures, 1944). Special Collections, USC Cinema and Television Library.

22. Letter from Joseph Breen enclosing report from the Pennsylvanian Censor Board (January 31, 1944), April 14, 1944. MPAA files for *Phantom Lady*. Special Collections, Margaret Herrick Library.

23. Ibid.

24. Porfirio, R. 1999. Dark jazz: Music in the film noir. In A. Silver and J. Ursini, eds. *Film Noir Reader* 2. New York: Limehouse Editions. p. 178.

25. Rózsa's "Main Title" cue ran to 2:32 minutes and "Dix's Demise" ran to 3:17 minutes. The music details for *The Asphalt Jungle* are listed in a document from the music copyright department of Loew's Incorporated, titled "Musical Compositions Recorded in a Production Entitled: THE ASPHALT JUNGLE," March 7, 1950. Special Collections, USC Cinema and Television Library.

26. Screenplay for *The Asphalt Jungle*, October 12, 1949, scenes 206–8, p. 123. Arts Special Collections, UCLA.

27. "Musical Compositions Recorded in a Production Entitled: THE ASPHALT JUNGLE," March 7, 1950. Special Collections, USC Cinema and Television Library.

28. Porfirio, R. 1999. Dark jazz: Music in the film noir. In A. Silver and J. Ursini, eds. *Film Noir Reader* 2. New York: Limehouse Editions. p. 180.

29. For a detailed discussion of the enforced changes to *Paris Blues,* see the chapter on Duke Ellington in Gabbard, K. 1996. *Jammin' at the Margins: Jazz and the American Cinema*. Chicago: University of Chicago Press. Alternatively, David Hajdu's biography of Billy Strayhorn contains a short but fascinating section on the film: Hajdu, D. 1997. *Lush Life: A Biography of Billy Strayhorn*. London: Granta. pp. 206–11.

30. Nash, J.R., and Ross, S.R., eds. 1986. *The Motion Picture Guide: H-K 1927–1983*. Chicago: Cinebooks, Inc. p. 1431.

31. Sidran, B. 1995. *Black Talk: How the Music of Black America Created a Radical Alternative to the Western Literary Tradition*. Edinburgh: Payback Press. p. 105.

32. Interoffice communication from Jerry Wald to Steve Trilling, June 23, 1947. Box 29: *Young Man with a Horn,* Jack L. Warner Collection, Special Collections, USC Cinema and Television Library.

33. Screenplay for *Young Man with a Horn*, undated first draft by Carl Foreman. Scene 142, p. 60. Arts Special Collections, UCLA.

34. Amy is given this description in an official review of the film (September 7, 1949) that was enclosed in a letter from Joseph Breen to Jack Warner granting the film its Certificate of Approval, September 21, 1949. MPAA files for *Young Man with a Horn*. Special Collections, Margaret Herrick Library.

35. Screenplay for *Young Man with a Horn,* undated first draft by Carl Foreman. Scene 284, p. 121. Arts Special Collections, UCLA.

36. Interoffice communication from Steve Trilling to Roy Obringer, May 6, 1949. Box 29: *Young Man with a Horn*. Jack L. Warner Collection, Special Collections, USC Cinema and Television Library.

37. Becker, H.S. 1963. *Outsiders: Studies in the Sociology of Deviation*. New York: Free Press. pp. 82–83.

38. Lees, G. 1991. *Waiting for Dizzy*. New York: Oxford University Press. p. 131.

39. Kemp, A. 1996. *The Musical Temperament: Psychology and Personality of Musicians*. Oxford: Oxford University Press. p. 189.

40. Pfeil, F. 1993. Home fires burning: Family *noir* in *Blue Velvet* and *Terminator 2*. In J. Copjec, ed. *Shades of Noir*. London: Verso. p. 229.

41. Ibid.

42. Becker, H.S. 1963. *Outsiders: Studies in the Sociology of Deviation*. New York: Free Press. p. 119. Becker notes that the family, as institution, "demands that the musician behave conventionally, creates problems for him of conflicting pressures, loyalties and self-conceptions. His response to these problems has a decisive effect on the duration and direction of his career." Rick Martin's response to these problems is, arguably, disastrous.

43. Robertson, J.C. 1993. *The Casablanca Man: The Cinema of Michael Curtiz*. London: Routledge. p. 144. Robertson observes that the choice of Curtiz as director of a number of early socially realistic Warner's films was made because "cynicism tended to surface in such films with action plots centered upon the law and law breakers, and Curtiz was undoubtedly selected for such movies because they were perfectly suited to his cinematic style and personality." Canham, K. 1973. *The Hollywood Professionals, Volume One*. London: Tantivy Press; New York: A.S. Barnes & Co. pp. 52–53. Similarly, Kingsley Canham cites cynicism as being a feature of Curtiz's work and one of the factors that has enabled his cinema to "live on."

44. Synopsis enclosed with the film's Certificate of Approval, in a letter from Joseph Breen to Jack Warner, September 21, 1949. MPAA files for *Young Man with a Horn*. Special Collections, Margaret Herrick Library. Foreman's script, which also begins with the taxicab accident, is held by the Arts Special Collections, UCLA.

45. Cook, P. 1993. *The Cinema Book*. London: BFI. p. 93.

46. Review by Meta Arenson for Warner Bros. Pictures, Inc. Story Department, June 27, 1938. Box 29, *Young Man with a Horn*. Jack L. Warner Collection, Special Collections, USC Cinema and Television Library.

47. Screenplay for *Young Man with a Horn*, undated first draft by Carl Foreman. Scenes 317–19, p. 137. Arts Special Collections, UCLA.

48. Robertson, J.C. 1993. *The Casablanca Man: The Cinema of Michael Curtiz*. London: Routledge. p. 103.

49. Undated original synopsis from Warner Bros., Burbank, California, HO 9-0221 (marked revcc 82249). MPAA files for *Young Man with a Horn*. Special Collections, Margaret Herrick Library.

50. Revised synopsis enclosed with the film's Certificate of Approval, September 21, 1949. MPAA files for *Young Man with a Horn*. Special Collections, Margaret Herrick Library.

51. *Reporter*, February 8, 1950.

52. *New York Herald Tribune*, February 10, 1950.

53. Copjec, J. 1993. *Shades of Noir*. London: Verso, p. 183.

54. At Benny Goodman's 1938 Carnegie Hall Concert, a "Twenty Years of Jazz" section was programmed. Harry James agreed to represent the absent Louis Armstrong, claiming he could replicate Armstrong's chorus on the tune *Shine*. The result was clearly James, but definitely in the spirit and style of Armstrong.

55. Gabbard, K. 1996. *Jammin' at the Margins: Jazz and the American Cinema*. Chicago: The University of Chicago Press.

56. Ibid., p. 144.

57. Ibid., pp. 139–40. Gabbard cites *Mo' Better Blues* (1990), *Young Man with a Horn, The Five Pennies* (1959) and *New York, New York* (1977) as containing examples of the symbolically castrated jazz musician.

58. Taylor, J.R. 1983. *Strangers in Paradise: The Hollywood Emigrés 1933-1950*. London: Faber & Faber Ltd. p. 209. Taylor notes that "producers of routine thrillers and us-and-them melodrama . . . found themselves impelled . . . to make key characters 'longhair' artists, writers and musicians. These 'longhairs' were no longer regarded as necessarily crazed merely because of their artistic calling. They certainly might be . . . but John Garfield as a tough violinist of working-class origins in *Humoresque* is carefully presented as all-man, and Paul Henreid as the cellist (of all things!) in *Deception* is by far the sanest character around."

59. Undated production notes on *Young Man with a Horn* from Warner Bros. Studio. Folder 665, *Young Man with a Horn*. Jack L. Warner Collection, Special Collections, USC Cinema and Television Library.

60. Ibid.

61. Ibid.

62. Ibid.

63. Interoffice communication from Jerry Wald to Jack Warner, April 8, 1947. Box 29, *Young Man with a Horn*. Jack L. Warner Collection, Special Collections, USC Cinema and Television Library.

64. Review by Meta Arenson for Warner Bros. Pictures, Inc. Story Department, June 27, 1938. Box 29, *Young Man with a Horn*. Jack L. Warner Collection, Special Collections, USC Cinema and Television Library.

65. Interoffice communication from Irene Lee to Sam Bischoff, June 30, 1938.

Box 29, *Young Man with a Horn.* Jack L. Warner Collection, Special Collections, USC Cinema and Television Library.

66. Ibid. Bischoff's response is written on his behalf on the same memo.

67. Interoffice communication from McDermid to Irene Lee, June 28, 1938. Box 29, *Young Man with a Horn.* Jack L. Warner Collection, Special Collections, USC Cinema and Television Library.

68. Alexander refers to a discussion he had with Trilling about the nature of the film's musical content. Letter from Willard Alexander to Ray Heindorf (the film's musical director), April 19, 1949. Box 29, *Young Man with a Horn.* Jack L. Warner Collection, Special Collections, USC Cinema and Television Library.

69. Certificate of Approval, sent to Jack Warner from Jospeh Breen, September 21, 1949. MPAA files for *Young Man with a Horn.* Special Collections, Margaret Herrick Library.

70. Interoffice communication from Collier Young to Steve Trilling, May 19, 1947. Box 29, *Young Man with a Horn.* Jack L. Warner Collection, Special Collections, USC Cinema and Television Library. Young suggested to Trilling that Welles "who I understand likes the subject, could direct this with great understanding."

71. Letter from Glaser to Trilling, May 17, 1949. Box 29, *Young Man with a Horn.* Jack L. Warner Collection, Special Collections, USC Cinema and Television Library.

72. Letter from Trilling to Charlie Yates, June 23, 1949. Jack L. Warner Collection, Special Collections, USC Cinema and Television Library. Box 29, *Young Man with a Horn.*

73. Gabbard K. 1996. *Jammin' at the Margins: Jazz and the American Cinema.* Chicago: The University of Chicago Press. An excellent discussion of Armstrong's film career.

74. Production notes on *Young Man with a Horn* from Warner Bros. Studio. Folder 665, *Young Man with a Horn.* Jack L. Warner Collection, Special Collections, USC Cinema and Television Library.

75. Sidran, B. 1995. *Black Talk: How the Music of Black America Created a Radical Alternative to the Western Literary Tradition.* Edinburgh: Payback Press. p. 99.

76. Sidran, B. 1995. *Black Talk: How the Music of Black America Created a Radical Alternative to the Western Literary Tradition.* Edinburgh: Payback Press. p. 96.

77. DeVeaux, S. 1997. *The Birth of Bebop: A Social and Musical History.* Berkekley and Los Angeles: University of California Press. p. 4.

78. Ibid., p. 269.

79. Ibid., p. 440.

80. Official (undated) press book for *Phantom Lady* (1944, Universal Pictures). Special Collections, USC Cinema and Television Library.

81. Porfirio, R. 1980. Phantom lady. In A. Silver and E. Ward, eds. *Film Noir.* London: Secker & Warburg. p. 226.

82. Dyer, R. 1993. *The Matter of Images: Essays on Representations.* London: Routledge. p. 56.

83. Tuska, J. 1984. *Dark Cinema: American Film Noir in Cultural Perspective.* Westport, Conn.: Greenwood Press. pp. 223–24.

84. Screenplay for *Young Man with a Horn,* undated first draft by Carl Foreman. Scene 78, p.30. Arts Special Collections, UCLA.

85. Ibid., Scene 112, p. 44.

86. Sidran, B. 1995. *Black Talk: How the Music of Black America Created a Radical Alternative to the Western Literary Tradition.* Edinburgh: Payback Press. p. 102.

87. Ibid.

88. *New York Times,* February 10, 1950.

89. *Reporter,* February 8, 1950.

90. *Motion Picture Daily,* February 8, 1950.

91. *Down Beat.* vol. 20, no. 17. August 26, 1953. p. 3.

92. Emge, C. 1951. "Strip" Is Adjudged Best "Jazz Film" To Date. In *Down Beat.* vol. 18, no. 22, November 2, p. 6.

93. Ibid.

94. Ibid.

95. Robertson, J.C. 1993. *The Casablanca Man: The Cinema of Michael Curtiz.* London: Routledge. p. 104. It is unlikely that such a claim could be made for *Young Man with a Horn* today.

96. Screenplay for *Young Man with a Horn,* undated first draft by Carl Foreman. Scene 78, p. 30. Arts Special Collections, UCLA.

97. Ibid., Scene 263, p. 118.

98. Ibid., Scene 105, p. 40.

99. Ibid., Scene 106, p. 41.

100. Ibid., Scene 134, p. 54.

4

Touch of Kenton
Jazz in 1950s Film Noir

By the beginning of the 1950s, jazz was becoming increasingly fragmented, with styles ranging from those of New Orleans and Chicago to swing, bebop and cool. Jazz no longer had the wide appeal that it had enjoyed in the Swing Era of the late '30s and early '40s. Film noir, however, had just reached its peak with several years of its classic period still to come. Although jazz's status as a popular music was declining, its acceptance as "art" music was slowly increasing. Yet the respectability being accorded to jazz that encouraged its use in film music was seldom reflected by the films themselves. Styles of jazz were predominantly used to underscore the film noir or films that involved crime and immorality. In this chapter, I discuss the development of the jazz-inflected score during the 1950s. The focus will be on David Raksin's score for *The Big Combo* (1953), the 1955 social problem film *The Man with the Golden Arm* and the late noir entries *The Sweet Smell of Success* (1957) and *I Want To Live!* (1958). I will argue that the most influential jazz musician on the music's use in film during this period was the white bandleader Stan Kenton. Exploring the possible reasons for Kenton's influence in Hollywood and why Duke Ellington, generally accepted as the finest composer in jazz, did not provide this influence, I will demonstrate that the "progressive" jazz Kenton championed was echoed in Elmer Bernstein's jazz-inflected scores for *The Man with the Golden Arm* and *The Sweet Smell of Success* and directly influenced Henry Mancini's score for *Touch of Evil* (1958).

A SOUNDTRACK NAMED DESIRE:
JAZZ IN THE EARLY 1950s FILM SCORE

Jazz relied on a clear justification for its use in a film. The use of a romantic-symphonic orchestra continues to be considered acceptable for a film set in a time and place where such a form of musical accompaniment would be unlikely, if not impossible. As the composer and jazz musician Lennie Niehaus notes, however, this allowance for musical anachronism is not easily extended to jazz:

> Jazz in film must be utilized with great care. Obviously in a Western or any period movie, jazz would not be appropriate. An upbeat jazz tune is basically a happy sound and would not be appropriate for many movies.[1]

As I later discuss, it was not the "happy sound" of jazz that came to the fore in the 1950s. In order for jazz to be used in a film score of the 1940s and early 1950s, there had to be a logical reason for its presence on the soundtrack. As seen in the previous chapter, this justification often came in the form of a jukebox or a band playing in a club. These on-screen explanations were limited to diegetic music, but the need to justify the involvement of jazz was equally extended to the nondiegetic score.

The rare instances of jazz being worked into a music score during the early 1950s occurred, in part, because the composers in question were waiting for a project in which they could incorporate jazz without having to justify its use. The trumpeter and composer Shorty Rogers would collaborate on a number of the pioneering jazz-inflected scores. As he revealed to Fred Steiner, both Elmer Bernstein and Leith Stevens (who scored, respectively, *The Man with the Golden Arm* and *The Wild One* [1953]) were keen to utilize jazz and were simply "waiting for the right piece of film to come along and they were ready to go."[2]

The setting of New Orleans, the birthplace of jazz, and the Four Deuces jazz club provided Alex North with the geographical justification for his jazz-inflected score for *A Streetcar Named Desire* (1951). North's music for *Streetcar* was a breakthrough for the use of jazz in a film:

> *A Streetcar Named Desire* is a landmark in the history of Hollywood music. It was a considerable departure from current concepts in scoring; it was, in fact, the first major jazz oriented score and its impact was instantaneous. Richly coloured with the sound of New Orleans jazz, the music wailed and stung, it pointed up Brando's coarse Kowalski and tinged the delusion and despair of Vivien Leigh's Blanche.[3]

This assessment of North's score is possibly overstating its significance somewhat. The music was met with great acclaim, as we shall see, but it did not trigger off a sudden explosion of jazz-inflected scores in the way that Elmer Bernstein's music for *The Man with the Golden Arm* would four years later. North's score was an important stepping stone, helping to pave the way for future jazz-related projects, but its blending of jazz and classical idioms was perhaps too subtle to have an immediate and broad impact on film music. Whereas Bernstein's music for *The Man with the Golden Arm* would result in the release of a song that was successfully constructed to have hit potential, tellingly, North's score did not (although a record of the music was made available). Instead, North was encouraged to preserve it in a form "other than background for a picture," namely, to adapt it into a concert suite.[4]

There had been jazz-inflected scores before *A Streetcar Named Desire*. Kathryn Kalinak offers a more cautious acknowledgment of North's music:

> As early as 1937 George Antheil included elements of jazz in his score for *The Plainsman* as did David Raksin in his 1948 score for *Force of Evil*. But it was the early fifties that saw the institutionalization of jazz through the success of such films as *Panic in the Streets* (1950) . . . (and) *A Streetcar Named Desire* (1951).[5]

North was no stranger to jazz. Having been commissioned by Benny Goodman to write a concerto for clarinet and orchestra in which he tried to "simulate jazz in a classical structure," North applied the same approach to *A Streetcar Named Desire*.[6] He was clearly sympathetic to the idiom. Born in America of Russian parents, he traveled to Russia (officially as a telegraphic engineer) to further his musical education at a Moscow conservatory, but was drawn back to America by his love of jazz:

> I gradually got homesick for American music. I remember one night playing a recording of Duke Ellington's *Mood Indigo* and breaking into tears. As a kid working in Atlantic City I used to go to the Steel Pier and listen to Paul Whiteman, Coon Sanders and Ted Weems. I soaked up all kinds of jazz, and suddenly it hit me in Moscow. I had to go home.[7]

Despite a genuine appreciation of jazz and a decision to incorporate it into the film's score that was not an attempt to take advantage of its commercial possibilities (indeed, North was congratulated on his "almost uncommercial" jazz!), North's music for *A Streetcar Named Desire* could not escape the conventions that would determine where and when jazz was employed in the classical Hollywood score.[8] Caryl Flinn argues that Hollywood films have sought, through music, to create the possibility of a utopian space for the audience. The chosen sound of this utopian promise was provided by the symphonic orchestra rooted in romanticism (Flinn specifically refers to the influence of Wagner).[9] Jazz, however, as Chapter 2 discussed, was used in the classical Hollywood score as the sound of "otherness" and a threat or opposition to the utopian symphony orchestra. The "landmark" use of jazz by North may have given a greater focus to the music, but, as Gorbman notes, it did so without contradicting any of the values of the dominant classical Hollywood score:

> However unconventional or avant-garde a Hollywood musical score might be, the film always motivates it in conventional ways. Thus there is little that's progressive or subversive about jazz in the milieu of drug addiction in *The Man with the Golden Arm*, the electronic sounds that waft over the strange *Forbidden Planet* or the electronically generated music complicit with the alcoholic dementia of Ray Milland in *The Lost Weekend*.[10]

Similarly, for *A Streetcar Named Desire* and its tale of sexual desire, rape and insanity, the use of jazz can be comfortably accommodated by the dominant ideology of the Hollywood score. Even North, who argued for an acceptance of jazz by the "serious" musical establishment, consistently referred to jazz's potential to underscore the seedy and immoral throughout his score for *A Streetcar Named Desire*. The manuscripts of the score reveal a clear intention to use jazz elements as the sound of sex. For the music underscoring reel 3, part 1, North includes the advice "sexy, virile" and the instrumentation features muted trumpet.[11] Mutes are not exclusive to jazz, but their use was a feature of jazz brass musicians and was particularly associated with the growling "jungle" sound of the Ellington orchestra. From bar 13 onward in this section, the instrumentation is that of the conventional jazz group: trumpets, saxes, piano and drums. Reel 5, part 4 contains a cue titled "Mitch and Blanche on staircase," which is scored for muted trumpets, trombones, piano solo and plucked bass and carries the advice "slow, freely in blue style." Most explicit is the theme titled "Lust" that runs from bar 42 in reel 13, part 1 into reel 13, part 2. Scored, again, for muted trumpet, the recommendation for the musician in this cue is simply one word: "dirty." Significantly, Blanche's fantasies and dreams of a nobler, purer life dispense with jazz voicings. Reel 7, number 1, for example, features a cue called "Belle Reeve," which, in bars 11-12, is scored for solo viola, celesta and solo cello with the instruction "magic-like, shimmering."

Even the best efforts of a composer seeking to free jazz from its association with clichés of sex and immorality could be undermined by a film's overall form and tone. David Raksin made considerable use of jazz elements in many of his scores (several of which predated *A Streetcar Named Desire*) and was aware of the codings applied to jazz. For the 1944 film noir *Laura*, Raksin had opposed director Otto Preminger's wish to use Duke Ellington's "Sophisticated Lady" as a theme for the film's eponymous mystery woman. The association of jazz with a woman of sexual experience, such as Laura, was something that Raksin was keen to avoid. As Kalinak discusses:

Raksin objected to "Sophisticated Lady," precisely because it embodied what he has called "the usual Hollywood approach to a woman of relatively easy virtue." . . . Because Laura had had lovers in the past, she was a woman of sexual experience which required a certain type of music to characterize her. Raksin argued for an original theme and Preminger gave him the chance to compose one. What Raksin produced became the melody immortalized as "Laura," a theme which represents a direct reaction against the classical score's formulaic conventions for the representation of female sexuality. . . . At least part of the film's ambivalence toward Laura's sexuality can be attributed to the tension between the image track and the music track.[12]

The coolness of the "Laura" theme moved it away from the "oleaginous saxophones" that might have been expected to underscore a character like Laura. Raksin's "Laura" nevertheless became a hit and was, ironically, interpreted by a number of leading jazz musicians such as Dave Brubeck and Stan Kenton.

A decade after *Laura*, Raksin provided a score for another classic noir, *The Big Combo* (1953). Directed by Joseph H. Lewis, *The Big Combo* is a visceral story of organized crime and obsessive love. Detective Leonard Diamond is attempting to arrest the enigmatic Mr. Brown, the head of a crime syndicate, but cannot find a means of proving Brown's guilt. Obsessed with putting Brown in prison, Diamond becomes equally obsessed with Brown's girlfriend, Susan Lowell, whom he originally sees as a means of capturing Brown. As the film progresses, Diamond falls in love with Susan and neglects Rita, his stripper girlfriend whose fate is to be shot by Brown's thugs.

Raksin furnishes *The Big Combo* with a driving score that makes excellent use of jazz voicings. The opening theme is clearly jazz-inflected. For the credits sequence of an overhead shot of the city lights at night, Raksin introduces a theme that recurs throughout the film. This central theme is played by a solo soprano saxophone over rich brass orchestration with big band textures. It was not unusual for Raksin to incorporate elements that were so obviously jazz-derived. Kalinak provides a neat summation of Raksin's compositional style and its acceptance of jazz:

Raksin seldom adopted the symphonic medium of the thirties score, using instead the pared down and smaller ensembles more characteristic of twentieth-century music. The dominance of strings, and indeed the very concept of melody, is not characteristic of Raksin's music. If anything, the instruments of jazz—brass, woodwinds, percussion—dominate his work.[13]

The significance of the soprano saxophone theme soon becomes apparent. In an early scene, Diamond's growing obsession with Susan is pointed out by one of his colleagues who tells him, "I'm not in love with her, Leonard; you are!" At this point the opening theme, played, again on the soprano saxophone, is heard on the score creating an association between the saxophone theme and Susan. The following scene takes place in a restaurant where a small jazz combo is playing (bass, piano, electric guitar and drums). Susan is eating at a table with Fante and Mingo, Brown's henchmen. The piano is playing the opening theme for soprano saxophone, thus confirming its status as Susan's theme. Susan asks an old man to dance with her, to her theme, but collapses, uttering that she thinks she is dying. Susan's siren song, that draws Diamond deeper into Brown's world, may suggest love, but it is a love that is doom-laden, as all those around Diamond and Susan come to a violent end. This theme propels Diamond further on his quest into Brown's lair. As Diamond drives through the city by night the theme returns, without drums, as rhythmic figures are provided by the brass. After the final encounter with Brown in an aircraft hangar shrouded in mist, the soprano saxophone theme is heard for the last time as the silhouette of Susan crosses to that of Diamond and their two shadows walk away, disappearing into the same mist that the criminal Brown has just been marched off into by the police. The music on the score swells in volume as the film comes to an end, echoing the brassy, big band sound of the opening credits.

Raksin's music and his decision to underscore Susan with a jazz-related theme creates an ambiguity concerning the film's representation of its two main female characters in a way not dissimilar to Kalinak's argument for Raksin's central theme in *Laura*. Ostensibly, *The Big Combo* presents yet another of Hollywood's virgin/whore oppositions in the characters of Susan and Rita. Rita, Diamond's girlfriend, is cast as the fallen woman. Her appearance contrasts starkly with that of Susan. Rita has dark hair and wears dark clothes and, not surprisingly, works as a stripper performing to brash jazz music. Susan is blond and wears white, speaks with a soft and anxious educated accent and listens to modern classical piano. Susan is privileged by the lighting, notably in the scene at a solo piano recital where she is picked out in white light. As Richard Dyer has extensively demonstrated, whiteness in Western art and popular culture has traditionally been equated with purity and the ideal woman.[14]

For the majority of the film, Susan is effectively owned by Brown. Brown makes demands of Susan that anticipate the efforts of James Stewart to shape Kim Novak into his perfect woman in *Vertigo* (1958). It is Brown who requests that Susan wears white, even though she does not want to. Brown clings to Susan's purity as if to cleanse himself of the memory of his wife. When Susan questions Brown about his wife, he becomes disgusted at the thought of the drunken "lush" she has degenerated into. "Leave me some pride," he says to Susan. Susan's only escape from her miserable existence with Brown is through her music. Brown does not like her taste in music and tells her to stop playing it. The modern classical piano that she listens to, performed on the soundtrack by Jacob Gimbel, is coded as being intellectual and thus another example of Susan's purity and perfection. It is placed in sharp opposition to the big band jazz to which Rita performs her striptease routine. When Diamond meets Rita backstage at the strip club, the jazz band can be heard as she is about to go on stage. "That's my music," says Rita, and she embraces Diamond almost as if she is performing part of her routine for him. The jazz music filtering through from the stage orchestra suggests that Diamond only thinks of Rita in sexual terms as a performer and does not really love her.

In this simple clash, classical music is presented as being superior to jazz. Jazz is most strikingly used in the film in the scene where Brown and his cohorts torture the captured Diamond by using the amplifier on a hearing aid to blast the "crazy drums" solo from a bop-oriented big band radio broadcast into Diamond's ear at full volume. In this scene, jazz is used as a weapon. Nowhere else in film noir is the association of jazz with violence and confusion so explicit. But if Susan's liking for modern piano is coded as being superior to jazz and beyond the comprehension of Brown, the film is careful not to assert that everybody should listen to a healthy dose of dissonant contemporary music. Susan's appreciation of this music is ultimately seen to be excessive and unnatural. As she listens to the piano concert she says to Diamond, "I live in a maze . . . and all the twisting paths lead back to Mr. Brown." The pianist on stage is performing in near darkness, and his recital comprises fast runs and discordant passages that suggest the fear and anxiety of Susan's life. But when Diamond tells Susan that his superior thinks that Diamond loves her, the piano music becomes softer and less technically complex.

Diamond, the film's male lead, must rescue Susan not only from Brown but from her intellectual music as well and assert the authority of the ideal heterosexual romance. (Notably, the gay couple Fante and Mingo, who act as Brown's heavies and torture Diamond with the "crazy" bop music, are destroyed by a bomb courtesy of their employer.) Possessed by Brown, the "fetishized" Susan represents Diamond's inferiority to Brown. In psychoanalytical terms, Susan is the phallus that Diamond lacks and for which he envies Brown. To gain control of the "phallicized" Susan, Diamond has to conquer Brown and the music that Brown could not prevent Susan from listening to. Diamond achieves these aims, of course, and his masculinity is not called into question by the end of the film.

The opposition between jazz and classical music, however, is not reflected by Raksin's score. In fact, Raksin blurs the crude parallel between jazz and classical music that the rest of the film presents. All of the jazz music used for Rita and the torture scene is source music that does not emanate from Raksin's nondiegetic score. Despite the filmmakers' decision to associate Susan with classical music and Rita with jazz, precisely the kind of distinction that Raksin fought against in *Laura*, Raksin again subverts this simple contrast by developing a bluesy soprano saxophone theme for Susan that seems to be at odds with the "pure" Susan that the rest of the film goes to great lengths to construct. Raksin's theme for Susan acts in almost an inverse way to his theme for Laura. Whereas Raksin opposed the simple and obvious equation of jazz with a "woman like Laura," his main theme in *The Big Combo* disrupts the simple and obvious construction of Susan as being emblematic of purity in part through her liking for modern classical music. By scoring Susan's theme as a jazz-inflected piece, Raksin draws on the film's crude coding of jazz as the seedy music of a stripper (Rita) and turns it on the film's privileged female character. In "tainting" Susan with jazz, Raksin suggests the impossibility of her constructed image of purity and gives her a sexual life that the film seems to be denying. Raksin also makes it clear why Diamond is so intent on possessing Susan and undermines any possibility of there being a noble concept of love and the chivalrous knight rescuing the damsel in distress from her vile captor, which is entirely appropriate for the cynicism of film noir. Raksin may have been aware of Hollywood's treatment of jazz in the classical era and actively resisted or subverted it, but his music in *The Big Combo*, despite adding depth to the film's basic opposition of jazz and classical, still linked jazz with sex.

But no matter how they were manipulated to ideologically support the dominance of the classical Hollywood score, these early jazz-inflected scores were essential for making jazz more widely accepted in American film music. The score for *A Streetcar Named Desire*, for example, received a favorable critical response, and its use of jazz elements did not go unnoticed. The film's director, Elia Kazan, was fulsome in his praise and told North that the film was lucky to have had him working on it.[15] Samuel Goldwyn wrote to North after seeing the film to congratulate him on his "simply beautiful" music and express his hope that they would work on a project together.[16] Beyond Hollywood, the reaction to the music was equally impressed. *Cahiers du Cinéma* noted that the:

> . . . use of a music admirable in itself is quite extraordinary. It is impossible not to be sensitive to the heavy and corrosive anguish which these jazz-themes distill when Blanche du Bois periodically sinks into the maelstrom of her vice.[17]

Jazz may have been used as the sound of "corrosive anguish," and so the values of the classical Hollywood score were maintained, but the fact that it was granted the opportunity to feature on the musical score to such an extent was significant. It was not simply the fact that North was using jazz elements that was important. It was how and where he incorporated jazz that was equally unusual. Russell Lack's discussion of North's score highlights its advances for jazz in film music, noting that the composer sought through small group arrangements to "link as much as possible the narrative underscore with the omnipresent jazz that filters from the Four

Deuces Café, giving the main score of the film opportunities to develop from the musical cues given on screen."[18]

Had *A Streetcar Named Desire* been made earlier or by a different production team, it is possible that jazz would not have been woven so integrally into the film's score. In other hands, the Four Deuces club setting, which is not entered into during the film, but is, as Lack puts it, "omnipresent," may have been seen as an opportunity to present a jazz sequence. Such a sequence, possibly performed by a leading black musician such as Louis Armstrong, would provide the film with its dose of otherness, but could easily be cut out to appease racist exhibitors while a symphonic classical Hollywood score would flow on unaffected by the jazz club. North's use of jazz is not so obviously inserted, but runs throughout the film.

Perhaps the most significant praise for North's music came from a major jazz musician. Four years after the release of *A Streetcar Named Desire*, the black trumpeter and composer Miles Davis was interviewed by jazz writer Nat Hentoff for *Down Beat* magazine. Davis was a forward-thinking musician who provided fresh directions for the development of jazz throughout his career. For the Hentoff interview, Davis was asked to give his opinion on his contemporaries and who he thought were the most interesting musicians in jazz. Discussing the merits of the various big bands, Davis made an interesting association between Stan Kenton and Alex North:

> Do you know the best thing I've heard in a long time? Alex North's music for *A Streetcar Named Desire* (Capitol LP P-387). That's a wild record— especially the part Benny Carter plays. If anybody is going to be able to write for strings in the jazz idiom or something near to it, it'll be North. I'd recommend everyone hearing that music. Now as for Kenton, I can't think of anything he did original. Everything he did, everybody else did before. Kenton is nowhere in the class with somebody like Duke (Ellington). Duke has done more for jazz than anyone I could name.[19]

Davis did not give his praise to other musicians lightly, and his genuine enthusiasm for North's score would be reflected in a series of musical projects that he collaborated on with the composer and arranger Gil Evans over the course of the following years. *Miles Ahead* (1957), *Porgy and Bess* (1958) and *Sketches of Spain* (1960) would pair Davis' solo trumpet and flugelhorn with rich orchestral settings that created evocative sound worlds not unlike film music. But why should Davis speak of the bandleader Stan Kenton in a discussion about North's film music? As I argue in the next section, the connection is not such an unusual one.

ARTISTRY IN NOIR:
STAN KENTON AND PROGRESSIVE JAZZ

Stan Kenton is a controversial figure in jazz history. Born in 1911, Kenton formed his first band in 1941; a fourteen-piece unit titled the

Artistry in Rhythm Orchestra. By the mid-1940s, the Kenton band had acquired a large following and its popularity was reflected in its success in
the polls of jazz magazines such as *Down Beat*. The response of jazz critics
and musicians to Kenton's band was less enthusiastic, however. Fellow
bandleader Charlie Barnet asserted that Kenton "killed the dance-band
business," while guitarist Eddie Condon noted that "music of his school
ought only to be played close to elephants and listened to only by clowns."[20]

Alternatively, bassist Howard Rumsey claimed that Kenton had "the
greatest influence on jazz since Gershwin!"[21] Over twenty years after his
death in 1979, the accepted critical view of Kenton has become more bal-
anced, acknowledging both his flaws and his virtues:

> A vast band, a colossal legacy, and an outsize personality at the helm:
> Kenton's achievement is possibly the 'biggest' that jazz has ever seen or will
> see. How much of it is truly worth listening to is harder to evaluate. Kenton
> seemed to believe in principles which often had little to do with musical sub-
> stance: volume, power, weight, noise. Nobody ever had bigger-sounding big
> bands, and nobody ever went to such pretentious lengths as Kenton could.[22]

The point at which Kenton began to draw vastly different responses to
his music was with the formation of his Progressive Jazz Orchestra. Crucial to this band's sound were the arrangements of Pete Rugolo, a composer
and arranger who would go on to have a career in Hollywood film music,
as would other writers for the "progressive" Kenton bands. Progressive jazz,
or "third stream" music, was a fusion of jazz and modern classical music.
Charges frequently leveled at the Kenton band were that it was pompous
and self-consciously grandiose. Kenton was accused of sensationalism, incorporating techniques and theories from twentieth-century classical music into the big band setting without any real understanding or attempt to
sensitively blend the two together. The area in which Kenton's Progressive
Orchestra was felt to be most seriously lacking was its ability to swing: an
almost indefinable quality that marks one band from another. A big band
that did not swing was committing the worst possible crime. Kenton, however, did not disguise the fact that he was no longer leading a conventional
big band that was fundamentally designed to play dance music:

> When it comes to music for dancing . . . bands like Lombardo, Kaye and Carle
> are tops. Our band is designed for creating moods and excitement. Our band
> is built to thrill.[23]

Kenton was enough of a businessman to realize that he could not play
progressive jazz all the time and hope to maintain a living as a bandleader.
The progressive arrangements were kept for concert performances or interspersed with more traditional big band charts for those instances when the

band played in a dance venue. The progressive music of the Kenton orchestra, full of dissonance, atonality and brash effects, often evaded the simple categories of jazz or classical music. If critics were reluctant to term Kenton's music jazz or discuss it on the same level as "serious" classical works, however, one category to which it has often been likened is film music. Taking a retrospective view of the 1956 Kenton album *Cuban Fire*, the *Penguin Guide to Jazz on CD* (1996) makes the assessment that "much of it sounds like mood or movie music."[24] For what kind of imaginary film was the Kenton orchestra providing a soundtrack? In his history of modern West Coast jazz, Ted Gioia provides a description of Pete Rugolo's arrangements for the 1940s progressive Kenton orchestra that relates them to film noir:

> Too often Rugolo's conception of modern music in the mid-1940s boiled down to making jazz sound like a movie score, an ambitious score to be sure but one that seems to be supporting a series of visual images to which we are never privy. His "Elegy for Alto" could well be the background to a hard-boiled mystery movie set in the 1940s. As such, it would be quite successful, but as a jazz piece it falls flat. Rugolo's "Impressionism," recorded a month later on October 22, 1947, is similarly ponderous.[25]

Gioia's likening of this music to a 1940s "hard-boiled mystery movie" is a little premature. There were no films noir in the 1940s that sounded quite like anything that Kenton and Rugolo were doing with the Progressive Orchestra. During the 1950s, however, there were a number of films that did sound like Kenton's progressive music and, in more than one instance, specifically cited Kenton as an influence. Lack's description of the kind of jazz that was beginning to appear in the film scores of this period notes that:

> It was very often then more of a "jazz style" that was being played with rather than anything one was likely to stumble across in a club. The styles of jazz that did make it on to the film soundtracks were derived from the sounds of the big touring bands of the 1940s—Stan Kenton, Woody Herman—brash themes that perfectly caught the personality of the modern man likely to be a character in the new, European-influenced cinema.[26]

When the composer Henry Mancini was appointed to provide the score for the Orson Welles–directed *Touch of Evil* (1958), it was to Kenton that he looked for the basis of the sound he wanted to use in the film.

THE INFLUENCE OF STAN KENTON ON FILM MUSIC IN THE 1950s

The soundtrack for *Touch of Evil* developed out of a "meeting of the minds" between composer and director. Welles was quite specific as to the kind of music he wanted in the film and outlined his choice in a letter to Joseph Gershenson, the film's musical director. When Mancini met the director, it quickly became clear that Welles and Mancini had "both been thinking of the same thing at the same time."[27] Welles's instructions were extensive:

> It is very important that the usual "rancheros" and "mariachi" numbers should be avoided and the emphasis should go on Afro-Cuban rhythm numbers. . . . Also, a great deal of rock 'n' roll is called for. Because these numbers invariably back dialogue scenes, there should never be any time for vocals. This rock 'n' roll comes from radio loudspeakers, juke boxes and, in particular, the radio in the motel. . . . What we want is musical color, rather than movement—sustained washes of sound rather than tempestuous melodramatic or operatic scoring.[28]

Mancini would faithfully adhere to Welles' guidelines. The majority of the music is diegetic, and the underscoring is largely confined to brief musical "stings." The exception is an extended theme that occurs twice in the film and is, arguably, the most memorable musical motif (although the lilting pianola theme for Tanya is also significant). This theme is used to underscore two of the most visually striking sequences in the film, the much-praised opening tracking shot and Detective Quinlan's murder of Grandi, and is clearly influenced by the Kenton orchestra.

Kenton had been making significant use of Cuban percussion since the mid-1940s, when the integration of Latin and Cuban rhythms into jazz groups became prevalent, especially with the big band led by Dizzy Gillespie. Just prior to *Touch of Evil*, Kenton had returned to a focus on Cuban percussion with his *Cuban Fire* album, and Mancini is almost certain to have been aware of this recording. Mancini had no doubts about looking to the ranks of the Kenton band:

> I went into my boss and said, "Joe, our band can't cut this." We had a staff band. It was a good band for the middle-of-the-road kinds of scoring . . . westerns and all of that. . . . But they couldn't blow like the Kenton band, which was my prototype for this.[29]

The Afro-Cuban tinged big band that Mancini specifically assembled for *Touch of Evil* drew heavily on musicians who had worked with Kenton. Drummer Shelly Manne, percussionist Jack Costanza, trombonist Milt Bernhart and trumpeter Pete Candoli were all noted (ex) Kenton sidemen and helped to give the score its drive.

If one compares a Kenton recording such as the Rugolo composed *Cuban Carnival* (1947) with Mancini's cue "Background to Murder," from *Touch of Evil*, there is a striking resemblance. Both pieces open with showers of percussion that are soon joined by the horns playing the central theme. The two pieces develop through a series of percussion breaks, after each of which the rest of the band returns to reprise the central theme, but in a slightly different form. As the "Background to Murder" cue reaches its climax and Quinlan strangles the gang leader, Grandi, the trumpets screech in the extreme upper register, as they do at the end of *Cuban Carnival*. This histrionic playing of the trumpets was a feature of the Kenton orchestra, especially when trumpeter Maynard Ferguson joined the band in the early 1950s, which was noted for its brass section that dominated the band's sound, often at the expense of the reeds.

Mancini's score was deemed a success. Although the film would be taken out of Welles' hands by the studio and much of his work was cut and his suggestions ignored, particularly for the sound design, he was nevertheless pleased with Mancini's score, feeling that the composer had done a "fine job."[30] Universal was also impressed enough with Mancini's work not to order any re-scoring. Mancini's combination of jazzy rock 'n' roll (the jukebox/radio music is not pure rock 'n' roll, utilizing a number of leading jazz musicians and big band textures) and Afro-Cuban-tinged big band was one of the few aspects of the film where commercial and artistic considerations coincided. The rock 'n' roll aspects of Mancini's score meant that *Touch of Evil* had a sound that would not have been out of place in any number of films that were then being targeted at the youth audience craze for rock 'n' roll.

Why should Stan Kenton have provided the prototype for Mancini's *Touch of Evil* score? Why did Duke Ellington not offer such a model? The reason for Kenton's influence is more complicated than the sound of his music alone, although this connection is significant. After the Progressive Orchestra, Kenton left music briefly in 1949 due to ill health, but returned with an even bigger ensemble titled the Innovations in Modern Music Orchestra. This band numbered forty-three musicians, including a string section as well as a larger and more varied wind section than that of a conventional big band. The scope of the Innovations band was unheard of in jazz. It was incredibly costly and Kenton ultimately lost money on the project, dissolving the band after two nationwide tours in 1950 and 1951.

The Innovations Orchestra alienated jazz and classical audiences alike, as well as the general public. Kenton was seeking to utilize the strings in a modern jazz setting, and it is in relation to this venture that Miles Davis was probably comparing Kenton with the jazz-inflected use of strings by Alex North in *A Streetcar Named Desire*. The broad instrumental palette that the Innovations in Modern Music Orchestra made available to Kenton and his arrangers gave the band a symphonic range of sounds and textures. The only other form of music that was producing a comparable diversity of instrumental sounds and styles was film music.

The instrumental range of the Innovations Orchestra provided a priceless opportunity for Kenton's arrangers to work with textures that would normally not be available in jazz. For Kenton arranger Shorty Rogers, the Innovations band offered on-the-job experience writing for instruments like French horn, tuba and strings; experience that would prove invaluable when he would later come to write scores for movie soundtracks.[31]

Rogers is an excellent example of the indirect influence that Kenton would have on film scoring in the 1950s. Rogers collaborated on many of the pioneering jazz-inflected scores of the early 1950s, including *The Wild One* (1953), *Private Hell 36* (1954) and *The Man with the Golden Arm.* Although Kenton himself would not score a film, many of the arrangers who worked for him did go into film work and brought with them the experiences and influences of their time with Kenton. The thumbprint of Kenton's Progressive or Innovations in Modern Music Orchestra can be heard in the film music of Shorty Rogers or Pete Rugolo. The big bands of the 1930s and 1940s required a constant diet of fresh arrangements and compositions, and so the bandleaders employed writers to ensure that this demand was met. This situation provided many young composers, who might not necessarily have chosen to work in jazz but appreciated the offer and experience of work, with a forum in which to develop their skills. As the 1940s progressed and the big bands began to die out, these writers found themselves in a position and with the experience to sell their services to film and television. Additionally, this new generation of composers and arrangers would find that there were opportunities waiting for them in Hollywood as the tradition for symphonic film scores proved increasingly costly:

> The breakthrough came with the more or less coincidental emergence of the small independent motion picture producer and the skilled and literate jazz composer-arranger, the latter a product, in turn, of the requirements of the highly polished big bands of the 'forties and 'fifties—Stan Kenton, Count Basie, Woody Herman, Shorty Rogers, and many others. It also coincided with the early maturity of television, which brought with it a new and insatiable demand for effective underscores written in a contemporary and colloquial idiom. The economics of film production also played a part. With the cost of a symphony orchestra of upward of fifty musicians rising from year to year, producers, and especially the smaller and more adventurous, were well disposed to a new approach to scoring, particularly if it could save—or even make—money.[32]

An early example of this new breed of composer, open to, and experienced in, a wide range of musical styles was David Raksin who went to Hollywood with a degree in music as well as the skills and knowledge acquired from big band work with the likes of Benny Goodman. The writers of film music who emerged in the 1950s were similarly conversant in a variety of styles. When Hollywood deemed that public tastes had changed and the symphonic film score could no longer be relied upon, composers like Mancini were able to survive in an increasingly competitive business.

REASONS FOR KENTON'S INFLUENCE IN HOLLYWOOD OVER DUKE ELLINGTON

Despite his huge ambition to develop jazz and take it into new areas, Kenton has never been considered by the majority of jazz musicians and critics to be on the same level as Duke Ellington. Ellington was receiving acclaim from the classical establishment long before Kenton's "progressive" projects. For many, Ellington remains the greatest composer in jazz. Yet Ellington would have to wait until 1959 and Otto Preminger's *Anatomy of a Murder* before he was allowed to score a Hollywood film. Sounds that would be familiar to a follower of the Kenton orchestra had formed the basis of jazz in Hollywood films for nearly ten years prior to Ellington's first assignment, however. Why did Ellington not provide this basis?

A key factor in the emergence of jazz scores during the 1950s was the transition of jazz from music performed in clubs and theaters to "respectable" concert venues. This transition was enforced on many large jazz orchestras by the decline of the big bands and the necessity of acknowledging that jazz was perceived as art music for listening to and not entertainment primarily for dancing. The composers Laurie Johnson and Lennie Niehaus have both cited this shift as helping to legitimize jazz in the perception of the Hollywood studios. As Niehaus suggests, the transition to the concert stage, by musicians such as Dave Brubeck and Miles Davis, as well as Kenton and Ellington, helped jazz to acquire a "status it never had in the past."[33] Kenton was particularly conscious of "elevating" jazz to the concert hall, and presented the original version of Robert Graettinger's *City of Glass* at the Chicago Opera House in 1948. Yet Ellington had performed in Carnegie Hall as early as January 1943, when he premiered *Black, Brown, and Beige,* his "tone parallel to the American Negro." He had also earned the respect and admiration of many in the field of classical music long before Kenton took his band into the concert arena at the end of the 1940s.

Ellington's dearth of film projects was not due to lack of interest on his part. His band had featured in a number of both short- and full-length films. In *Black and Tan* (1929) and *Symphony in Black* (1935), short films that showcased Ellington and his music, Ellington was presented as an urbane, intellectual composer and artist, a rare positive image of a black performer in films of that time. Ellington's early involvement in film was generally to provide a few numbers for a jazz sequence, but he was keen for the opportunity to do the score for an entire film. During the lengthy course of the production of *Young Man with a Horn* (1950), the possibility of Ellington being offered the composing duties was put forward to the film's musical director, Ray Heindorf, and Warner Brothers employee Steve Trilling. Negotiating on behalf of Ellington was the agent Willard Alexander who, in a letter to Heindorf, was keen to stress Ellington's eagerness to provide a score:

> Yesterday I talked with Steve Trilling on long distance phone re Duke Ellington for the *Young Man with a Horn* picture. . . . Steve explained to me that the studio had not made a decision as to what it was going to be—a musical, or a dramatic story with incidental music, and if it were the latter that possibly it would not be interesting to Ellington. I pointed out that Duke is so anxious to do this type of thing that he would be willing to do incidental or certain specific musical assignments in the picture. . . . *Duke would be willing to consider a reasonable offer, rather than a lot of money, as it would be his first assignment of this kind and he has been extremely anxious for years to do this type of thing. I know I don't need to tell you of his ability, and I am sure whatever musical requirements you need that Duke would do an outstanding job and would not only be willing to consider a reasonable price, but feels that this is a field for him to explore that he has never up to now undertaken and he is extremely desirous of establishing himself in this phase of the business . . .* I am sure you would be extremely pleased with Duke's work, as he really has a lot of material and ideas which he has not even touched for this kind of thing [emphasis mine].[34]

Clearly, Ellington's reputation and stature as a performer and artist were not enough to simply speak for themselves and secure his involvement on the film. Alexander's letter labors the point of Ellington's "anxiety" to work on a film project and repeatedly refers to Ellington's willingness to work for a "reasonable price."

Ellington was not offered *Young Man with a Horn*. Several weeks after his first letter, Alexander had not received a reply and wrote again to Heindorf asking whether a decision had been made as to the participation of Ellington on the film.[35] There was no further written correspondence between Alexander and Heindorf, and the possibility of Ellington working on the film seems to have simply faded away. Ultimately, the producers of *Young Man with a Horn* opted for a balance between a "musical or a dramatic story with incidental music." The finished film takes the form of a dramatic story, but there are many musical interludes. That incidental music that is used, as observed in Chapter 3, is more in keeping with the lush symphonic tradition of the classical Hollywood score and barely reflects the film's narrative of the rise and (softened) fall of a jazz musician. Instead of Ellington, or any number of talented jazz composers and arrangers, the production team acquired the services of a star performer, the white trumpeter Harry James. James was employed as both musical advisor, teaching the lead actor Kirk Douglas to finger a trumpet convincingly, and the trumpet soloist who is heard playing with the orchestra on the nondiegetic score, as well as dubbing Douglas's performances in the various diegetic band sequences. I have already shown how racism influenced the involvement of black musicians in *Young Man with a Horn*, and it is likely to have also affected the decision not to employ Ellington. Racism is undoubtedly a factor in the lack of scoring offers made to Duke Ellington by the Hollywood studios. In his liner notes for the recording of Duke Ellington's music for *Paris Blues* (1961), Patrick McGilligan asserts that:

> Although Ellington was established as a seminal figure of American music— an acknowledged "master in our time of the small form, the miniature, the vignette and the cameo portrait," in Gunther Schuller's words—racism, along with his exhausting schedule of recording and touring, had limited his involvement in Hollywood production.[36]

In both the areas that McGilligan cites as reasons for Ellington's absence from Hollywood, Stan Kenton held the "advantage." First, Kenton was white. Jazz was beginning to find the acceptance that would encourage its use in a Hollywood film score. Yet, the notion of a high-profile black composer providing the music for a film that focused on white characters, as *Young Man with a Horn* did, would still have been a difficult one for a Hollywood studio to entertain. When modern jazz musicians began to be featured in films throughout the 1950s, such as *The Man with the Golden Arm* and *I Want To Live!*, they were almost invariably white and not leading black artists like Dizzy Gillespie, Miles Davis and Thelonious Monk. As the previous chapters have discussed, a leading black performer of the older generation of jazz musicians, Louis Armstrong for example, could be featured in a Hollywood film because he was deemed to be an entertainer and did not present an intellectual stance that challenged Hollywood representations of blackness. Kenton, and many of the musicians who came out of his band or were a part of the related West Coast scene, provided the white modern jazz fan with a visible figure with whom they could identify. As Gabbard observes, in his discussion of the character of a white jazz musician in *Sweet Smell of Success*, Kenton (alongside musicians such as Stan Getz, Dave Brubeck, Gerry Mulligan and Shorty Rogers) was representative of a trend in America during the 1950s to "idealize white jazz musicians," especially when white audiences might have "felt threatened in some way by black male artists."[37]

If a Hollywood film of the 1950s called for a jazz score, it would also be likely to feature a sequence of jazz musicians actually playing diegetically. As I argued at the beginning of this chapter, jazz usually required a narrative justification if it was to be used in a film's score. Thus the jazz-inflected score of *The Man with the Golden Arm* is reflected by the central character, Frankie, who is a drug addict seeking to become a professional jazz drummer. In one scene, Frankie auditions for the Shorty Rogers Orchestra, and it is not surprising that it is musicians from Rogers' band that perform the jazz parts of Elmer Bernstein's nondiegetic score. Similarly, the protagonist in *I Want To Live!*, Barbara Graham, is a devoted follower of the music of Gerry Mulligan and Shelly Manne. Both of these musicians are featured in the opening scene set in a jazz club, as well as being heard on the nondiegetic score and diegetic recordings emanating from a radio or record player.

In part, what is involved here is a cost-cutting exercise, but it is one that works in partnership with racism. If a film's score was provided or played by black jazz musicians, the restrictions of racism would make it unlikely for the same musicians to be featured diegetically alongside the white protagonists. To avoid the mingling of black and white performers, another white band or white "fake" musicians would probably have to be incorporated. This strategy would result in additional expense that the producers might be reluctant to make allowances for. A jazz score that was performed by white jazz musicians also meant, however, that the musicians could "double-up" and appear in the film, effectively as themselves, for any scenes requiring the presence of jazz musicians. This practice also helped prevent any of the perceived tensions of black and white characters mixing in the same location.

The second of McGilligan's explanations for Ellington's few Hollywood scores is more practical. Ellington was not based in Hollywood, but in New York, and was in demand throughout the world for concert performances and tours, making it difficult for him to commit to a film project. Ellington's geographical distance from Hollywood does not seem as convincing a reason for his lack of film projects as the racism that was active there. In fact, during the decline of the Swing Era in the late '40s and early '50s, maintaining a big band was increasingly difficult, and Ellington was reduced to performing in a number of undignified venues, such as aquacades, in support of lesser talents who were in vogue. During this period of his career, Ellington survived on the royalties of his past successes and compositions. The offer of a film score would have been gratefully accepted for financial as well as artistic reasons. As Willard Alexander's letter to Ray Heindorf outlined, Ellington's desire to work on a film score was such that it seems likely that had an appropriate project been offered, he would have been able to accommodate it into his schedule. Indeed, when Ellington and Billy Strayhorn, his long-term cowriter, were asked to provide the score for *Paris Blues*, Ellington overcame his notorious fear of flying so that he could be present for much of the actual shooting of the film.[38]

Kenton, however, was based in Los Angeles and was a major figure in the contemporary West Coast jazz scene. He and his musicians were literally on the doorstep of the Hollywood studios. If a film required the collaboration of jazz musicians, then the ranks of the Kenton orchestra would have been a familiar and immediately accessible resource. Not surprisingly, the jazz-inflected scores of the 1950s consistently featured the playing of current or former Kenton musicians. The most prolific of these musicians to work in Hollywood was the drummer Shelly Manne, who was a mainstay of the Kenton bands between 1946 and 1951. Manne would become the ubiquitous sound of Hollywood drums in those films that incorporated jazz, working on jazz-inflected scores for, among others, *The Wild One, The Glass Wall* (1953), *The Man with the Golden Arm, I Want To Live!, Some Like It Hot* (1959), *The Subterraneans* (1960) and *Too Late Blues* (1961). Although he did not have a major career as a composer for Hollywood, Manne would eventually provide a number of scores for films such as *The Proper Time* (1959), *The Trial of the Cantonsville Nine* (1972) and *Trader Horn* (1973).

It was through the various composers and arrangers who had worked for him that aspects of Stan Kenton's music were able to manifest themselves in Hollywood film scores of the 1950s. Aspects of the Duke Ellington band were not so easily transplanted to Hollywood. The sound of the Duke Ellington Orchestra was one consistently provided by Ellington and Strayhorn. Ellington rarely performed music written by anybody else. Instead, Ellington and Strayhorn wrote specifically for the individual musicians in the band, shaping pieces around a musician's unique tone and personality. This compositional technique was helped by the fact that the musicians who played with Ellington tended to do so for many years. Baritone saxophonist Harry Carney would stay with Ellington for his entire career. As a result, the Ellington Orchestra had an easily identifiable sound. To bring a distinctly Ellington sound into a film would have meant getting Ellington, Strayhorn and a good proportion of their musicians to participate on the project.

Kenton, however, did not have a specific sound, but rather a specific volume. Although he did compose for the band, most of the Kenton Orchestra's output came from the pens of writers Pete Rugolo, Bill Russo, Bob Graettinger, Shorty Rogers, Bill Holman and Johnny Richards. These writers provided Kenton's bands with their varying sounds. They also ensured that, however indirectly, the Stan Kenton Orchestra, in its differing guises, would have a lasting influence on film music. During their time with Kenton, Rugolo and Rogers would gain vital experience that would set them in good stead when they began to work in film. Similarly, the composer and alto saxophonist Lennie Niehaus, who has scored the majority of Clint Eastwood's directing projects since the mid-1980s, has acknowledged the writing opportunities available to him during his time with Kenton in the 1950s as being of help to his later career in film.[39] Bill Russo, who provided many of the arrangements and compositions for the Innovations in Modern Music Orchestra, also carried the Kenton connection with film music further when he taught the composer John Barry, now one of the most celebrated composers for film. Barry, who would establish a trade-mark brass and percussion-based sound for the action sequences in the James Bond films (a sound that is not far removed from Kenton's progressive music), studied with Russo via a correspondence course titled Harmony and Orchestration for the Jazz Orchestra.

Although it was Kenton's writers who moved on to careers in Hollywood and not Kenton himself, it would be wrong to remove Kenton entirely from the music that his staff of composers and arrangers were producing and which some of them would write for film. Kenton established the principles of the band. It was Kenton's openness to exploring new sounds and possibilities for the large-scale jazz band that gave the likes of Graettinger, Russo and Rugolo an opportunity to develop their music. Max Harrison has observed that it is unlikely that much of the music of Graettinger and his colleagues would have been heard without Kenton:

> [Kenton has] never received due credit for the most remarkable aspect of his career . . . the prominence he gave to the composers who wrote the finest of the music those bands played. People such as Pete Rugolo and Bill Russo would surely have found it more difficult to discover an audience for their music without Kenton's advocacy, and without him we surely would never have heard of Robert Graettinger.[40]

Kenton's personal artistic vision and ethos informs the vast majority of the music played by the Progressive and Innovations orchestras. It is Kenton's concept of jazz and what he sought to express through music that should also be considered when attempting to understand the influence of his progressive jazz in Hollywood. Kenton's Progressive and Innovations projects coincided with his growing fascination with psychiatry. In fact, such was Kenton's interest in this field that he temporarily retired from music at the end of 1948 to seek psychiatric help for his emotional and relationship problems and promptly developed the intention of becoming a psychiatrist himself. As Kenton biographer Carol Easton puts it:

> Psychiatry grabbed Stan as nothing had since his discovery of music. Since childhood, his thought processes had had an analytical bent. Here was a neat support system for a kind of logic which, if it couldn't resolve your hangups, at least offered endlessly fascinating illuminations of them. Psychiatry legitimized techniques Stan had been using for years. He was a master, for example, at psyching out his musicians. . . . He had an amazing facility for projecting an authority based on the sheer dazzle of his personality and enhanced by his acquisition of enough psychological jargon to hint at a superior intellect.[41]

When Kenton relaunched his career in music, it was with the Innovations in Modern Music Orchestra. This band reflected Kenton's angst and fixation with psychiatry more than any other unit that he led in his career. Kenton was quite open about his music's purpose:

> He began making statements like, "Jazz is neurotic," and told an undoubtedly bewildered *Down Beat* reporter, "The band reflects me as well as my musicians, and I have within me tremendous aggression and drive which have to be expressed in my music."[42]

Unimpressed critics would use this definition of jazz against Kenton. Writing in *Metronome*, George Simon felt that:

> Stan and Pete [Rugolo] and the men who play their music so well are deeply shrouded under a neurotic conception of jazz if not of all music. Their stuff is not mellow, but megalomaniacal, constructed mechanically of some of the familiar sounds and effects of modern composers, from Bartok to bongo drums, with little apparent feeling for the jazz medium and none at all for the subtleties of idea and emotion.[43]

But it is precisely the neuroticism and "tremendous aggression" of Kenton's concept of jazz that made it an appropriate musical model for the scores of 1950s film noir and social problem films. Spence refers to these aspects in his brief discussion of the use of modern jazz in films of the early 1950s:

> Feature films did not present modern jazz to a large audience. Its importance as an art form was overlooked. Yet not completely. The new music was more apt to turn up in some form as thematic underscoring in films. Employment of jazz musicians began to increase behind the camera while it steadily decreased in front of it. Many musicians unwittingly supported films that communicated mixed messages at best, clearly adversarial at worst.... The startling quality of the new music seemed fit for *film noir*, characterized by its brooding, somber, anxious nature.... A plethora of films alloyed psychological friction and neurosis with modern jazz. The zenith may have been reached in 1953 with *The Wild One*.... Teenagers were depicted as unmanageable (uncontrollable), perverted, twisted, "out for kicks," violent, unpredictable. *The Wild One* depicted youths as vagabond bikers, spoiling for a fight, disrupting a quiet town. And enjoying Shorty Rogers music.[44]

The dissonance that was typical of Kenton's bands at this time, especially those pieces written by Bob Graettinger, had already been introduced as a legitimate film scoring technique by Miklós Rózsa in his score for the classic noir *Double Indemnity* (1944). The classical Hollywood score could permit Rózsa's use of dissonance because of the immorality and cynicism of *Double Indemnity*. When jazz began to become established in film scores of the early 1950s, it was only the film noir and social problem films like *The Man with the Golden Arm* that could offer jazz scoring opportunities that would not be considered to undermine the values of the classical Holly-wood score. Asked in the early 1950s what jazz meant to him, Kenton's reply summed up much of the ethos of film noir:

> I think the human race today may be going through things it never experi-enced before, types of nervous frustration and thwarted emotional develop-ment which traditional music is entirely incapable of not only satisfying but expressing. That's why I believe jazz is the new music that came along just in time.[45]

Through pieces such as Graettinger's suite "City of Glass" (1952), Rugolo's "Conflict" (1950) and the Kenton-Rugolo "Abstraction" (1947), Kenton's music of this period often sounds like a 1950s noir score in search of a film.

If Kenton's neurotic and frustrated sound made an effective template for the atmosphere of film noir, however, the music of Duke Ellington and Billy Strayhorn was not so obviously rooted in a noir sensibility. Adjectives such as "thwarted," "neurotic," "megalomaniacal" and "nervous" could be readily applied to Kenton's bands, but the Ellington band was defined more through its warmth, joyousness and lyricism. Had Ellington been asked to score a film noir, he would doubtless have done so with great skill, but the familiar sound of his orchestra was not in tune with noir. Considering the associations that were being made by Kenton and his critics about the anxiety of his music and that of the other progressive groups, it seems un-likely that the Ellington Orchestra would have been seen as such an obvi-ous candidate to provide the score for a film noir. Despite Ellington's eminence as a composer, it was clearly "progressive" jazz that was the favored style in Hollywood scores of the 1950s.

CASE STUDY: *I WANT TO LIVE!*

Johnny Mandel's jazz-based score for *I Want To Live!*, a 1958 film noir, is an excellent example of a "progressive" jazz score and the tensions that such a score could create. The subject matter of *I Want To Live!* ensured that it would be a controversial film. The film questioned the ethics of the death sentence through the re-enactment of an actual case: the conviction for murder of Barbara Graham. Susan Hayward played Graham in a power-ful performance that earned widespread audience sympathy for her char-acter. Yet the police officials involved in the actual arrest of Graham were not pleased by the film, which they denounced as having an "unjustified premise that an innocent woman was driven to her death."[46] Not inciden-tal to the film was the fact that Graham was also a modern jazz fan.

Mandel's music was promoted as "anxiety jazz," a label that clearly referred back to Kenton's "neurotic" intentions for his Progressive and Innovations bands a decade earlier. Previewing the film, which was still not completed, the *L.A.Times* ran a short article on the film's intended score titled, "Anxiety Jazz Killer-Diller."

Jazz in movies is as old as the first sound tracks; employing it as a symptom, a symbol, of the times or playing it in counterpoint, ironic or hysterical, to enacted dramas, is newer. In *I Want To Live!*, new name for *The Barbara Graham Story*, they are calling it "anxiety jazz." *I Want To Live!* is no merry jive session. In it Susan Hayward is playing the convicted murderess, Barbara Graham. However, Robert Wise, who is directing, believes music can be used to "tell" her story. He defines anxiety jazz as "pre-Beat Generation jazz— but with a beat, nevertheless." Barbara's downward slide from petty crime as a teen-ager to the chamber at 32 was paced by the sort of music that came out of San Francisco's Tenderloin district, Wise says. The period was the late '40s. John Mandel, a trombonist once known as "the Bearded Bard of Basie's Band," was recruited to compose and arrange the anxiety jazz. Walter Wanger, the producer, is getting together an all-star quintet to play it—Shelly Manne on drums, Red Mitchell on bass and a trumpet, saxophone and piano player to be determined from a list that includes Dizzy Gillespie, Shorty Rogers, Gerry Mulligan, Stan Getz, Erroll Garner, André Previn and Oscar Peterson. Sounds like progressive jazz—but considering the subject matter it could well be regressive.[47]

The article's final comment suggests an awareness of the frequent association of jazz with crime and degeneracy and the efforts of modern jazz to rid itself of such associations.

Mandel's music is excellent but there appears to have been a lack of agreement between the director, Robert Wise, and the producer, Walter Wanger, as to what the use of jazz in the film suggested about the character of Barbara Graham. The first part of the film establishes Barbara and her reckless lifestyle of partying, drinking and casual sex. Wise does not attempt to ignore Barbara's wild behavior and both negative and redeeming aspects of her character are revealed. The Protestant Motion Picture Council classified the film as being "objectionable" and stated that "detailed accounts of her sordid life are given so realistically as to be offensive."[48]

The "sordid" parties and nightclubs that Barbara frequents all feature jazz groups heard diegetically, either as a band present on screen or emanating from a radio or record player. At first, the film appears to be making a clear connection between jazz and immorality. This link is confirmed by Nelson Gidding's screenplay for the film. The final shooting draft's account of the opening title sequence explicitly presents Gidding's concept of what jazz represents:

1. A RIBBON OF SMOKE
silver gray whorling sinuously against a black background. As it diffuses and drifts out of frame, more smoke keeps coming. Simultaneously with a crash of modern jazz, a series of stylized shapes and forms appear and

disappear behind the slowly rising smoke. OVER THESE THE MAIN
TITLE and CREDITS FADE IN. The music is the beat of the beat generation—real cool, cool jazz suggesting sex, speed, marijuana, hipsterism
and other miscellaneous kicks. (It will play an important part in the
mood of the picture, for the underscoring is to be carried through in this
style of modern jazz.) Synchronized with this music, the changing patterns of shape and form are also highly evocative of the fever and the
drive, the loneliness and craving, the furies and tenderness—even the
rebellion and religion—of BARBARA GRAHAM.[49]

The eventual realization of the title sequence, however, does not make
such an immediate and obvious association between modern jazz and "sex,
speed, marijuana, hipsterism and other miscellaneous kicks." The abstract
shapes and patterns that Gidding describes in his screenplay are not made
use of, and Mandel's opening "I Want To Live!" theme can be heard in any
number of ways without necessarily associating it with sex and drugs.

Instead of sinuous smoke and "stylized shapes and forms," Wise opts
for a stark and simple title sequence. The elegant title card for Figaro
Incorporated, accompanied by some delicate classical piano, suggests nothing of the gritty film to come. This card is then followed by a written statement from Edward Montgomery announcing that, "you are about to see a
factual story." Montgomery was a journalist who covered the Barbara
Graham case and is portrayed in the film. Initially pronouncing Barbara
guilty, Montgomery got to know Barbara personally and gradually changed
his opinion of her until his articles began to proclaim her innocence. This
statement of "truth" and "reality" fades to a black screen. There is a sudden "sting" of loud brass, and Susan Hayward's name appears in white
lettering. A Cuban percussion roll is followed by a loping bass line and the
"I Want To Live!" theme develops with baritone saxophonist Bill Holman
taking the lead. The title *I Want To Live!* appears in bright, white lettering then fades to gray and slowly recedes into the background and noth-
ingness as the other credits are superimposed. After the leading actors'
names have appeared, the entire jazz combo is credited. The naming of each
musician in the band was an unusual level of acknowledgment and remains
so today. In crediting each of the musicians, who appear in the on-screen
band, alongside the actors themselves, Wise appears to be suggesting that
they are central characters in the film and not merely playing on the
soundtrack. The respect that the band is accorded in the titles removes them
further from Gidding's association of jazz with sex and the sordid. In immediately following Montgomery's statement that the audience is about to
see a "factual story," the band is also coded as being the sound of "truth"
and "authenticity." That truth may appear to be sordid, but it does endow
the jazz heard in the film with the characteristics of being honest and rel-

evant. "This is what it really sounded like," is the message effectively being transmitted to the audience. The realization of the title sequence also distances the film's opening use of jazz from Gidding's interpretation of the music. Wise's chosen title sequence does not offer the audience any visual images with which to lead them in their interpretation of the jazz score. Gidding's suggested sequence, of sinuous smoke and abstract shapes in partnership with modern jazz music, however, would undoubtedly have led much of the audience into making associations between the audio and visual information. Wise's titles are much more ambiguous.

The clichéd connotations of jazz and coiling smoke would have immediately established the jazz score as the sound of seedy nightclubs and included the very associations that Gidding refers to in his screenplay. Wise, however, appears to have interpreted Barbara Graham's love for modern jazz, especially the music of Dave Brubeck, Shelly Manne and Gerry Mulligan, as a redeeming aspect of her character and not another example of her corrupt and immoral life. Clearly concerned by the criticism the film was receiving from the authorities regarding its sympathetic portrayal of a woman executed for murder, Wise released a statement that expressed his opinion of the significance of Barbara's love for jazz:

> First, we wanted to tell the story of Barbara Graham, the woman, rather than the story of the Barbara Graham *case*. . . . As we methodically poured over the research material we had gathered we grew to know Barbara Graham very well, and in many ways to like her a great deal. Human beings, whether good or bad, don't come in clearly definable shades of black and white. They come in grays, and often the shades of gray are all but indiscernible. . . . How could we grow to like a convicted murderess? Because Barbara was generous, if misguidedly so. Generous enough to spend a year in prison for lying to help a friend. Wrong, yes, but pathetically loyal and selfless. And we liked her because she was intelligent and sensitive. She loved good writing and in her short lifetime read an enormous amount of it with fine understanding and appreciation. And she loved good music, from Brahms and Bach to Manne and Mulligan. She loved her child as deeply and tenderly and as fiercely as any mother I know.[50]

Although Wise would term "good music" as ranging from "Brahms and Bach to Manne and Mulligan," the producer, Walter Wanger, does not seem to have shared Wise's view of the role of jazz in the film. During the shooting of the film, Wanger sent a memo to Wise that made no secret of his questioning of the merits of jazz. Congratulating Wise, Gidding and Hayward for their work in the first two weeks' rushes, Wanger expressed his concern that the character of Barbara was still lacking something. Although he felt that Hayward was "wonderful as the 'Peck's Bad Boy,' the delinquent, the hoyden," Wanger stressed that it was vital that the audience did not perceive Barbara as "just another bum—this is a bum with something plus."[51] But whereas modern jazz was felt by Wise to be part of the "something plus" in Barbara's character, Wanger seems to have associated jazz as confirming Barbara's status as "just another bum." Wanger suggested that the use of jazz might be responsible for the film not properly expressing the dignity of Barbara's character. Wanger felt that the unusual quality that they were hoping to express in Barbara's character, an aspect that was on record and noted in many of the interviews relating to the actual case, was not helped by the fact that they had replaced classical music with jazz and had "no reference to her good taste in music and literature."[52]

Wise did not agree with Wanger about the inadequacy of jazz. His copy of the Wanger memo is marked with numerous handwritten responses to Wanger's thoughts and suggestions. The notion that classical music should possibly have been used instead of jazz is met with the simple comment "nonsense." For Wanger, the jazz score and Barbara's numerous references to her knowledge and appreciation of the music of Manne and Mulligan ("I know all his sides by heart," says Barbara as she confidently identifies Mulligan's playing on the radio in her cell. "Now they'll announce it. See if I'm right.") did not count as references to her good taste in music. Wanger felt that Barbara's artistic taste could be better expressed through references to poetry and music other than the modern jazz of someone like Dave Brubeck. Wanger referred to Gidding's original script and an opening scene where Barbara asks a boyfriend if he knows anything about poetry, and he responds with a limerick. For Wanger, this example was a more effective means of illustrating Barbara as a "bum plus," instead of a scene where she was to play a recording by Brubeck. Concerned that all they had as evidence of Barbara's "good" taste in culture was a reference to Omar Khayam, Wanger noted that if the Brubeck record was replaced by something "decent," in other words a non-jazz recording, then the scene might still work.[53] Wise was unimpressed by Wanger's argument, and he responded to the suggestion that the Brubeck record is not "decent" with the written comment, "what do you mean?"[54] Wise stood by the decision to use a jazz-score and Barbara's references to modern jazz musicians. In fact, in view of the aspersions Wanger cast on the validity of jazz, Wise's decision to name the jazz combo in the credits can be seen as something of an affirmation of his faith in the ability of jazz to underscore the film and suggest Barbara's appreciation of culture.

Despite Wise's defense of the Mandel score and the Mulligan-Manne band, *I Want To Live!* still delivers conflicting messages about jazz. Regardless of whether modern jazz represents Barbara's higher qualities or not, she is nevertheless portrayed as a prostitute, a gambler, a heavy drinker, a member of a criminal gang and a woman executed for murder. The association of jazz with immorality is still there for the audience even if Wise's intentions were against this relationship. Just as Gorbman has argued that the use of jazz in *The Man with the Golden Arm* was acceptable to Hollywood because the film dealt with a heroin addict, Gabbard notes that the same film acquired much criticism for its depiction of drug use, but little objection to its association of jazz with such a theme.[55] Jazz seemed to be the most natural music to imply urban turmoil and immorality. Similarly, although *I Want To Live!* acquired the condemnation of the Los Angeles Police Department for its "half truths and propaganda," nobody condemned the use of modern and progressive jazz to underscore Barbara Graham's lifestyle and her eventual downfall.

An analysis of Mandel's music, however, reveals that there is not a causal link being made between crime, immorality and jazz. The aspects of jazz that are heard throughout the film can be separated into three basic categories. First, there is Mandel's jazz-inflected nondiegetic score. This music is played by an orchestra of leading West Coast jazz musicians, many of whom had worked at some point with Stan Kenton, including Bill Holman, Red Mitchell, Al Hendrickson, Pete Jolly, drummers Shelly Manne and Mel Lewis, trumpeters Jack Sheldon, Al Porcino and Ed Leddy, and trombonists Milt Bernhart, Frank Rosolino and Dave Wells. The second category of jazz heard in the film comprises the performances of the Mulligan-Manne band. This band is featured in the film's opening scene set in a jazz club. They are also heard at various times on the radio. The final category of jazz used in the film consists of a number of miscellaneous recordings that are heard, diegetically, on the radio, jukeboxes, record players and so on. There are clear differences between the nondiegetic score and the Mulligan-Manne band, as Gidding specified in his screenplay. Jazz is not one vast, sprawling category, and Barbara clearly has her preferences. When she is in her cell undergoing the death-watch process, she responds sharply to some sweet dance music on the radio, instructing the nurse to "turn off that schmaltz!" Barbara does not simply listen, unthinkingly, to any music and has a criterion for what makes "good music."

After the title sequence has ended, the first people that we see and hear are the jazz combo. The film's first sequence takes place in a jazz club where a band is in the midst of a set. A tilted shot of a draped ceiling tracks down to reveal the jazz combo playing on stage in a club. Gidding's instructions are followed with key exceptions:

2. INT. THE NEW FRISCO CLUB—FULL SHOT—NIGHT
Crowded and jumping, it's a San Francisco hot-spot. The varied characters who frequent it are having themselves a whale of a time. The small JAZZ COMBINE on the stand blows something closer to bop than the progressive music at the opening. No dancing, just jazz—REAL jazz.

3. GROUP SHOT—JAZZ COMBINE
A low, crazy ANGLE, FAVORING the drum which is littered: GOLDEN CATERS. The COLORED ALTO-SAX PLAYER preaches up a storm a la Charlie Parker.

4. CLOSE SHOT—TWO COOL TYPES standing by the men's room door exchanging a stick of tea. They blow the smoke into the ventilator just above their heads.[56]

Wise did shoot the majority of the club sequence through a variety of tilted camera angles that seem to be intended to create a sense of distorted perception, possibly due to the marijuana, in partnership with the jazz band. The sense of having entered a world of transgression is also suggested through the club's clientele. Mixed-generation couples are visible, as well as black audience members, although they are always in the background. The "two cool types" that Gidding refers to are included and are coded for seediness, seen smoking in a corridor as the musicians play.

It is the musicians who are the focus of this scene. The first musician to take a solo, however, is not the "colored alto-sax player, a la Charlie Parker" but the white baritone saxophonist Gerry Mulligan. The camera generously features Mulligan during his solo, and it seems unlikely that a black musician would have been accorded such a level of attention. In fact, after Mulligan, the next soloist is the black trumpeter Art Farmer, who is not given anything like the on-screen time that Mulligan enjoys. Given the concern expressed over the portrayal of a mixed-race band in *Young Man with a Horn,* the representation of a mixed-race and, significantly, modern band in *I Want To Live!* is something of a progressive step for the depiction of black musicians in a Hollywood film. Farmer is no "entertainer" in the manner of Louis Armstrong. But it is still the photogenic white musician who is privileged. As I have already noted, Mulligan was typical of what Gabbard calls the "cult of the white jazz artist" of the 1950s. Although he was an exponent of modern jazz and an excellent composer, Mulligan's image was unusual in its rebelliousness. Unlike the sophisticated artist look that many of the black bop musicians had adopted as they sought a higher status for their music, Mulligan offered an alternative model:

> The crew-cut, square-jawed Mulligan became a kind of icon, in sharp counter-definition to the long-hair, goatee and beret image of jazz.[57]

There is a marked difference between the representation of Mulligan and his colleagues in the *I Want To Live!* band. The jazz style that the band plays in is bebop, and the musicians are clad in the standard bop attire of smart suit and tie, with the exception of Mulligan. Mulligan is not dressed in a suit, thus emphasizing his rebelliousness and individuality, but wears instead a white shirt that hangs open at the neck and is streaked with sweat. Mulligan's appearance seems to be designed, in part, to affirm his masculinity. Some of the other musicians are also given traits or props that signify their opposition to the perceived effeminacy and pretensions of the male artist. The trombonist, for example, swigs from a bottle of beer as he waits between solos, and Shelly Manne drums with a cigarette drooping from his mouth. Farmer, however, is not given any such characteristics, and although he takes the second solo, the camera quickly cuts away after the introductory statement of his improvisation.

The pool of musicians that the *L.A. Times* announced Walter Wanger would be considering for the *I Want To Live!* band raised the possibility of a more equal balance of black and white musicians than actually appeared on screen. Trumpeter Dizzy Gillespie and pianists Erroll Garner and Oscar Peterson were all major black artists. Gillespie, however, was one of the founders of the bebop movement, and it is unlikely that he would have been happy with playing such a secondary role to Mulligan in a band performing a style of music that he had helped to create. Whatever the reasons for Gillespie not being hired to play in the band, it was Farmer, who did not have anything like the status of Gillespie, who was chosen as the trumpeter. The band's eventual personnel comprised Farmer, Mulligan, Frank Rosolino, Bud Shank, Pete Jolly, Red Mitchell and Shelly Manne. Farmer is the only black musician.

After the opening club sequence, the band is not seen again. Yet its presence is felt throughout, haunting Barbara, either from the radio or the nondiegetic score. Although several of the musicians in the club do not actually play on the nondiegetic score, it often functions as a twisted version of the diegetic music that Barbara loves so much. It partly achieves this effect through the "I Want To Live!" theme, initially stated by Bill Holman's baritone saxophone (which represents Mulligan and the importance of his music for Barbara) over the title credits, that recurs at key moments in Barbara's life. Barbara is not present in the opening club sequence. Her absence is perhaps unusual considering that it is her favorite musicians who are playing in the band. Instead, Barbara is in a hotel room above the club, sleeping with a man who, it is suggested, is paying for her services. The Mulligan-Manne band can still be heard playing in the club below, however, and Barbara wakes up as the trombonist begins his rousing solo. Barbara is linked with the musicians below through this juxtaposition. It is almost as if the trombonist is alerting her to the imminent arrival of the authorities. The music continues to be heard from below as a detective enters the room. The man with Barbara is on the brink of being arrested for bringing a woman, Barbara, across state lines for immoral purposes when Barbara comes to his defense at her own loss. Telling the detective that she was responsible for paying for the room, Barbara is charged instead of the man, fully aware of the consequences of her action. "Isn't life funny?" says the man, to which Barbara responds "Compared to what?" This scene immediately establishes Barbara's character. She is introduced as an immoral woman, but one who also has a bizarre loyalty, sacrificing her own freedom so that her client can walk away. Barbara's cynical humor, suggesting a life of experience, combined with her perverse but admirable loyalty, make her a likeable character even if the audience does not approve of her lifestyle. Present in the audience's consciousness as it begins to form its first impressions of Barbara is the modern jazz that is heard throughout this scene. The audibility of the jazz music being performed in the club below transforms it from diegetic music to nondiegetic. Effectively, the Mulligan-Manne band functions in the same way as Mandel's nondiegetic score in this scene, and the distinction between the two categories of music is blurred. The Mulligan-Manne music is established as the soundtrack to Barbara's life and thus, by extension, all the conflicting associations and interpretations that go with it. Like Barbara, it may be superficially presented as being sleazy and unworthy, but it also contains many attractive and redeeming qualities.

Mandel's nondiegetic score generally functions as a statement of the reality of Barbara's plight. There is also a suggestion, however, through the use of drums and Cuban percussion, that Barbara is not in control of her life and that she is being helplessly driven on to the gas chamber by the music. The encounter that introduces her involvement with criminals, and another prison sentence, takes place at a rowdy soldier's party. An alto saxophone is heard playing a heavily inflected blues. The tone and phrasing of the saxophonist is typical of the "oleaginous saxophones" that have come to be associated with sleaziness and immorality in Hollywood film. A bongo player, who is actually present at the party, starts to play as two of Barbara's old associates turn up at the party. The criminals, fresh from a robbery on a delicatessen, have come to ask Barbara if she will provide them with an alibi so that they can avoid arrest. Barbara agrees and returns to the party to dance to the bongos, which are increasing in intensity. The screenplay, and its realization on film, suggests that Barbara's dance to the bongo player reflects the pace of her life and that she is being carried forward by forces beyond her control:

23. INT. LIVING ROOM—CLOSE ON THE BONGO PLAYER

now beating up a storm on his skins. He's a real cool type—faded blue jeans, sandals.

26. MED. SHOT

Barbara, ringed by an excited GROUP of men, dances almost frenziedly to the driving rhythm of the drums.

27. CLOSE SHOT

The drummer's hands flailing the skins faster and faster.

28. HEAD CLOSEUP—BARBARA

reacting more and more excitedly to the increasing tempo. In a sudden crash of abrupt silence, we . . .

STRAIGHT CUT TO:

29. INT. COURTROOM—CLOSE SHOT—A GAVEL—DAY—pounding the bench in loud, measured strokes.

29A. INSERT—A SMALL NEWSPAPER ARTICLE

GOODTIME GIRL GETS YEAR FOR PERJURY

The sound of our jazz underscoring will lead to a . . . SLOW DISSOLVE TO. . . .[58]

The sudden cut from Barbara dancing at the party to the announcement of her prison sentence creates the impression of the music taking over her life and thoughts. When the music abruptly stops, the audience discovers that Barbara is going to prison. Clarity and reason have returned. There is a trace here of the loss of thought and "jungle fever" that Meltzer notes was associated with jazz since the 1920s.[59] The headline of Barbara's guilt, however, is underscored with a melancholic muted trumpet and electric guitar. The bongo rhythms suggest that Barbara's love of a particular kind of music contributed to her downfall, that she was too busy having a good time to think about the consequences of her actions. Yet the nondiegetic jazz that is heard when her guilt of perjury is announced is sympathetic to her situation.

Mandel's nondiegetic score often provides a comment on the angst and impending doom in Barbara's life. The "I Want To Live!" theme refers to Barbara's futile plea that she makes in one of her letters while awaiting execution. In this sense the theme acts as a harbinger of Barbara's death. Heard over the film's opening titles, the theme returns for the final time when Barbara is executed. As Barbara sits in the gas chamber with the pressmen swarming at the windows to see her death throes, the theme is heard again in a haunting arrangement. In contrast to the brassy and defiant interpretation it receives when Barbara is arrested, the theme is heard distantly, played softly by a single piccolo in its lower register, lending it a childlike quality that, Mandel observed, did not actually sound like a piccolo, but gave the impression of a person's dying breath.[60] This fragile statement of the theme is drowned out by a drone that increases in volume until the life drains out of Barbara's body. The "I Want To Live!" theme has pointed to this moment from the beginning of the film.

Mandel's nondiegetic score is doom-laden, and his progressive jazz seems fully aware of Barbara's fate. There is no utopian promise or suggestion that a better life might have been possible for Barbara. The size of the jazz combo and its presentation as a working band, as well as the size of the nondiegetic score band, furthers the sense of perspective that the film has about Barbara's life. A standard Hollywood score of sweeping symphonic strings would, arguably, have been too big for *I Want To Live!* and not as effective in creating the threat and claustrophobia that is evoked by Mandel's music. Yet, again, there was a lack of consensus between Wise and Wanger regarding the scale of the Barbara Graham story. Wanger seems to have been seeking to elevate Barbara to a much more grandiose and epic level. In the same memo to Wise of April 11, 1958, Wanger stressed again how impressed he was by Susan Hayward's performance, but that they had still not managed to elevate Barbara beyond a gangster's moll, and thus she would not be able to become a "great character in drama and history," which for Wanger was "the difference between a very fine picture and a great picture."[61]

The suggestion that Barbara might possibly become a "great character in drama and history" is a portentous one, and Wise's copy of this memo comments on Wanger's hyperbole with the expression "Oh, come on now!"[62] The use of a progressive jazz-based orchestration (the majority of Mandel's instrumentation for the nondiegetic score would be found in a big band) helps to keep *I Want To Live!* firmly grounded as a contemporary, urban and American story. This kind of story was obviously not enough for Wanger, who felt the film lacked a soul, but Wise seems to have been satisfied with the direction in which the film was heading. If Wanger was hoping for a "great picture," as opposed to a "very fine" one, Wise's memo bears the comment that "I'll settle for this" in reference to the film being merely "very fine." The film's ending does not employ heart-wrenching scoring designed to inform the audience that they should be upset at Barbara's "tragic" demise. Wise and Mandel do not glorify Barbara. Mandel was particularly conscious of this tone during the execution scene and explained that he did not want the score to become melodramatic. Instead, he opted to create an anticlimax as Barbara slowly succumbs to the cyanide, and the music gradually fades away with her.[63]

After the execution, the final scene of the film features the journalist, Montgomery, waiting outside the penitentiary where Barbara's death has taken place. Having initially condemned Barbara in his newspaper articles, Montgomery has become convinced of Barbara's innocence and campaigned for her release. He is informed of Barbara's death and receives a last letter in which she thanks him for all his efforts. As the journalists pour out of the penitentiary and clamor to get away in their cars, Montgomery is visibly disgusted by the behavior of his colleagues and turns off his hearing aid so that the sound of the press-men's car horns is no longer audible. With a look of relief he gets into his car and drives off. The nondiegetic score plays an upbeat jazz theme, "Black Nightgown," with Mulligan's baritone saxophone to the fore, thus making the link to Barbara and her favorite music. The music does not imply a sense of loss or tragedy and is almost anempathetic in its pragmatic feeling of "getting on with things." Life continues without Barbara.

The music ends with a similar "sting" of brass to that which opened the film and is followed by a revised version of Montgomery's statement of authenticity, now assuring the audience that they have "just seen a factual story." As the favored sound of Hollywood's fantasies of utopia, a classical symphonic score would not only have detracted from the film's realism, but would also have made it more obvious to the audience as to how they should feel about Barbara's guilt or innocence. Had the techniques of the standard classical Hollywood score been used for Barbara's story, then, as the film's protagonist, she would have been more explicitly coded as guilty or innocent. In fact, critic Vincent Canby congratulated the film on its avoidance of "several of the most important conventions of moviemaking," which increased its impact:

> By the very fact that they have utilized as their "innocent" victim of this practice (capital punishment) such an amoral and anti-social character as Barbara Graham, they have stripped the issue of all false sentimentality and fuzzy romanticism. They are saying, in effect, that all God's creatures, including the perjurers and the prostitutes, deserve the same compassion.[64]

Wise was aware of the danger involved in presenting Barbara as clearly guilty or innocent and had responded to police criticism about the film's perceived bias in favor of Barbara's innocence with the statement that:

> We maintained as objective and as neutral a position with regard to the guilt or innocence of Mrs. Graham and to the punishment the people of California inflicted upon her, *as was possible within the dramatic boundaries of her story.*[65]

Mandel's music supports Wise's claim of neutrality concerning Barbara's guilt and generally confines itself to expressing the bleakness of the scenario. Considering the film's origins in a real case and its claim that "you are about to see a factual story," had Wanger's aim to turn Barbara into "a great character in drama and history" been realized through standard Hollywood techniques of scoring and narrative, then the film would have been endowed with exactly the "false sentimentality and fuzzy romanticism" that could have opened it up to greater criticism from the authorities.

RESPONSE TO MANDEL'S SCORE FOR *I WANT TO LIVE!*

There were mixed reactions to the film. The condemnation of the Los Angeles Police Department aside, critics and reviewers differed in their interpretation of how objective the film had been about Barbara's case. *Reporter* noted that:

> It leaves the final question of her guilt or her innocence tactfully unresolved. But in its harsh eloquence, the picture, by virtue of Miss Hayward's great and many-faceted performance, goes beyond the question of innocence to the more haunting and profound one of mercy.[66]

Variety, however, was certain that the film, despite Wise and Wanger "purposely stacking the cards against themselves," had revealed its opinion on Barbara's guilt even though it had not avoided portraying the immorality of her life:

> There is no attempt to gloss the character of Barbara Graham. . . . The woman apparently lived a completely sordid life. She had no hesitation about indulging in almost any form of crime or vice if they promised excitement on her own, rather mean terms. To describe her depravity, it is easier to say what she was not. She was not a narcotics addict and, according to a psychiatrist, she was incapable of physical violence. Although Wanger's production, through Wise's superb direction and the perceptive Gidding-Mankiewicz screenplay, is rather blunt in stating that Miss Graham was not guilty of the murder for which she was executed, this is not a crucial point of the picture.[67]

The "official" verdict on the film's objectivity came in a letter from Geoffrey Shurlock, of the Production Code Administration. Writing to Mr. F. K. Johnston of Figaro Incorporated, Shurlock noted that in depicting Barbara's crimes of prostitution, perjury, forgery and robbery and her being charged, convicted and executed for an unseen murder, the film both enlisted and distanced the audience's sympathy for "the criminal."[68]

The film's use of jazz received a considerable amount of acknowledgment from reviewers. While some critics considered it as being simply evocative of the sordid story and Barbara's immoral lifestyle, others were impressed by its original use. *Variety* commented that it was "the first time jazz has been used for scoring on a major picture of this type, and the nervous beat strongly underscores the starkly realistic scenes."[69] This response is unusual considering that *Reporter* had noted the "exciting and pioneering use of jazz for the purpose of dramatic emphasis" in *The Man with the Golden Arm* three years earlier.[70] Perhaps what these conflicting reports on the "first" use of jazz, as an element in film music, reveal is that such was the rarity of an obviously jazz-based score that when one appeared it was still considered "pioneering" even if an earlier film had gotten there first. It does seem to suggest that jazz was not perceived as dominating Hollywood film music in the 1950s in quite the way that some writers have claimed. There is possibly some ambiguity in these early references to a jazz score with some writers differentiating between pure jazz music and jazz-inflected music and other writers referring to a "jazz score" even if the amount of improvisation involved is extremely small. *I Want To Live!* incorporates a purer jazz score than *The Man with the Golden Arm.*

Dick Williams, the entertainment editor of *Mirror News* offered a more perceptive appreciation than most critics of Mandel's score, albeit one that still combines pure jazz with jazz-inflected music:

In my original review space limitations forced a deletion of one of the un-usual aspects of the picture which added to its effectiveness. This is the Johnny Mandel jazz score played by Gerry Mulligan, Shelly Manne and crew. A moody, at times harsh and jarring jazz score accompanies the entire film. I recall only one other picture, the French-Italian coproduction of *No Sun in Venice*, which featured the Modern Jazz Quartet, which has used a complete jazz score. Actually there is a place for jazz in many films. Moviemakers should strike out and experiment more with its use, instead of always fall-ing back on the large symphony orchestra playing the standard kind of score. Jazz is not only hot, cool, bluesy and lowdown; it can be amusing, roman-tic, tender, bizarre, nostalgic as well.[71]

Williams's observations are interesting in their apparent awareness of the qualities traditionally associated with jazz, "hot, cool, bluesy and low-down," and which he seems to suggest *I Want To Live!* perpetuates. Although he was supportive of Mandel's score, Williams does not seem to have recognized Wise's intention of expressing Barbara's redeeming quali-ties through her love of modern jazz. It may be that Wise's intentions were too subtle and most viewers of the film considered the use of jazz to be re-flective of her sordid and criminal life. Even if the jazz that Barbara en-joyed was acknowledged as being representative of her taste and culture, it was, nevertheless, the taste and culture of a prostitute and perjurer.

LOWDOWN AND BLUESY OR HIGH BROW AND DINKY?

I Want To Live! offers a perfect example of the changing associations being applied to jazz during the 1950s. Although Wanger disagreed with Wise and could not consider jazz as being "decent" and "good music," he still wanted to exploit the film through the release of a theme song with lyrics. Again, Wise was strongly opposed to the decision of his producer. After speaking to Gidding and Mandel, Wise wrote back to Wanger, urg-ing him not to go ahead with the song:

We all feel the same way and have to go on record in the strongest fashion against the idea of this kind of song. Considering the subject matter of our picture and the meaning of "I WANT TO LIVE!" *any lyric,* no matter how well written, could not escape being in the worst possible taste. It makes no difference that it's not used in the picture. It would work against every bit of reality and honesty that we've struggled so hard to get into the movie. An instrumental "I WANT TO LIVE!" theme is a must and Mandel certainly has plenty to draw on for that . . . and it can be a real hit. But, *please,* let's not louse it all up now with a tasteless, cliché title song. Surely we have enough to sell the picture on without going to that extreme.[72]

Wise managed to convince Wanger not to release a title song. Instead, a soundtrack record was made available that sold relatively well. Wanger's thoughts about the effectiveness of jazz reflect two opposing perceptions of the music. On the one hand, Wanger did not feel that jazz was sufficiently "decent" and high brow enough to impart Barbara's unusual dignity and good taste in culture. However, Wanger also seems to have deemed jazz as being not commercial enough to provide a successful hit tune with which to promote the film.

These differing readings of jazz can be found in any number of films from the 1950s that made use of the music. In 1953, the rebellious youths of *The Wild One* were listening to bebop and the progressive jazz of Shorty Rogers, who had recently left the Stan Kenton Orchestra. Yet, only two years later, *The Blackboard Jungle* (1955) presented disaffected youths destroying the jazz recordings of their teacher, Richard Kiley. Kiley's tastes in music were cited as including Stan Kenton, but, in this film, Kenton was anathema to the teenagers. As Gabbard has noted, the musical tastes of these youths had moved on to Bill Haley and rock 'n' roll.[73]

As I have demonstrated with the example of *I Want To Live!,* tensions surrounding Hollywood's use of jazz were frequently present within an individual film text. For many, the desperate life of heroin addict Frankie Machine (Frank Sinatra) was perfectly expressed by Elmer Bernstein's jazz-inflected score for *The Man with the Golden Arm.* The interpretation of jazz as being the sound of Frankie's addiction, and thus a negative element, is easily taken from the film. Indeed, Bernstein's reasoning that jazz could speak readily of "heroin, hysteria, longing, frustration, despair and finally death" supports a negative perception of the music.[74]

The film's title theme is a brash blues played by the Shorty Rogers Orchestra. This theme is used on several occasions throughout the film. Bernstein's nondiegetic score, featuring, again, the skills of leading West Coast and ex-Kenton musicians such as Shelly Manne, Pete and Conte Candoli, Buddy Childers, Frank Rosolino, Milt Bernhart, Harry Betts, Bud Shank and Bob Cooper, repeatedly uses progressive big band textures and effects in association with Frankie's addiction. The film's controversial drug-use scene is preceded by Frankie succumbing to the wiles of his pusher, Louis. Frankie is "clean," having just come out of a rehabilitation center, yet Louis constantly tempts him to use again. When Frankie goes to his local bar, Louis walks past him, without speaking but making his presence felt. Leaving the bar, Louis heads over the road to his apartment. Frankie is fully aware that Louis is tempting him with the offer of a fix. The nondiegetic score reflects the conflict that takes place within Frankie through the return of the opening blues theme for big band. As Frankie finally snaps and follows Louis to his apartment, the trumpets screech histrionically in the upper register.

Once inside the apartment, Louis prepares the heroin and needle for Frankie. As each implement is placed on a table, it is scored with a loud brass "sting." There is an extreme close-up on Frankie's eyes as Louis injects the heroin into him, and Bernstein again makes use of the trumpets "screaming" in what is almost a free jazz style. Once Frankie has received his fix, however, the music becomes soothing and the aggressive brass is replaced with tranquil woodwinds. "The monkey won't climb on my back again," says Frankie, and it is clear that the "monkey," Frankie's addiction, is being represented, nondiegetically, through the harsh jazz-inflected music. Similarly, when Frankie subjects himself to a period of cold turkey and is locked in a room, his torment over his craving for heroin is represented on the score through a drum solo and the return of the title theme.

The film also represents jazz as being an escape route for Frankie, however. Desperate to get away from the slums, Frankie is trying to become a professional drummer with a band. He eventually gets an audition with the Shorty Rogers Orchestra, which plays the title theme, as well as contributing to Bernstein's nondiegetic score. The representation of the musicians is important and also quite at odds with Hollywood's traditional portrayal of jazz. The recording studio where the audition takes place is a bright, white, sanitized room. The musicians are all in clean, smart clothes and are thoroughly professional. Frankie, however, arrives at the audition in a terrible state, visibly suffering from his heroin addiction. Rogers asks him to sit in with the band and drum, but Frankie is not in any fit state to play, and his drumming is disastrous. Eventually Frankie leaves in shame, and Shelly Manne returns to the drums, demonstrating to the audience and Frankie how they should really be played.

This scene is important. It portrays successful jazz musicians as demanding high standards and discipline. It acknowledges that jazz requires a great deal of proficiency and skill to be played well. Neither is the band playing in Hollywood's traditional setting for the jazz musician of the shady nightclub. The film's visual representation of jazz creates a curious relationship with the jazz aspects of the nondiegetic score. Frankie's addiction is scored with jazz-elements and played by many of the musicians who are featured in the band for which he auditions. Yet it is his addiction that prevents him from joining the ranks of these musicians and escaping the hold of heroin. Although the audition scene provides a positive image of jazz, it is doubtful whether the overall impression created by the film is one that breaks the association of the jazz musician as being involved with drugs. Shortly after scoring *The Man with the Golden Arm*, Bernstein would provide another score that made a significant use of jazz elements. Yet, *The Sweet Smell of Success* left its audiences with an even more confused perception of what its use of jazz represented.

As with *The Man with the Golden Arm* and *I Want To Live!*, *The Sweet Smell of Success* combines Bernstein's nondiegetic jazz-inflected score with the on-screen music of a group of leading jazz musicians, in this case the Chico Hamilton Quintet. *The Sweet Smell of Success* is a story of sleaze and corruption set in New York. Burt Lancaster plays J.J. Hunsecker, a ruthless newspaper columnist who has the ability to create or destroy careers through his writing. Hunsecker is extremely possessive of his younger sister, Susan, and disapproves of her relationship with Steve Dallas, a young guitarist who plays in the Hamilton Quintet. Keen to see his sister's relationship with Steve terminated, Hunsecker employs his underling, Sidney Falco (Tony Curtis), to ruin Steve's reputation, but in such a way that Hunsecker's involvement does not become evident to his sister. After several unsuccessful attempts at separating Susan from Steve, Sidney plants marijuana joints on the guitarist in order to secure his arrest. The plan is not successful, however, and Susan tells her brother that Sidney assaulted her. Hunsecker turns on Sidney, but is ultimately left alone as Susan returns to Steve.

Originally in the form of a 1949 screenplay by Ernest Lehman, the film would not be approved until May 28, 1957, when a revised script by Clifford Odets met the recommendations of the Motion Picture Association.[75] By 1957, music tastes had changed, and there was a significant difference between Lehman's original script and the Lehman-Odets approved draft concerning the kind of music with which the character of Steve was associated. Lehman's original five-page synopsis for the film had described Steve as a promising nightclub entertainer and singer. Whereas Lehman's original script describes Steve as a popular performer and, significantly, an entertainer, with the associations between art and entertainment that I discussed in the previous chapters, the Lehman-Odets script clearly establishes Steve as an artist who plays modern jazz:

CAMERA lingers a moment on the guitarist, STEVE DALLAS. He is a youth of pleasant, intelligent appearance. He plays with the intent air of the contemporary jazz musician who takes his work very seriously indeed and affects a much greater interest in the music and his fellow musicians than in the listening audience.[76]

Steve's character is significant within the film where, as Gabbard has noted, he is the only person with any "integrity."[77] The script makes a link between the integrity and seriousness of his nature with his chosen musical style of modern, progressive jazz. The choice of the Chico Hamilton Quintet as the band that is featured with Steve is an unusual one, but supports his characterization. Hamilton's group was one of the rising bands in modern jazz when they were brought into *The Sweet Smell of Success*. Prior to the film, Hamilton had won the best new drummer poll in *Down Beat*, the leading jazz journal. *Down Beat* gave generous coverage to Hamilton, and its August 8, 1957, edition ran a special feature on both Hamilton himself and his band's involvement in the film. Hamilton's band was in vogue, and in selecting them, the film displayed a contemporary awareness that added to its authenticity.

The cover of *Down Beat* depicted Hamilton and the film's star, Tony Curtis, toasting each other with champagne against a backdrop of sky-scrapers and a crowd outside a cinema playing the film.[78] For *Down Beat*, the central interest in the film was the involvement of the Hamilton group. The band members are permitted a rare amount of screen-time both on and off the stage. Hamilton is given several short lines that establish him as a strong and "cool" presence. Although Steve leads the group for the pur-poses of the film, it is clear that Hamilton is a driving force and not a sub-missive sideman. This characterization is both unusual and important, in that Hamilton is black. The representation of a mixed-race group was more acceptable in the late 1950s than it had been for *Young Man with a Horn*, but Hamilton presents a striking difference from the, often, servile enter-tainers that formed the dominant image of the black musician in Hollywood film. Hamilton, in his brief moments on screen, reflects intelligence, author-ity and attitude. His band also blurs the distinction between the traditional opposition of black music, jazz, as being rhythmic, impulsive and anti-intellectual against white music, which was encoded as being serious, in-tellectual and therefore superior. Hamilton's band plays modern jazz with an unusual, for the time, instrumentation of drums, electric guitar, alto saxo-phone/flute, bass and cello. Although Hamilton, as the drummer, plays the most obviously aggressive and rhythmic role, and thus might conform to audience assumptions of the black musician, the coolness and intelligence of his off-stage persona presents a black musician that contemporary film audiences would not have been used to.

It is Chico who informs Steve that Susan is waiting for him in the court-yard behind the club. Susan has come to give Steve her reply to his pro-posal of marriage. Steve is clearly nervous about discovering Susan's response, but Chico reassures him. The final shooting script of the Lehman-Odets screenplay contains two versions of this scene (9F CONTINUED), one that provides Chico with more dialogue, but both give him a certain status of authority. In the first version, Chico is allowed to be more direct, telling Steve that, "you proposed to her, not me—go get your answer," whereas in the alternative scene he merely grins in sympathy and slaps Steve on the shoulder.[79]

The version that was utilized in the final cut of the film was the scene that leaves Hamilton without any dialogue. However, both versions and Hamilton's actual performance establish him as a man of experience, the inference being that he has a, presumably, sexual experience with women that Steve lacks, and one who the white lead looks to for support and re-assurance. Shortly after this scene, Sidney arrives backstage with the inten-tion of destroying Steve and Susan's relationship. Hamilton, however, and the rest of the quintet intimidate and delay Sidney enough to allow Susan and Steve time together. When Sidney finally gets to the two lovers and the situation threatens to become unpleasant, it is the arrival of Hamilton and his colleagues that encourages Sidney to leave. The rest of the film contains precious little business or characterization for Hamilton other than his musicianship. In the film's opening club sequence, however, Hamilton is given a prominence, a quiet presence, defending Steve and Susan against Sidney, which is, arguably, all the more striking through his lack of dialogue and the emphasis being, instead, on his gestures and cool demeanor.

In allowing the jazz musicians to be portrayed as serious artists, the film runs the risk of making its sympathetic characters too far removed from conventional depictions of masculinity. Hamilton's coolness creates an attractive attitude in those brief moments that he is on screen, but Steve is more problematic for the film. As the romantic male lead, Steve has to come across to the audience as being both desirable and serious, an intellectual artist, but one who is not pretentious and distanced from the youth audience who might be looking to identify with him. As I have noted, several Hollywood films had presented modern jazz as being too avant-garde and high brow for the liking of their youthful audience. *The Sweet Smell of Success* achieves its aim in a short scene where Steve is accosted by an earnest female jazz fan. The characterization of the woman is mildly satirical, but it reassures the audience that Steve is a "nice guy," lacking the perceived affectations and pretensions of the artist, but also being the source of female interest:

9F INT. CLUB
Steve has been trapped by a young woman in spectacles, a much-too-earnest devotee of progressive jazz.
DEVOTEE: I'm terribly interested in jazz—*serious* jazz. You studied with Milhaud, didn't you? This is such an interesting fusion of the traditional, classical form with the new progressive style, I just wanted to ask you how you came to form the group. . . .
CHICO
He comes through the curtains of the doorway, pausing as he sees that Steve is involved with the Intellectual Young Woman.
REVERSE ANGLE—(Existing)
Steve glances at Chico over the shoulder of the Intellectual Young Woman. Seeing that Chico has something to say to him, he wriggles out of the young woman's clutches by passing the buck to an unfortunate Fred Katz, who is descending from the bandstand behind him.
STEVE: Well, we just sort of got together (turning to introduce Fred). Maybe if you ask Mr. Katz. . . . He writes the stuff, you know.
FRED: (blankly) Huh?[80]

Fred Katz is the member of the Hamilton quintet most likely to be characterized by the film as the "intellectual one." Katz wears glasses and plays the cello, which was then considered a non-jazz instrument and still boasts few jazz exponents. The female devotee acts as confirmation of a certain kind of modern jazz fan, but also serves to remove Steve and Chico from an interpretation of their style of music that might characterize them as being aloof and affected. The female devotee is indicative of the film's awareness of the kind of music that it is featuring. Later in the film Sidney refers to Steve's band as being a "dinky jazz quintet." Sidney approaches a columnist rival of Hunsecker's, Otis Elwell, with the fabricated story of Steve's narcotic and communist activities. Elwell's column the following day features this story, which associates jazz with "sordid" behavior.[81] Elwell's description of Steve's band as being "high brow" sounds as if it is part of the accusation and that intellectual jazz is just as unsavory as marijuana or being a member of the communist party.

The jazz musicians in *The Sweet Smell of Success*, however, are positively portrayed. The review of the film in *Down Beat* was grateful:

> What a blessed relief to see jazz musicians depicted as honest human beings. In Lehman's original story there was no jazz combo, and the hero was a singer working single instead of a guitarist. Be it to the producer's credit, therefore, that an important place was made in this film for an established modern jazz group such as Hamilton's.[82]

For Gabbard, forty years after its initial release, the film remains "one of the American cinema's most unrelentingly negative portraits of U.S. culture at the same time that it is one of the most flattering portraits ever of a jazz musician."[83] *Down Beat* expressed frequent concern over the depiction of jazz musicians in Hollywood films of the 1940s and 1950s. Through its "Hollywood Music" and "Filmland Up Beat" columns, the journal offered comment on those films that incorporated jazz. When press releases announced that *The Man with the Golden Arm* was to feature a jazz drummer with a heroin addiction, *Down Beat*'s film correspondent, Charles Emge, or "Hal Holly" as he was otherwise known, interviewed the film's director, Otto Preminger. Preminger was asked if he was implying that "most exponents of modern jazz are just a few bars ahead of the police?"

> "No!" replied Preminger emphatically. And he was happy to explain at some length: "Our principal male character is very definitely a victim of narcotics, and he is also a drummer. But in emphasizing the jazz factor in the story, we will also show that narcotics brought his musical career to an end. One of the important sequences will show him failing in an audition directly as a result of what narcotics have done to him—wrecking his co-ordination and robbing him of all the ability he once had as a musician."[84]

Yet, as I have suggested, the overall impression and tone of the film is one that inevitably forges an association between jazz, drug addiction and a criminal lifestyle. Similarly, in *The Sweet Smell of Success*, jazz is associated with a ruthless and corrupt world despite the fact that the jazz musicians themselves represent the only characters with any decency. The "taint" of the decadent corruption that surrounds Steve and his band is so overpowering that the film's audience can easily recall Steve's progressive jazz as being emblematic of the corruption and not an antidote to it.

Spence discusses the film through its music where "Chico Hamilton's score sounded the alarm about America's trading authenticity for glitzy in the 1957 *Sweet Smell of Success*, a tale of power and corruption."[85] Mike Philips's account of the film also associates the music of the Hamilton band with the immorality presented by the film:

> [Tony] Curtis is brilliant, capturing the sleazy, jazzy glamour of '50s Manhattan in a performance which is echoed in Bernstein's score for the Chico Hamilton quintet, and the glassy skin-deep glitter of the interiors.[86]

Both of these references to the film's music confuse Elmer Bernstein's nondiegetic score with the music played by Chico Hamilton's quintet as being one and the same. This mistake was also made by contemporary reviews, and both *Variety* and *Reporter* refer to Bernstein's music as being played by Hamilton and his group.[87] In fact, as with *I Want To Live!*, the nondiegetic and diegetic personnel were quite different. The Chico Hamilton quintet did not play the entire score, but neither did Elmer Bernstein compose the music performed by the quintet. The Hamilton group is heard only in those sequences where they play diegetically. The nondiegetic score, however, was composed by Bernstein and performed by a studio orchestra. According to a *Down Beat* interview with Fred Katz, the quintet's cellist, Hamilton and Katz had nevertheless collaborated on composing the complete score for *The Sweet Smell of Success*.[88] A later Katz interview in 1986 confirmed that he and Hamilton had provided an entire score, but that it was almost entirely discarded when the studio brought Bernstein into the project.[89]

There is, however, a blurring between Bernstein's nondiegetic score and the music of Hamilton and Katz that mistakes the music of the quintet for being a reflection of the film's corruption. The film clearly portrays Steve and Chico's modern jazz as being removed from the immorality and decadence of the culture in which they perform. Yet Bernstein's jazz-inflected score is used as an expression of the negative aspects in the film's characters and narrative. Bernstein himself has always been adamant that his "jazz scores" have never been pure jazz but jazz-inflected. After the success of *The Man with the Golden Arm*, Bernstein was interviewed by *Down Beat* and, according to the journal, opined that "jazz isn't as progressed as it thinks." Bernstein was glowing about the contributions of Shorty Rogers and Shelly Manne, but remained doubtful about the merits of progressive jazz:

Modern jazz musicians, who place more emphasis on study and musical form than the traditionalists . . . are definitely making contributions to American music, especially in the things they are doing with small groups, like those of Shorty and Shelly. I hear much so-called modern jazz that is not modern, and, in my opinion not even jazz. I'm referring to things that are easily traceable to composers like Stravinsky, Schoenberg, and other pioneers of a generation ago.[90]

Bernstein's comments about modern jazz would seem to suggest that he was alluding to the Stan Kenton Orchestra. Ironically, the jazz-inflected film music that Bernstein composed during the 1950s sounds as if it is more closely related to Kenton's Progressive and Innovations bands than any other jazz group. The description of Bernstein's score for *The Man with the Golden Arm* in the *Down Beat* interview interprets it in such a way that could also be describing a Kenton piece:

Portions of it are in the nature of a symphonic extension of the music of an all-star band featuring Shorty Rogers and Shelly Manne, whose group in these portions is the nucleus of the 65-piece recording orchestra.[91]

By employing many of Kenton's key musicians and placing them in musical settings that blended the classical tradition with elements of jazz, Bernstein arrived at a hybrid music that could easily have been in the repertoire of Kenton's Innovations in Modern Music Orchestra. Even if he was not being consciously referenced, Kenton's concept of jazz flourished in Hollywood's use of the music during the 1950s.

Music loosely defined as progressive jazz is used in *The Man with the Golden Arm, The Sweet Smell of Success* and *I Want To Live!* to both evoke these film's immoral and criminal worlds and also represent the struggles and aspirations of those characters seeking to escape them. However, the choking atmosphere of film noir ensures that although the music of Shorty Rogers, Chico Hamilton and Gerry Mulligan is used to represent something nobler and higher, it is ultimately remembered by many as the soundtrack to the life of a drug addict, a corrupt journalist and a convicted murderer. As the next chapter suggests, the audience does not necessarily perceive the intentions of the composer and director.

NOTES

1. Lennie Niehaus, interviewed by the author, August 1999.
2. Steiner, F. 1976. An examination of Leith Stevens use of jazz in *The Wild One. Film Music Notebook.* vol. 2, no. 2, p. 32.
3. Thomas, T. 1973. *Music For The Movies.* South Brunswick, N.J. and New York: A.S. Barnes. pp. 181–82.
4. North was encouraged to adapt the score for a concert performance in a

letter from Milton Rosenstock dated August 3, 1951. The Alex North Collection, Margaret Herrick Library.

5. Kalinak, K. 1992. *Settling the Score: Music and the Classical Hollywood Film*. Madison: University of Wisconsin Press. p. 185.

6. Thomas, T. 1973. *Music For The Movies*. South Brunswick, N.J., and New York: A.S. Barnes. p. 182.

7. Ibid., p.181.

8. Letter from Harold Byrns to Alex North, December 19, 1951. The Alex North Collection, Margaret Herrick Library.

9. Flinn, C. 1992. *Strains of Utopia: Gender, Nostalgia, and Hollywood Film Music*. Princeton: Princeton University Press.

10. Gorbman, C. 1987. *Unheard Melodies: Narrative Film Music*. London: BFI. p. 153.

11. All references to the score's notes are from a copy of North's score included in The Alex North Collection, Margaret Herrick Library.

12. Kalinak, K. 1992. *Settling the Score: Music and the Classical Hollywood Film*. Madison: University of Wisconsin Press. p. 167.

13. Ibid., p. 160.

14. Dyer, R. 1997. *White*. London: Routledge.

15. Letter from Elia Kazan to Alex North, March 13, 1951. The Alex North Collection, Margaret Herrick Library.

16. Letter from Samuel Goldwyn to Alex North, May 18, 1951. The Margaret Herrick Library.

17. Review from *Cahiers du Cinéma*. no. 12, May 1952. The Alex North Collection, Margaret Herrick Library.

18. Lack, R. 1997. *Twenty Four Frames Under: A Buried History of Film Music*. London: Quartet Books. p. 200.

19. *Down Beat*. 1955. vol. 22, no. 22. November 2. p. 14.

20. Easton, C. 1973. *Straight Ahead: The Story of Stan Kenton*. New York: Da Capo Press. p. xii.

21. Ibid.

22. Cook, R., and Morton, B., eds. 1996. *The Penguin Guide to Jazz on CD*. London: Penguin. p. 739.

23. Easton, C. 1973. *Straight Ahead: The Story of Stan Kenton*. New York: Da Capo Press. p. 120.

24. Cook, R., and Morton, B., eds. 1996. *The Penguin Guide to Jazz on CD*. London: Penguin. p. 741.

25. Gioia, T. 1992. *West Coast Jazz: Modern Jazz in California 1945-1960*. New York: Oxford University Press. p. 151.

26. Lack, R. 1997. *Twenty Four Frames Under: A Buried History of Film Music*. London: Quartet Books. p. 197.

27. Stubbs, J. 1985. The shooting script(s). In *Touch of Evil*, Orson Welles, director. T. Comito, ed. New Brunswick, New Jersey: Rutgers University Press. p. 191.

28. Brady, F. 1989. *Citizen Welles: A Biography of Orson Welles*. London: Hodder & Stoughton. pp. 502–3.

29. Brown, R.S. 1994. *Overtones and Undertones: Reading Film Music*. Berkeley and Los Angeles: University of California Press. p. 299. Henry Mancini interview.

30. Welles, O. (with Bogdanovich, P.), and Rosenbaum, J., ed., 1993. *This Is Orson Welles.* London: Harper Collins. p. 304.

31. Gordon, R. 1986. *Jazz West Coast: The Los Angeles Jazz Scene of the 1950s.* London: Quartet Books. p. 58.

32. Pleasants, H. 1968. Jazz and the movies.*The World of Music.* vol. 10, no. 3, pp. 41–42.

33. Lennie Niehaus, interviewed by the author, August 1999.

34. Letter from Willard H. Alexander to Ray Heindorf, April 19, 1949. Box 29: *Young Man with a Horn,* Jack L. Warner Collection, Special Collections, USC Cinema and Television Library.

35. Letter from Willard H. Alexander to Ray Heindorf, May 12, 1949. Box 29: *Young Man with a Horn,* Jack L. Warner Collection, Special Collections, USC Cinema and Television Library.

36. McGilligan, S. 1998. Liner notes for *Paris Blues* Rykodisc RCD 10713.

37. Gabbard, K. 1996. *Jammin' at the Margins: Jazz and the American Cinema.* Chicago: University of Chicago Press. pp. 129–30.

38. Hajdu, D. 1997. *Lush Life: A Biography of Billy Strayhorn.* London: Granta. pp. 206–11. See Hajdu's biography of Billy Strayhorn for an account of the scoring of *Paris Blues.*

39. Lennie Niehaus, interviewed by the author, August 1999.

40. Harrison made this statement in the third episode of his program *Kenton's Innovations,* a four-part series broadcast on BBC Radio 3 throughout December 1997.

41. Easton, C. 1973. *Straight Ahead: The Story of Stan Kenton.* New York: Da Capo Press. p. 116.

42. Ibid., p. 122.

43. Ibid, pp. 118–19.

44. Spence, K.C. 1988. Jazz digest: From big band to be-bop. *Film Comment.* vol. 24, no. 6, November/December, p. 42.

45. Dyer, G. 1995. Tradition, influence and innovation. In James Campbell, ed. *The Picador Book of Blues and Jazz.* London: Picador. p. 385.

46. Interview with Police Chief Parker. *Los Angeles Evening Mirror News.* Friday, November 28, 1958. Box 14:14, *I Want To Live!* Robert Wise Collection, Special Collections, USC Cinema and Television Library.

47. Preview by P.K. Scheuer of the score for *I Want To Live! L.A.Times.* April 14, 1958. Robert Wise Collection, Special Collections, USC Cinema and Television Library.

48. Assessment of the Protestant Motion Picture Council, December 1958. PCA Files for *I Want To Live!,* Margaret Herrick Library.

49. Screenplay for *I Want To Live!* Shooting final draft, March 14, 1958. Scene 1, p. 1. Arts Special Collections, UCLA.

50. Undated statement from Robert Wise outlining the objectivity of the film. Robert Wise Collection, Special Collections, USC Cinema and Television Library.

51. Memo from Walter Wanger to Robert Wise. April 11, 1958. Box 14:12, *I Want To Live!* Robert Wise Collection, Special Collections, USC Cinema and Television Library.

52. Ibid.

53. Ibid.

54. Ibid.

55. Gabbard, K. 1996. *Jammin' at the Margins: Jazz and the American Cinema.* Chicago: University of Chicago Press. p. 134.

56. Screenplay for *I Want To Live!* Shooting Final Draft, March 14, 1958. Scene 2, p. 1. Arts Special Collections, UCLA.

57. Cook, R., and Morton, B., eds. 1996. *The Penguin Guide to Jazz on CD.* London: Penguin. p. 955.

58. Screenplay for *I Want To Live!* Shooting Final Draft, March 14, 1958. Scene 23–29A, p. 15. Arts Special Collections, UCLA.

59. Meltzer, D., ed. 1993. *Reading Jazz.* San Francisco: Mercury House. pp. 22–23.

60. Quoted in the liner notes for *I Want To Live!* Rykodisc RCD 10743.

61. Memo from Walter Wanger to Robert Wise. April 11, 1958. Box 14:12, *I Want To Live!* Robert Wise Collection, Special Collections, USC Cinema and Television Library

62. Ibid.

63. Quoted in the liner notes for *I Want To Live!* Rykodisc RCD 10743.

64. Canby, V. 1958. Review of *I Want To Live! Motion Picture Daily.* October 28.

65. Undated statement by Robert Wise. Box 14:14. *I Want To Live!* Robert Wise Collection, Special Collections, USC Cinema and Television Library.

66. Moffitt, J. 1958. Review of *I Want To Live! Reporter.* October 28.

67. *Variety.* 1958. Review of *I Want To Live!* October 28.

68. Letter from Geoffrey Shurlock of the Production Code Administration to F.K. Johnston of Figaro Incorporated. October 2, 1958. PCA Files for *I Want To Live!* Special Collections, Margaret Herrick Library.

69. *Variety.* 1958. October 28.

70. Moffitt, J. 1955. Review of *The Man with the Golden Arm Reporter.* December 14.

71. *Los Angeles Mirror News.* 1958. December 2.

72. Memo from Robert Wise to Walter Wanger. September 2, 1958. Box 14:12, *I Want To Live!* Robert Wise Collection, Special Collections, USC Cinema and Television Library.

73. Gabbard, K. 1996. *Jammin' at the Margins: Jazz and the American Cinema.* Chicago: University of Chicago Press. p. 9.

74. Bernstein, E. 1956. *The Man with the Golden Arm. Film Music.* vol. 15, no. 4, Spring, p. 3.

75. Letter from Joseph Breen of the Motion Picture Association to Robert Lord of Santana Pictures. May 16, 1949. PCA Files *The Sweet Smell of Success.* Special Collections, Margaret Herrick Library. The Motion Picture Association did not grant the project their approval on three main counts: the suggestion of incest between Hunsecker and his sister, the planting of marijuana cigarettes on an innocent, and the final scene in which "the girl strips herself, accuses the lead of rape, and (apparently) brings about his murder at the hands of her enraged brother—which constitutes murder without any indicated punishment."

76. Ernest Lehman-Clifford Odets final shooting script (dated December 14, 1956). Scene 9C. PCA Files for *The Sweet Smell of Success.* Special Collections, Margaret Herrick Library.

77. Gabbard, K. 1996. *Jammin' at the Margins: Jazz and the American Cinema.* Chicago: University of Chicago Press. p. 129.

78. *Down Beat.* 1957. vol. 24, no. 16, August 8.

79. Ernest Lehman-Clifford Odets final shooting script (dated December 14, 1956). Scene 9F (revised January 31, 1957). PCA Files for *The Sweet Smell of Success.* Special Collections, Margaret Herrick Library.

80. Ibid.

81. Ibid., Scene 50A (revised December 26, 1956).

82. *Down Beat.* 1957. vol. 24, no. 16, August 8, p. 35.

83. Gabbard, K. 1996. *Jammin' at the Margins: Jazz and the American Cinema.* Chicago: University of Chicago Press. p. 128.

84. *Down Beat.* 1955. vol. 22, no. 22, November 2, p. 46.

85. Spence, K.C. 1988. Jazz digest: From big band to be-bop. *Film Comment.* vol. 24, no. 6, November/December, p. 42.

86. Philips, M. 1997. *The Sweet Smell of Success.* In P. Hardy, ed. *The BFI Companion to Crime.* Berkeley and Los Angeles: University of California Press. p. 316.

87. Reviews in *Variety* and *Reporter.* 1957. June 19.

88. Fred Katz interviewed by Don Gold. 1957. *Down Beat.* vol. 24, no. 20, October 3, p. 27.

89. *The Cue Sheet: The Newsletter of the Society for the Preservation of Film Music.* 1986. vol. 3, no. 2, April, p. 18. Fred Katz interviewed by Leslie T. Zador.

90. *Down Beat.* 1956. vol. 23, no. 2, January 25, p. 11. Elmer Bernstein interviewed by Charles Emge.

91. Ibid.

5

The Last Syncopation

Jazz in Contemporary Film Noir

The tender swing of the jazz melody from *Taxi Driver* (1976) is typical of a tendency in films of the last twenty years to use jazz as the sound of the past. As I discuss in this chapter, the anachronistic jazz cue of *Taxi Driver* serves to heighten Travis Bickle's alienation from contemporary New York by evoking an earlier age. Yet, one of the perceived benefits of the emerging jazz-inflected scores in the 1950s was that they endowed their respective films with a modern, "the time is now" sound. At the time of his initial success with a jazz-based score, for the Blake Edwards television series *Peter Gunn* (1958–1961), Henry Mancini reportedly believed that "jazz is the only music to use for a contemporary story."[1] In this chapter I look first at the proliferation of "crime jazz," with a particular focus on Henry Mancini, before considering how film noir of the 1970s, '80s and '90s, has used jazz. I will suggest that many of these later (pseudo) noirs, such as *Farewell, My Lovely* (1975), *Body Heat* (1981) and *Blue Velvet* (1986), make a nostalgic use of jazz as a signifier of the classic noir phase in order to assert their own noir credentials. In John Dahl's *The Last Seduction* (1994), however, there is a fresh use of jazz to underscore traits and situations that would not have been possible for a jazz score of the 1950s.

THE COMMERCIAL SUCCESS OF THE JAZZ SONG

Chapters 3 and 4 discussed the somewhat narrow range of jazz that was used in film noir of the 1940s and '50s. It was not until the mid- to late 1950s that modern styles of jazz began to be featured in Hollywood films. "Hal Holly," the film correspondent of *Down Beat,* responded enthusiastically to the 1957 film *The Wild Party*, which featured piano solos by Pete Jolly and the quartet of bop clarinetist Buddy DeFranco, considering the film to be:

> . . . one of the best attempts so far to combine a jazz flavor with a movie melodrama and is just about the first time the moviemakers have caught up with the fact that the music is no longer completely synonymous with New Orleans, Dixieland, or Benny Goodman.[2]

Holly's journalese is a little misleading, and he has overlooked the film appearances of modern musicians such as Shorty Rogers and Shelly Manne in *The Man with the Golden Arm* (1955) or *The Wild One* (1953). Nevertheless, Holly's statement was roughly accurate, and the jazz used in Hollywood films of the time tended to be those styles that were felt to be less commercially and ideologically threatening. *The Wild Party*, however, was no advance for the narrative use of jazz, and Holly referred to the film's "shaky premises," which included "the one that good jazz musicians nowadays work in dives as sordid as those found in this picture."[3] What *The Wild Party* did reflect was the increase in jazz's currency in Hollywood, an increase that Holly had predicted in 1955.

The reasons for this increase in the use of jazz were primarily financial rather than the artistic merits of scores written by composers such as Elmer Bernstein, Alex North and Leith Stevens. Holly attributed the source of this change in jazz's fortunes to the success of *Pete Kelly's Blues* (1955). Previewing Otto Preminger's forthcoming *The Man with the Golden Arm*, Holly claimed that:

> Those still-soaring box-office figures set by *Pete Kelly's Blues* have made Hollywood extremely jazz conscious. And among the first of the moviemakers to spot the trend and its possibilities is, not surprisingly, Otto Preminger.[4]

Set in Kansas City, *Pete Kelly's Blues* was a Warner Bros. picture that displayed many of the approaches to jazz that Warner's earlier picture *Young Man with a Horn* (1950) used. In fact, certain lines of dialogue and platitudes about jazz are repeated almost verbatim as if they were official Hollywood doctrine. In the earlier film, Rick Martin's girlfriend tells him that he is married to his trumpet. Similarly, in *Pete Kelly's Blues*, the cornet-playing hero played by Jack Webb, who also directed the film, expresses a reluctance to go through with his proposed marriage. Pete is informed by his fiancée, Ivy, "You don't want to get married, Pete, unless you find a girl who looks like a cornet." Despite both films focusing on the lives of jazz musicians, the scoring duties were largely entrusted to the conventional symphonic orchestra. There is also a lack of anything other than a token and indirect acknowledgment of the presence of black musicians in the development of jazz. *Pete Kelly's Blues* does feature the black singer Ella Fitzgerald, but more emphasis is given to the white singer Peggy Lee. Lee also plays a leading role in the film. *Pete Kelly's Blues,* despite its title, is a more vibrant film than the darker *Young Man with a Horn*. Shot in Technicolor, the film presents a less convoluted plot than *Young Man with a Horn* and closes with an unambiguously happy ending. The villain is vanquished, Pete and Ivy's romance is rekindled and the nondiegetic orchestral score joins with the joyful Chicago jazz of Pete's band.

The film contains a number of original songs with vocals. Arthur Hamilton provides the music and lyrics for two songs, "He Needs Me," and, most famously, "Sing a Rainbow," both of which are performed by Peggy Lee. The central theme, however, is "Pete Kelly's Blues," with lyrics by Sammy Cahn and music by Ray Heindorf, the musical director for *Young Man with a Horn*. This song dominates the score in a number of instrumental arrangements, and its one vocal rendition is, significantly, by Ella Fitzgerald. The film's endorsement of these songs, just like that of *Young Man with a Horn*, is a compromised one. Pete Kelly's Big Seven play instrumental Chicago jazz, but Pete is forced by a gangster to employ a female vocalist, Rose Hopkins (Peggy Lee). Pete protests, "We don't carry a singer; it's not that kind of band. . . . It's jazz. The people here they come for the noise." Rose is hired, but one of Pete's musicians objects that, "We don't need a singer, we agreed." Nevertheless, it is the various bands' performances that feature a vocalist that are given the most extensive coverage by the camera. The instrumental numbers are usually shot as they come to a close and are never portrayed in their entirety.

The potential commercial benefits of a film possessing a hit theme song had been made clear by the success of *High Noon* (1952). Wherever possible, as demonstrated in Chapter 4 by the example of *I Want To Live!* (1958), certain studios and producers would press for a vocal song, even though it might be inappropriate for a particular film's theme, in the hope of emulating the financial rewards of the song "Do Not Forsake Me, O My Darlin,'" sung by Tex Ritter in *High Noon*. Elmer Bernstein claimed that "the death of the classical film-music score began in 1952" with *High Noon*.[5] He also acknowledged his own role in the demise of the symphonic score through the commercial success of a song based on his music for *The Man with the Golden Arm*.

The Man with the Golden Arm was heavily exploited through a commercially released song that was not featured in the film itself. With lyrics by Sammy Cahn and vocals by Sammy Davis, Jr., the song, "The Man with the Golden Arm," was founded on the film's score by Elmer Bernstein and made use of the film's featured jazz musicians.

Advertisements for the film, "An untouchable theme! An unforgettable motion picture!" announced that it also had "a great new song by a great singer!"[6] The most fulsome piece of advertising, however, came in the form of a "letter," apparently written by the film's star, Frank Sinatra, to the song's vocalist, Sammy Davis, Jr., in which Sinatra raved about the song and the certainty of its success:

> Dear Sammy,
>   I just lifted the needle off a Decca side you cut called "The Man with the Golden Arm." When the odds are laid on this wax, the price is a fat thousand to one you'll have one of the largest hits ever pressed.
>   As you know, I had my heart set on recording this tune, but after talking it over with Otto Preminger, director and producer of "The Man with the Golden Arm," we both decided that due to the type of role I play in the picture, it would be a shade out of character for me to do it.
>   Whatever the story, you've done a magnificent job and the cat that doesn't dig this record needs hospitalization.
>   Once again, congratulations and a gillion thanks for one of the most thrilling two minutes and fifty-five seconds of my young and swingin' life.
>   Sincerely,
>   Frank[7]

The letter advertisement also reveals some of the producer's concern over the way in which *The Man with the Golden Arm* was being received. The film had been denied a seal of approval by the PCA for its depiction of a heroin addict as its central character.

The song itself was a success and, following the impressive box-office fortunes of *Pete Kelly's Blues,* appears to have cemented the jazz song, if not the jazz score, as being a commercially viable proposition. Not long after *The Man with the Golden Arm* came *Nightmare* (1956), a film noir that was adapted from a Cornell Woolrich story and directed by Maxwell Shane, who had already directed a version of the story in 1947. Shane's remake moved the action to New Orleans and made use of jazz arrangements by the bandleader Billy May. May was featured in the film, as was the black boogie-woogie pianist Meade Lux Lewis and an underscore by music director Herschel Gilbert that sought to "catch the jazz flavor in the story." Yet Hal Holly saw the film's use of jazz as being indicative of the music's perceived commercial value:

> *Nightmare* is another sign of the times in Hollywood—to ride the jazz wagon for all it's worth while it's hot box-office. And it may be the first big break for singer Connie Russell, who is also likely to come out of it with a very big record of the title song, "Nightmare Blues," due for heavy promotion with the picture.[8]

The increase of jazz's profile in Hollywood films of this time was reflected by the increase in jazz musicians who were signed to the film studio's staff orchestras. In March 1956, *Down Beat*, in an article headlined "Film Studios Grab Off More Jazzmen," noted that a "steady infiltration of jazzmen, including some prominent exponents of avant gardism, into film studio staff orchestras continues." The financial benefits in 1956 for jazz musicians who joined the studio's ranks were cited as being a minimum guarantee of $6,990 a year for 500 hours work, with the added freedom of being able to undertake casual engagements and recording dates should they arise.[9]

Not surprisingly, this offer of security was tempting for many jazz musicians who might have tired of long tours spent on the road for a not-especially substantial financial reward. Once jazz musicians began to become more prevalent in Hollywood, they helped to break down the long-held belief of some of the studios that jazz musicians were inferior to their classically trained counterparts. As Henry Mancini discusses:

> The film studios used jazz musicians with great reluctance, only if they had a score that called for jazz. They had the idea these men couldn't read music, they thought they would be lost when faced with classical pieces. Well, they eventually found out the classical pieces were the easiest for these fellows—they read anything, play anything.[10]

Although the initial innovative impact of the early jazz-inflected scores could not last, and their perceived commercial appeal with the record-purchasing youth market was superseded almost immediately by the rise of the rock 'n' roll film, jazz was established in Hollywood film music. The progressive jazz-inflected scores of the mid- and late 1950s found a niche in film noir, thrillers, social problem films and tales of disaffected youth such as *The Beat Generation* (1959) and *The Subterraneans* (1960). It was television and the music of Henry Mancini, however, that would standardize the presence of jazz in film scoring and the popular consciousness.

HENRY MANCINI AND THE CRIME JAZZ BOOM

Mancini's partnership with the director and producer Blake Edwards resulted in a lasting and popular jazz sound for screen music. Edwards approached Mancini to score the private detective series that he had created, titled *Peter Gunn*. Mancini had just completed working on *Touch of Evil* (1958), discussed in Chapter 4, and Edwards was impressed by that film's mixture of big band and rock 'n' roll. The music for *Peter Gunn* was in a similar vein to that of *Touch of Evil*. Mancini returned to the pool of musicians he had utilized on the film, including drummer Shelly Manne and saxophonist Ronny Lang, who would go on to perform the "melody in the head" for Bernard Herrmann's *Taxi Driver* score.

The *Peter Gunn* music was a huge success. Two soundtrack albums were released and subsequently won eleven Grammy award nominations. Mancini and his band were selected by the trade publications *Billboard* and *Cashbox* as the "most promising" band of the year, and the score itself was nominated for an Emmy as the "best musical score of the season." The series ran for three years until 1961, and Mancini's music was crucial to its identity. Midway through the series' original broadcast run, Edwards stated that fifty percent of *Peter Gunn's* success was due to Mancini's music.[11]

What were the reasons for this success? The *Peter Gunn* sound was a fresh one that incorporated a number of innovations in film and television scoring. An important factor was that the program featured original music. Prior to *Peter Gunn*, it was standard practice for many American television series to make use of library music for their scores. This decision not to commission new music was a financial one based on the policies of the musicians' union. James C. Petrillo, then head of the American musicians' union, taxed television producers five percent of their overall budget whenever they employed musicians. In order to avoid this taxation, many producers decided to simply dispense with musicians and fashion scores from existing music in their studio's archives. Although there were music editors who skillfully cut library music to the needs of a particular show, it was difficult for a television program to develop its own musical identity. Nor did the music editors have the creative freedom of the composer to shape a score to blend naturally with the visuals. According to one television commentator of the day:

> Most background music on TV dramas and comedies has been poor in quality and bears no more relationship to the visual action than Spike Jones playing for a High Lama convention in Tibet.[12]

When Petrillo left the musician's union in the autumn of 1958, the situation eased somewhat. The five percent tax rule could still be enforced, but it was now possible for producers to obtain a "letter of consent" that granted them temporary exemption from taxation on the employment of musicians.[13] Blake Edwards took advantage of this opportunity and hired Mancini to compose original music for each installment of *Peter Gunn*. The resulting scores would have been striking to the ears of the program's audience. Hal Humphrey, then the television and radio editor of *Mirror News*, noted that "even those critics who panned the opening show itself were impressed with the music."[14] The music's success, however, was not simply due to the fact that it was composed specifically for the program. Mancini's music made use of several groundbreaking elements, some of which were born of necessity. The *Peter Gunn* scores had an unusual instrumentation that dispensed with the usual string section and made extensive use of bass and alto flutes. In total, Mancini employed a thirteen-man band, comprising a rhythm section of piano, bass, guitar, vibraphone and drums, four trombones and one trumpet and three flutes that alternated between bass and alto. Mancini has stated that the band's instrumentation came about because the budget would not permit a larger range of instruments and the conventional textures of the strings. The financial benefits of hiring a smaller jazz band proved irresistible to the Hollywood producers. As David Meeker explains:

Well, why it [the use of jazz in film] took off? It took off because jazz was cheap! It did. I mean, jazz didn't actually take off in films until the TV series *Peter Gunn*, which was, what, '59. *Peter Gunn* was such a success you can't believe what a success it was now . . . they were just churning out LPs all the time, going back in the studio again and again . . . I mean it was so big that it immediately had an effect on other TV series so the guys, mostly from [Stan] Kenton, people like Pete Rugolo, they immediately started churning out jazz scores for the Hollywood producers. Mainly for television to start with, and the producers loved it because it was cheap. They didn't have to hire an eighty-piece symphony orchestra anymore. You could have a jazz trio, quartet, sextet: dirt cheap. All the lower budget film producers immediately got on that bandwagon as well. So a lot of the, particularly the second, features in those times, invariably have jazz scores. Why? Because they only had to hire four musicians instead of eighty. And so for a while, jazz was very, very popular but it was just exploiting them [the musicians]![15]

The popularity of the Mancini style resulted in a number of shows that made use of jazz in a similar fashion. *77 Sunset Strip* (1958–1964), *Richard Diamond* (1957–1960), *Mike Hammer* (1958–1959), *M Squad* (1957–1960), *Naked City* (1958–1963) and *Johnny Staccato* (1959–1960) all used big band jazz themes and scores. Significantly, all of these shows were also centered on the escapades of private detectives and the police force. A retrospective label has been applied to this music, which seems entirely appropriate: crime jazz. The film jazz of the 1950s was darker in tone, but as the 1997 Rhino Records compilation *Crime Jazz: Music in the First Degree* notes, Mancini's variant was brighter and more accessible:

. . . swinging, blaring, compelling jazz that substituted scripted notes for improvisation and placed boundaries on its experimental tendencies. What made crime jazz magical was the purity of its sound combined with its pop sensibility. Here was fun jazz. You didn't really have to "understand" it. The horn section was swinging. The bass line walked with a stealthy pace. The closing-time piano solo continued to back a vibrating and lazy tenor sax. The muted trumpet signaled an uncertain turn of events. The brushes caressed the snare drum, and the ta-ta-tsssss, ta-ta tssssss of the hi-hat cymbal heralded the story line's quickened pace. Moving, moody, stark and bluesy, crime jazz was the soundtrack of action for more than a decade.[16]

The combination of streamlined jazz with these crime shows is probably where the jazz and film noir connection became firmly rooted in the popular consciousness. These programs reached millions of people and often ran for several years, numbering hundreds of episodes with the possibility of repeat runs. They were able, therefore, to become entrenched in their audience's memories in a way that would not have been possible for comparatively seldom seen films such as *Phantom Lady* (1944), *The Big Combo* (1955) or *I Want To Live!* (1958). Despite being small screen productions, these programs, with their assortment of hard-boiled detectives and private investigators, were direct descendants of film noir. If it took film noir almost until the end of its classic phase before it could fully realize its relationship with jazz, television noir was able to be much more "pure" in its use of the music. The use of jazz in these shows was, as with their big screen counterparts, often to underscore violence, sexual desire and the notion of the "outsider." In discussing the *Peter Gunn* episode "Lynn's Blues," James Ursini notes that blues and jazz are "traditional signifiers in noir. Here they are used to signify the alienation and despair of the main character."[17] The connection between jazz and these themes was readily identified by critics of the day. Hal Humphrey referred to the "jazz idiom" of Mancini's *Peter Gunn* scores as being:

> . . . a type of beat which, when heard by itself, leaves many Welk-weaned music lovers cold. But by artfully blending the off-beat blast of a trumpet to a punch on a hoodlum's nose, and the wail of a sax to a sexy feminine shape, Mancini manages to get his message across to the squarest of so-called squares.[18]

Mancini's own views of the potential of jazz to signify or suggest certain taboo themes are entirely consistent with the way in which jazz was usually employed in a film or television score:

> People want to be smart, and when they listen to jazz with a modern story, they start to get the feel, even though they don't know what they are doing. Any emotion can be inspired by jazz. It has a lot of sexual drive, and this is one way TV can employ sex in its stories without being questioned by the censors.[19]

Mancini was not the first composer to have employed big band jazz in a crime series. In fact, *M Squad*, which starred Lee Marvin as Sergeant Frank Ballinger, made use of a Count Basie theme tune and scores by Benny Carter and a pre-Spielberg John Williams. The series debuted three nights before the first episode of *Peter Gunn*. It was Mancini's music, however, that received most attention and the status of being groundbreaking. Inevitably, walking bass lines and big band arrangements became a trademark feature of television detective programs, but the Mancini sound spread further than the crime genre. Looking back on the influence of *Peter Gunn*, Mancini acknowledged that its success also came with undesirable side effects:

> We've become a nation of followers when it comes to fashionable trends. Scoring *The Graduate* with a string of songs by Simon and Garfunkel was an excellent device for that particular film, but it set off repercussions, just as I did myself with the use of jazz in *Peter Gunn*. For years after that, jazz was used in films for which it wasn't suited. Now, everything is geared to the swinging youth scene. Sometimes it works well, sometimes it doesn't. As for integrity—we have the music departments thinking about the record album even before the picture is scored! It's the kind of thing where the tail is wagging the dog. I don't think the craft of film scoring is being furthered by this particular development.[20]

Yet, there were positive changes to film and television scoring brought about by the success of *Peter Gunn*. During the 1960s, a new generation of film composers came to the fore with strong jazz credentials. The demand for their jazz skills was largely generated by the impact of Mancini and the crime jazz programs. Composers such as John Barry, Quincy Jones and Lalo Schifrin, alongside Mancini, provided an era-defining sound. The crime jazz of the early 1960s was followed by the more comic book and action-oriented jazz themes for television series, such as *Mission: Impossible* (1966–1973) and *The Man from UNCLE* (1964–1968), and films such as *Bullitt* (1968), *The Split* (1968) and the *James Bond* sequence. Barry, Jones, Mancini and Schifrin were skilled in a variety of musical styles, and their respective film careers demonstrate that they could not be categorized as simply jazz composers, with all of them going on to compose scores in idioms beyond jazz. Yet it was their jazz sensibilities that helped them to become established in the 1960s, and that owed a lot to Mancini's achievements with *Peter Gunn*. When Mancini was asked in an interview by Royal S. Brown, "What do you feel your place is in the overall picture of film music?" he suggested that his most important contribution was in paving the way for other jazz-based composers to work in film:

> I think maybe that through the success at the beginning, of *Peter Gunn* and then that time that followed, it maybe made it easier or made it less of a hassle for people who came from where I came from. I'm talking about people like Dave Grusin, Quincy Jones. It became acceptable to have roots on the jazz side or on the popular side.[21]

In 1949, Duke Ellington's international reputation as a composer of importance was not enough to convince the producers and music director of *Young Man with a Horn* that he was an appropriate choice to score the film. Ten years later, attitudes toward jazz had changed enough for another black composer, John Lewis, to be commissioned to compose the score for Robert Wise's late film noir entry *Odds Against Tomorrow* (1959). Lewis was leader of the Modern Jazz Quartet, an important and much respected group, still in existence at the time of writing, that brought something of a classical sensibility to their performances. Lewis expanded the Modern Jazz Quartet's standard personnel (Lewis himself on piano, Milt Jackson on vibraphone, Percy Heath on bass and Connie Kay on drums) with a twenty-piece ensemble. The score was heavily featured, and Brown suggests that it was possibly "the first score to use jazz idioms in a series of cues composed to be closely coordinated with the action," although the Johnny Mandel score for Wise's earlier *I Want To Live!* is also important in this respect.[22] Unlike Ellington a decade earlier, or the guarded use of jazz in films such as *Pete Kelly's Blues* or *Sweet Smell of Success* (1957), Lewis was extensively involved during the film's shooting stage and actively encouraged by Wise, who told the composer that he was "damned glad we have you doing it."[23] Wise drew Lewis' attention to the film's ending and how "extremely much we are drawing on the underscoring in this last section, and I think this will give you a chance to make a far greater contribution to the end result than the composer ordinarily has."[24] The extent of Lewis' role in a Hollywood film, as a black composer of modern jazz, would have been extremely unlikely ten or even two years earlier. Such was the change in Hollywood attitudes toward jazz by the end of the 1950s that Lewis' status as a jazz composer was seen to be an asset for the film's marketing and exploitation possibilities. Discussing the final advertising billing for *Odds Against Tomorrow*, Gabe Sumner informed Joseph Gould of United Artists, "we have added a music credit for John Lewis, based on his preeminence in the modern jazz field."[25] In addition to this credit for Lewis, Sumner also sought to exploit Lewis' involvement through a tie-in article with *Down Beat*:

> Based on John Lewis' immense stature in the jazz musical world, we have sold *Down Beat*, the leading jazz publication, on covering Lewis' scoring *Odds Against Tomorrow* at Reeves Sound Studios. Likewise, freelance photographer Kurt Gunther will cover the scoring session on spec to see if we can get additional mileage out of it.[26]

This interest in Lewis was extremely unusual for a film composer, whatever their idiom, and demonstrates the perceived commercial possibilities of the jazz score in the late 1950s and early 1960s. It was the crime jazz of *Peter Gunn* that drew the attention of the studios to those possibilities and helped to finally secure the use of jazz in Hollywood scoring. *Peter Gunn* also secured the association of jazz, and notably modern jazz, with the noir world of private detectives, criminals and femmes fatale. The effect of Mancini's music on the public perception of jazz was anticipated at the time. The liner notes for the second RCA album of music from *Peter Gunn*, released in 1959, proposed:

> If modern jazz becomes indelibly linked with manslaughter, murder, may-
> hem, wise-cracking private eyes and droll policemen the brunt of the respon-
> sibility must be borne by composer Henry Mancini. Because of him the point
> is rapidly being reached where no self-respecting killer would consider pull-
> ing the trigger without a suitable jazz background.[27]

Despite predicting an indelible link between jazz and urban crime drama,
Bill Olofson, the writer of the album's liner notes, stressed the positive ben-
efits that *Peter Gunn* would have for the public's perception of jazz.
According to Olofson:

> Mancini feels that the whole thing is leading the public toward an ever greater
> acceptance of jazz as an art form, benefiting the listener and the musician.
> Never before have so many people been actively aware of modern jazz. This
> form of music has found a new medium of exposure.[28]

There was no doubting the wider audiences that jazz could reach through
its extensive use in television of the late 1950s and early 1960s. This period enabled a particular form of jazz to acquire a popular base while
maintaining a strong level of jazz content, thus overcoming the perennial
problem for the music: "its inability to gain mass acceptance without selling itself short."[29] The swing variant of jazz, for example, which was incredibly popular in the 1930s and 1940s, ultimately became standardized
and streamlined at the expense of much of its jazz sensibility. As Olofson
predicted, modern jazz also became standardized as the soundtrack to crime
drama. This form of music may well have found a "new medium of exposure," but, as the next section will discuss, it is a medium of exposure in
which jazz in general has become entrapped.

JAZZ AS SIGNIFIER OF CLASSIC NOIR IN
CONTEMPORARY FILM

The generally accepted cut-off point for the classic phase of film noir is
Orson Welles' *Touch of Evil* (1958). It is a convenient boundary, but one
that is far from being firm. *Odds Against Tomorrow* (1959), for example,
is a film noir that does not fit within the established parameters of *The
Maltese Falcon* (1941) and *Touch of Evil*. What becomes evident, however,
if one studies the film noir reference guides is that the number of films considered to be films noir, or demonstrating a significant noir sensibility, drop
markedly after 1957. Taking Alain Silver and Elizabeth Ward's 1980 survey of film noir as a basic guide (and a broad one, as the editors include
films from 1927 to 1976), it is possible to gain a rough picture of the rise
and fall and partial rise again of film noir.[30] According to those films identified by Silver and Ward, film noir peaked, in terms of annual output, in
the late 1940s. During this time the Hollywood studios were releasing more

than twenty films each year that could be considered film noir. The high
point, based on Silver and Ward's selections, was in 1950, with the release
of thirty-one films noir. In 1952, the number of films noir released dropped
noticeably, Silver and Ward identifying only fourteen such films, before sta-
bilizing somewhat for the following five years. Nine films are included in
Silver and Ward's list for 1957, but the following year brought a second
slump and a total of three films. These figures, of course, give only a crude
approximation, and there are some surprising omissions from Silver and
Ward's survey. *I Want To Live!* (1958), for example, is not included, dem-
onstrating how subjective the defining of noir is. There is, nevertheless, a
dearth of film noir throughout the 1960s: Silver and Ward identify only
eleven films for the entire decade, with some years providing no additions
at all to their noir canon.

It is beyond the scope of this book to discuss why film noir declined
during the 1960s. In the 1970s and early 1980s, however, a number of films
were released that specifically referenced the classic period of film noir,
either through their iconography, narrative or both. Many of these modern noirs sought to accurately re-create the world of their inspiration, but
in doing so amounted to little more than, at worst, pastiche or, at best, homage. *Farewell, My Lovely* (1975) faithfully represents Raymond Chandler's
Los Angeles of the 1940s and, in Robert Mitchum, an icon of classic noir,
has an excellent Marlowe, but still failed to convince many critics it was a
genuine film noir. For Kim Newman, the film may have looked and sounded
"right," but only at the expense of its noir soul:

> The problem is that the period trappings (pastel colours, neon signs, careful
> set decoration, a sinuous jazz score) overlay Chandler's gritty, gutsy story with
> a veneer of nostalgia that makes this a far less effective version of the author's
> tone than the much more radical betrayals of Robert Altman's *The Long
> Goodbye*.[31]

Newman was not alone in making such comments, but it is interesting
that David Shire's "sinuous jazz score" is included in the list of "period
trappings" of classic film noir. It should not need to be stated by now that
no film noir of the 1940s, nor much of the 1950s for that matter, would
have featured a score remotely like Shire's. Michael Stephens, however,
offers a different interpretation of the film, but one that still confuses Shire's
jazz as being evocative of the classic noir phase:

> The film is also an interesting and successful attempt to recapture the classic
> look of film noir in color. Shot on location in Los Angeles, with many night
> scenes, it is a neon-drenched, eerie film. The ambiance is enhanced by an
> excellent jazz score by David Shire.[32]

Two contrasting responses to *Farewell, My Lovely*, yet both citing jazz as being characteristic of original film noir. What were Newman and Stephens listening to in the cinema when they saw *Murder, My Sweet* (1944), *Double Indemnity* (1944) or *Out Of The Past* (1947)? Their responses to the film's music seem to suggest more what they thought they were listening to, or even what they felt they would have been listening to had they inhabited the screen world of Philip Marlowe and Phyllis Dietrichson. Newman and Stephens, and arguably Shire and his colleagues, are possibly responding to a cultural memory of what film noir sounded like, or should have sounded like. It is a memory that would have been clouded by time and influences beyond the actual films and their music. Jazz may have become associated with film noir simply by being contemporaneous. As Reid and Walker surmise:

> Apart from *film noir* and bebop, the post-war forties enjoy remarkably little purchase on what passes for popular memory.[33]

The fact that film noir and many jazz styles originated and flourished in the same historical period is crucial when considering why they have often been cast together in recent decades. Barry Keith Grant notes that:

> It is true that we tend to "anchor" music with images (often in the form of memory of specific events or places when we had heard the music in the past), which is why music yoked with film images is so capable of overpowering us emotionally. Hence the nostalgic attraction of American Graffiti-type movies, the kind that appeal to the "historical" fantasy of "the good old days," in which the songs are visually contextualized within their specific historical moment. Sometimes the pairing is so effective that it becomes difficult to think of them separately, as, now, say, with Wagner's "Ride of the Valkyries" and the helicopters flying in formation over the Vietnamese jungle in Francis Coppola's *Apocalypse Now* (1979).[34]

The historical relationship of jazz and film noir would be further suggested by those relatively few films noir where jazz did make an appearance. The jazz-inflected scores of the mid- to late 1950s and the crime jazz of countless television episodes would add to this suggestion. The popular myths of the jazz life, as well as the writing of the original noir authors, such as Cornell Woolrich, which often referred to jazz as a feature of the city, also contributed to a connection being made between jazz and film noir. It is not surprising then that contemporary filmmakers and critics of film noir have often assumed that jazz was indeed the actual soundtrack to classic noir. This perception is the result of *retrospective illusion,* a term I concentrate on in the next section.

THE MELODY IN THE HEAD: THE RETROSPECTIVE
ILLUSION OF *TAXI DRIVER*

Michel Chion establishes the term *retrospective illusion* in his book, *Audio-Vision*.[35] Chion discusses this phenomenon in terms of an audience's memory of a film and offers examples in the form of the responses of some of his students to a screening of *La dolce vita* (1960). Chion found that the students often described sounds and music that they had not actually heard in the film, but that had been inferred instead:

> We also find false memories, for example memories of sounds that were only suggested by the image and the general tone of the sequence. In an aerial shot of St. Peter's square crammed with people one student heard the "acclamations of a crowd." This sound does not exist; it was created . . . by the sight of the crowd and by the grand chiming of churchbells heard with the image. In addition, sounds that do exist and are even quite prominent seem to have evaporated in some memories. One student noted an abrupt silence in the shot of the women in bathing suits. He totally blocked out Nino Rota's swing music; apparently all he retained from that moment was the fact that the helicopter's hum is interrupted.[36]

Many of the critical responses to *Taxi Driver* (1976), and its score by Bernard Herrmann, display this effect of retrospective illusion in their lack of understanding of the music and the extent and nature of its use of jazz.

Herrmann's decision to incorporate a jazz melody into what would prove to be his final score might appear to have been unusual. As Herrmann's biographer, Steven Smith, has noted, this selection seemed to some to be "an odd choice for a musician who had little good to say about the jazz idiom."[37] When David Meeker asked Herrmann whether a jazz bassist had worked on his score for Alfred Hitchcock's *The Wrong Man* (1957), the composer revealed a contempt for jazz:

> "Jazz musician on *my* scores?!" He said, "Asking a jazz musician to play *my* music would be like asking Cilla Black to sing *Aida!*" That's what Bernard Herrmann was like, so even if he did know (the identity of the bassist) he wasn't going to tell me. Anymore than he could tell me about the jazz sequence in *Citizen Kane* (1941). He told me, "Oh I dunno. Orson (Welles) went out onto the street and picked up these musicians; I didn't have anything to do with it!" . . . But nevertheless, it was ironic that what he's remembered for by the kids today is a blues theme played by Ronny Lang when he was so rude about jazz. *So* rude to me, except that Bernard Herrmann was like that, you never knew whether to believe him or not. But of course he never did write jazz scores, as you know. Composers who need jazz cues in their scores, like in jukebox sequences or whatever, would get someone else to do it.[38]

The composer Laurie Johnson, however, found Herrmann to be an admirer of jazz. Herrmann had been particularly impressed by Johnson's composition "Synthesis" (1969) that combined the jazz and classical idioms.[39] According to Johnson, Herrmann was against the use of "jazz for jazz's sake," or any musical style where it did not advance the film and was incorporated instead for commercial purposes.[40]

The composer who developed the jazz melody in *Taxi Driver* was Christopher Palmer. Acknowledging his lack of ability in the jazz idiom, Herrmann approached Palmer to develop a piece of his existing music into an appropriate jazz cue. Palmer selected as his raw material the first four bars of a soprano solo, "As the Wind Bloweth," from a Herrmann composition called "The King of Schnorrers." Developing the melody line further, Palmer titled the resulting piece of music "So Close to Me Blues," a romantic ballad for solo alto saxophone and small band, consisting of trumpet, trombone, acoustic bass, drums, piano and vibraphone, with string accompaniment. Smith notes that Herrmann was "so delighted with the result that the theme became a key part of the score."[41] In fact, the jazz melody is used fourteen times in the film. Yet Palmer's shaping of the jazz theme should not call into question the extent to which Herrmann's decision to feature it was his own. Herrmann acknowledged to the director, Martin Scorsese, and Laurie Johnson that the use of jazz in *Taxi Driver* was a first for him, in a film.[42] Indeed, Herrmann commented to Johnson that *Taxi Driver* was a film in which, for once, he was going to have to "cool down" the story through the score.[43] It was Herrmann's feeling that the "hard-edged" nature of the story required jazz, possibly to offset the film's brutality or make the audience all the more horrified when it did occur.[44]

The project clearly appealed to Herrmann and his artistic inclination that was drawn to the darker aspects of human existence. He described the script to Scorsese as "most compelling and exciting."[45] In discussing Herrman's score for *Vertigo* (1958), Smith outlines Herrmann's favorite dramatic themes as being "romantic obsession, isolation and the ultimate release of death."[46] All three of these elements formed the core of *Taxi Driver*. The central character, Travis Bickle (played by Robert DeNiro), is a former marine who cannot adjust to life in the city. Travis is a psychotic, alienated and unable to connect with society (he describes himself as "God's lonely man") and the "perfect" woman, Betsy (played by Cybill Shepherd), with whom he is obsessed. When Betsy rejects him, Travis responds by expressing his alienation through the disgust he feels toward the city's lowlife, pimps and pushers—scum that he reasons it is his calling to clean off the streets. Travis carries out his calling at the film's climax—a bloody and graphic assault on a pimp and his associates.

On paper, the overall impression of the *Taxi Driver* score is the predominance of brass and percussion. This is reflected by the instrumentation employed, where there is a shortage of strings and the complete absence of a violin section. The orchestra required for the score consisted of eight celli, four basses, two harps, four French horns, four trumpets, four trombones, eight woodwinds, four percussion and two tubas.[47] Herrmann's score makes extensive use of this instrumentation, but it is the repeated use of the jazz theme that has featured in many critics' memories. Michael Adams, for example, has referred to "the haunting jazz score by Bernard Herrmann" as being perfect for the film.[48] Even those who have just seen *Taxi Driver* often conveniently summarize its music as being "jazz-type."[49] But there is only one jazz theme in a score that is otherwise dark, brooding, non-melodic and orchestral.

What is clear is that although the score makes memorable use of jazz, Herrmann does not provide the "jazz score" that has been so frequently referred to. The jazz cue comes in the form of a yearning melody that is heard throughout the film, making it easier for the audience to recall it after the film has finished. The melody lingers in our consciousness far longer than the rest of the score, which consists of harp glissandi, insistent percussion and variations on Herrmann's trademark short phrases and use of the ostinato device. These aspects do not lend themselves to being whistled on the way home from the cinema. As Tom Shales observed, in his criticism of the Arista album of the score that dispensed with most of Herrmann's music, Herrmann's score was "not supposed to be easy listening. It was supposed to help scare people speechless."[50] Within the context of the film, it is disturbingly effective.

Herrmann's horror music is not something that we would normally want to remember. It is the sound of our fears and nightmares, the most unsettling example being the shrieking violins of the "terror" cue from the shower scene in *Psycho* (1960). Surrounded by Herrmann's stormy orchestral music, the audience clings to the moments of tender jazz both in its experience of the film as the narrative unfolds and in their memory of it afterward. The jazz offers a haven from the sense of impending doom that the rest of the score creates. So effective are Herrmann's orchestral themes as the sound of Travis Bickle's degeneration and the violence to come that it is easy to cease to think of them as music. They are, as Scorsese said of the score as a whole, an integral aspect of the audience's experience of the film.[51] Many of the critical responses to Herrmann's music, which suggested that it was a jazz score and evoked the sleaze and violence of the city, are thus examples of retrospective illusion. As Chion observed of his students' discussion of the soundtrack to *La dolce vita*, "the plot situation rubbed off on the music as the students remembered it."[52] This effect is certainly true of *Taxi Driver*, where the jazz melody has often been described as "sleazy" and, most extremely, suggestive of the "appearance of Satan."[53] It is unsurprising then that someone who has experienced *Taxi Driver* and attempts to recall it can often only think of the music in terms of its jazz cue. The remainder of Herrmann's score has often been "blocked out," as Chion phrases it, in favor of the jazz melody. Everything else is the noise made by a psychotic preparing to go on the rampage and ultimately bloodily doing so.

Instead of being expressive of the sleaze of the city, an analysis of the use of the jazz theme reveals that it highlights Travis' alienation from the "scum" of his surroundings and his yearning for romantic love. Martin Scorsese has often stated that Travis was somebody who did not listen to any music and was only conscious of his own internal voices.[54] Travis actually confesses to Betsy that he does not really know anything about music. The official music timing notes for the production also instruct, however, that at the end of the film as Travis, seemingly rehabilitated after the shootout in the brothel, stops for a customer in his taxi who turns out to be Betsy, he "*hears* [emphasis mine] 'melody in head.'"[55] There are numerous instructions in the music timing notes that request the score to represent Travis' feelings in a particular scene:

SEQUENCE: R4/5 P5/1 STARTS At: 826 FEET 13 FRAMES

:00   Day ext. City street. M.S. Travis walking. Note: This scene in Travis' mood.

Narration begins: I REALIZE NOW HOW MUCH SHE IS JUST LIKE THE OTHERS, COLD AND DISTANT. . . .

:10 ½   E.O.R./S.O.R. &n CUT to M.S. Travis, seated at his desk, writing in his journal.

His voice is narrating as he writes. NOTE TO MR HERRMANN: PLAY TRAVIS' MOOD THROUGHOUT.

Narration: June eighth. My life has taken another turn again.[56]

The association of the music, and the jazz melody in particular, with Travis is immediately made in the film's opening sequence. A black screen and silence are broken by the militaristic sound of a snare drum and a two-note theme for brass and woodwind. This theme increases in volume as it announces the appearance, in slow motion, of a yellow taxicab, bursting through the steam and fog. This theme is distinctly martial and almost heroic, a dark fanfare heralding a call to arms, but the sinister quality of the woodwinds, playing in the lower register, gives an indication of the horror to come. Another wave of steam washes across the screen, and the camera dissolves to a close-up of a pair of eyes, gazing in all directions. This is Travis. A shot of the blurred neon and swarming crowds is revealed to us as Travis' distorted point of view of the city he is driving through. It is with the dissolve to his eyes that the jazz cue/saxophone theme is first heard, for just over thirty seconds. The camera dissolves again to Travis' point of view as he watches people crossing the street. The music segues from the jazz theme back to the darker opening theme for brass, percussion and woodwind. This brief shot dissolves to another close-up on Travis' eyes, which is underscored again with the jazz theme. The direct association of the jazz theme with Travis is explicit. The audience, however, is not yet certain of the nature of that association. Travis is established as a loner, watching other people. The solo saxophone of the jazz cue perfectly complements this sense of loneliness. The individual soloist's voice draws on the popular urban mythology of the jazz musician as an outsider. Jazz, as a minority form of music not appreciated or understood by the majority, works as a particularly effective metaphor for Travis' isolation from society. The jazz is a tender theme, and this style encourages the audience to place its sympathies with Travis. The jazz melody is later used to underscore a lengthy sequence of Travis at work, driving through the city at night, watching prostitutes ply their trade and men pick up women. Travis is both fascinated and disgusted by the city. He is in the wrong place and the wrong time, and the jazz theme effectively supports this sense of displacement. The style of jazz used is not contemporary but in the swing tradition of the 1930s and 1940s. This style therefore sounds out of place underscoring the night life of 1975 New York that transfixes Scorsese's camera/Travis' gaze. Whereas a funk or modern jazz/pop soundtrack, both of which were in vogue at the time, would connect Travis with the world he is in, the nostalgic swing of a bygone age further expresses his alienation.

The opening sequence's combination of musical themes also acts as a warning that all is not well with Travis, however. The extreme split in Travis' thinking and that he is alone against the world is also established by the music as it segues between stark musical opposites. Travis is underscored with the romantic jazz, but his view of other people is underscored by the dark militaristic music of the orchestra. Although the jazz music draws the audience into siding with Travis, the entire opening musical sequence provides an indication of his insanity. The signs are all there, but the audience is not yet aware of them. As the camera dissolves from Travis' point of view to a shot of him entering the taxi depot, where he is applying to become a cabbie, Herrmann closes the opening musical sequence with a rumbling three-note theme for woodwind that finishes on a discordant note. The uncertainty of this theme's final note creates a sense of incompletion. This theme suggests unfinished business. The camera closes in on Travis' face as he enters the depot, and the music swells ominously in volume. Yet, before it can reach a "satisfactory" thematic resolution, it is brought to a halt by a roll on the snare drum. This intervention by the percussion creates the sense of a military procession being stalled as it surveys its new surroundings. But the procession will start up again. The sequence has not ended with the tender jazz, but with the unresolved darkness of the woodwinds. Herrmann makes it clear where Travis is heading.

The two aspects of the score, the tender jazz and martial music, are kept separate for the majority of the film. The jazz melody flourishes at first, representing Travis' romantic longing for Betsy, and is heard when he first sees her and then narrates their date for "coffee and pie." The cue returns immediately after this scene when Travis goes to buy Betsy a Kris Kristofferson record that she refers to in the coffee bar. Travis finally seems to be making a genuine connection with another human being. He carries it through by doing something that "normal" couples do: the giving of gifts to each other. Yet, when Betsy rejects Travis, the martial music comes to dominate the score as his obsessive personality seeks revenge in destroying the city's scum.

The growing relationship between Travis' romantic and violent impulses is crucially set when a young prostitute is pulled out of the back of Travis' cab against her will by her pimp. It is Iris (played by Jodie Foster) and Sport (played by Harvey Keitel). Shouting "bitch, be cool" to Iris, Sport urges Travis "to forget about this" and tosses him a crumpled twenty-dollar bill. It is an important scene. From this point on, the second of Travis' obsessions develops, and he becomes convinced that he must "save" Iris from her "evil" pimp-oppressor. The crumpled money acts as a symbol of his mission to cleanse the city, and he will not use it until Iris has been avenged. Significantly, the jazz cue is used to underscore this fateful meeting with the other woman in Travis' life and fades in on the soundtrack as Sport throws his money into the cab. The jazz theme is thus not exclusive to Betsy, but represents Travis' idealized and impossible perception of love. As Michael Bliss has observed:

> The two women's equivalent status in his (Travis') life is only further affirmed by Bernard Herrmann's astute use of the same romantic love theme to accompany many of the scenes in which they appear.[57]

When Travis' relationship with Betsy collapses, after his unthinking suggestion of a date in an adult cinema, the jazz cue is used again to suggest his isolation. The melody is heard after he has just spoken to Betsy on the phone to no avail. As Travis apologizes to Betsy and tries to arrange another meeting, the camera pans to the right of him to reveal a long empty corridor stretching away. Friedman describes this shot as portraying Travis "on the rack of his loneliness, a loneliness rendered now so painful that, led by the pitying camera, the viewer too flinches from the sight/site."[58]

The jazz melody continues in the next scene, and it is now that it begins to appear to be out of sympathy with Travis and his situation. The camera cuts to Travis' dingy flat that is full of decaying flowers, his rejected gifts to Betsy. Although Travis' voice-over and the images it accompanies are about sickness ("The smell of the flowers only made me sicker. The headaches got worse. I think I've got stomach cancer."), the jazz cue persists.

Combined with these images and words, the jazz melody now takes on a
sick feeling itself. It plays relentlessly despite the breakdown in Travis' head
and relationships. The use of the jazz at this point implies that Travis is
blind to what is happening to his life. He cannot see where he is going
wrong, and his impossible idyll of the perfect love, as represented by the
romantic jazz, remains. It is a classic example of what Michel Chion has
termed "anempathetic music." As Chion explains, this music exhibits:

> Conspicuous indifference to the situation, by progressing in a steady, un-
> daunted and ineluctable manner . . . the anempathetic impulse in the cinema
> produces those countless musical bits from player pianos, celestas, music
> boxes, and dance bands, whose studied frivolity and naiveté reinforce the
> individual emotion of the character and of the spectator, even as the music
> pretends not to notice them.[59]

The individual emotion of Travis is loneliness. In using the romantic jazz
with images of his rotting relationship, his isolation is intensified. Even the
jazz cue, which for so long has been expressing Travis' humanity and our
sympathy for him, has abandoned him in this sequence and is almost mock-
ing him as it plays dreamily over the dead flowers. Travis' isolation is
complete.

Freed from his romantic obsession with Betsy, another fateful meeting
sets Travis on a new and shocking course of action. Driving at night, Travis
collects a passenger (played by Scorsese himself) who begins to behave
strangely. He directs Travis' gaze to a window in a block of flats where a
woman, the man's wife, can be seen in silhouette. Informing Travis that a
"nigger lives there," the passenger tells Travis that it is his intention to kill
his unfaithful wife with a .44 Magnum. It is after this encounter, which
Friedman suggests is "perhaps the moment that turns him into a killer,"
that Travis begins to "get organized."[60] In a pathetic attempt to reach out
for help and communication, Travis tries to express his feelings to the senior cabbie, Wizard. Travis is aware of what is happening to him ("I got
some really bad ideas in my head"), but Wizard misinterprets him and cannot offer any meaningful help. As soon as Travis drives away from Wizard,
the score returns with the snare drum and a cymbal pulse providing a sense
of acceleration as Travis is now truly heading to a violent outburst. A sinister four-note theme, repeated again and again, becomes prevalent, constantly propelled by the snare drum and cymbals.

When Travis almost accidentally runs over her in his cab, Iris becomes
the source of his obsession, and he determines to save her from her sordid
life. The only way that he reasons he can achieve this quest, however, is
through violence. Travis must destroy Iris' "captors" so that love and order can return. Numerous commentators on *Taxi Driver* have discussed the
film's conflation of sex/love and violence/death. The most obvious paral-

lels are drawn between the gun and the penis. Friedman refers to Paul Schrader's script "relentlessly pressing the sex/violence analogy," but the music also provides a link.[61] Travis actively begins to prepare himself for his onslaught, rigorously exercising and getting rid of all the unhealthy things in his life so that there is "total organization. Every muscle must be tight." The next step for Travis is the assemblage of an armory and the perfecting of his shooting skills. This sequence, which Schrader titled "Travis gets organized," is a lengthy one, and the jazz melody is absent from the soundtrack for nearly thirty minutes as it develops.

The score makes the symbiosis of love and death/sex and violence chillingly apparent in the lengthy tracking shot through the brothel after Travis' onslaught. The audience is shown the full effect of Travis' madness on his victims. As the camera tracks back through the blood-splattered corridors, the score finally fuses the martial orchestral music of the brass, woodwind and percussion with the jazz melody. The horns quote the "melody in the head theme" that Smith notes is "particularly symbolic," and he refers to an important anecdote from the film's co-producer, Michael Philips:

> Benny explained that the reason he did it [quote the jazz cue] was to show that this was where Travis' fantasies about women led him. . . . His illusions, his self-perpetuating way of dealing with women had finally brought him to that bloody, violent outburst . . . I had never thought of it in terms of what Benny said, but Bobby [DeNiro] and I both said, "God, he's right." Absolutely. Perfect.[62]

Herrmann's music for Travis' violent intentions is spare and mechanical. It strips away emotional content to a minimum. As Travis says, "every muscle must be tight." During the "Travis gets organized" sequence, there is no place in the score for the jazz melody. Scorsese has said that, for these scenes in particular, Herrmann wanted to suggest the strength and indomitable qualities of Travis's character through the emphasis on brass and percussion.[63] Stern has convincingly argued that *Taxi Driver*, although it "doesn't assert that the body is a machine," portrays a "gradual charting of a defensive process, of a shoring up of the body by turning it into a machine."[64] Travis' doctrine of "total organization" and transformation of himself from lonely cabbie to killing machine is reflected by the music. Sharp and precise musical "blocks" of sound replace the dreaminess of the jazz cue: sudden harp glissandi, harsh brass and rolls of percussion. The various aspects of this section of the score sound as if they are produced through the pressing of a button, the flick of a switch and the activation of a device. There is no human warmth.

Although Herrmann seems to have crucially realized that Travis' obsessions of love and violence were bound up with each other, and clearly demonstrated this connection in the music for the "after the slaughter" sequence, he provided a musical thread between the two impulses throughout the entire score. Despite the fact that there is only one distinct "jazz cue" (the "melody in the head"), the suggestion of jazz is present in other aspects of the score. As Smith has observed, "the jazz idiom pervades the film, as Travis's taxi rides and monologues are echoed by the pulsating rhythm of cymbal and snare."[65] The score links rhythm with sex and violence. Smith suggests that the ever-present ticking of rhythm is possibly the score's "most psychologically astute element," and that it works "on several levels."

The increasingly brutal battery of percussion could mirror the steady tick of Travis's meter, his throbbing mind ("twelve hours of work and still I can't sleep"), the meaningless beat of the passing city dwellers or simply the mounting tension that Scorsese methodically builds.[66]

There is also the added suggestion of repressed sexual and violent desire. I have already discussed in Chapter 2 the Eurocentric perception that equates rhythm with sex. The use in films of rhythm and percussion as a metaphor for sex, as we have seen particularly with the orgiastic drum solo in *Phantom Lady* (1944), is a consistent one. The music for *Taxi Driver* perpetuates this metaphor. Initially, the ticking percussion on the score, for those cues other than the jazz melody, is slow and steady, but insistent. It certainly does not "swing," as jazz percussion would. Travis is just managing to keep his thoughts and desires under control. Yet, as particular events befall him, the rhythm breaks out of its repressed beat at key moments. After his futile attempt to express his feelings and seek the help of Wizard, the snare and cymbals on the score play at a distinctly quicker tempo. The score suggests that he is now accelerating on his path to destruction. Similarly, when Iris has abruptly appeared in his life for the second time, when she steps out in front of his cab, Travis follows her as she walks along the sidewalk with her friend. Iris and the other prostitute meet two clients, and at this point Travis suddenly drives off. The snare and cymbals return, accompanied by a steady, insistent bass pulse, which suggests not only the literal acceleration of Travis' cab, but also that something has been set in motion in his thoughts. It is after this incident that Travis' obsession with rescuing Iris takes hold of his life.

Shortly after this encounter, Travis meets the gun salesman, Easy Andy, who will equip him with the tools for his bloody destiny. As Travis' voice-over comments that "suddenly there is change" (once he has bought the guns, there is no turning back), the steady pulse of the snare and cymbals finally begins to break free and there is the suggestion of swing in their patterns. At each of these three significant points in his life (the failure to get help, the meeting with Iris and his encounter with the gun salesman), which will propel him that much closer to the carnage in the brothel, the steady tick of the drums quickens and carries Travis forward. "There never has been any choice for me," says Travis, and the drums, with the connotations of sex and violence, seem to drive him unthinkingly on.

Herrmann's score does not make a crude equation of jazz with sex. It is rhythm that is associated with sexual desire. Herrmann manages to suggest through the score, however, that Travis' sexual and violent impulses cannot be separated from his purer desires for love and meaningful connection with other people. Both the jazz/love theme and the martial "sexual/violent intent" theme are connected, in terms of orchestration, through the drums. The relationship of the jazz cue with the film's dominating themes of sexual and violent obsession has resulted in a number of critics and commentators referring to the music as being "sleazy" in its use of jazz. This observation seems to have been influenced by the prevailing Hollywood tradition of using "oleaginous saxophone tones for seduction scenes."[67] One of the most confused descriptions of the use of jazz in the film can be found in Bob Polunsky's review of *Taxi Driver* for the *San Antonio Light*. Commenting on the opening sequence ("One of the most amazing opening shots to a movie I've ever seen"), Polunsky observed:

> The scene is a shot of wet streets with steam billowing out of a man-hole. The steam fills the screen, and the taxi drives through and stops in center screen. At the same time *the jazz-type musical score makes it seem like an appearance of Satan* [emphasis mine]. It's a gripping sequence that sets the mood for the whole show perfectly.[68]

Polunsky does not explain how jazz casts Travis and his cab as Satan (possibly the claim of jazz as being the devil's music?). Both Michael Bliss and Lawrence Friedman, however, have discussed the opening sequence in terms of it being a visual metaphor for Hell. Friedman describes Travis in terms of Odysseus, Theseus and Aeneas in that he must journey into Hell in order to test his "heroic stature." Travis, argues Friedman, "already in Hell, must brave its nether regions to rescue Iris."[69] For Bliss, there is also the inference of Hell. The shots of Travis' cab:

> . . . slowly emerging from sewer steam suggest that he is, additionally, a messenger from Hell. However, since Travis (along with all of New York's occupants) is himself in Hell, it seems appropriate that it be one of the underworld's inhabitants who, in rebellion, attempts to effect a change.[70]

In the opening sequence, Travis' alienation from the city/Hell is indicated through the jazz melody. Rather than confirming Travis as an occupant of Hell, the use of jazz expresses his disgust at his surroundings and his desperation to do something about them. Unfortunately, this desperation manifests itself in such a way that ensures he will remain in Hell forever.

Amy Taubin has recently offered a brief but more considered reading of the use of the jazz melody. Taubin does not appear to succumb to the retrospective illusion that has affected many of the responses to the score discussed in this chapter. For Taubin, the jazz melody is not indicative of the sleaziness of the city, but its glamour and, as I have suggested, emphasizes Travis' alienation from his surroundings:

> I suspect, too, that many viewers respond not to Travis' alienation per se, but to Scorsese's own sense of being an outsider in a glamorous city—expressed not through character or narrative, but through mise-en-scène. Scorsese describes *Taxi Driver* as a mix of gothic horror and tabloid news, but it also has a heightened noir glamour. It's the glamour of New York that Bernard Herrmann's bittersweet theme expresses—a glamour that has rubbed off on the city from a hundred movies in which the sound of a soaring saxophone promises danger or love.[71]

The jazz melody does indeed promise Travis love, but only results in him delivering danger and death to others. Yet Taubin's comment reflects a different retrospective illusion, an illusion that is not of *Taxi Driver,* but the classic period of film noir and the extent of its use of jazz. Taubin cites Herrmann's "moody, jazz-inflected score" as being part of the film's stylistic relationship to American film noir.[72] It is certainly true, as the previous chapters have demonstrated, that jazz was more likely to be used in a film noir than any other genre of the 1940s and 1950s. But the contemporary perception that jazz was the dominant sound of the original films noir is less accurate, as I discuss in the remainder of this chapter.

JAZZ AND NOSTALGIA IN CONTEMPORARY NOIR

The perception that jazz was a consistent feature of 1940s and 1950s film noir is the result of retrospective illusion functioning on a grand scale: It is the retrospective illusion of not just a single film, but an entire film era. In fact, the retrospective use of jazz has become one of the main purposes for the music being employed in contemporary films. Inevitably, this use of jazz to create the feeling of the past has contributed to the rarity with which it has been featured in recent decades. Whereas in the mid- to late 1950s certain styles of jazz were considered entirely appropriate, if not essential, for a modern, urban film, jazz no longer seems to be considered relevant or vital for a film about "today." In the conclusion to his study of jazz in American cinema, Gabbard notes that the last twenty years have not been especially rewarding for collaborations between jazz and film, with the music largely being used to suggest an earlier decade or the nostalgia of a particular character.[73]

This use of jazz is not such a recent phenomenon. As I discussed in Chapter 3, *Young Man with a Horn* was promoted through its use of an older style of jazz to create a sense of nostalgia for the "only yesterday period when Jazz was Jazz."[74] Similarly, *Pete Kelly's Blues* returns to the same period, even though it was made at a time when the jazz-inflected score was coming into prominence. Both these films were made when modern jazz (bebop, cool, progressive or free in style) was in the vanguard of contemporary music and was literally new. By the 1970s, bebop was thirty years old, no longer avant-garde and had replaced swing as the mainstream style for jazz. The nostalgia for swing and Dixieland in the 1940s and 1950s, a nostalgia that Hollywood participated in, was due in part to a sense of alienation from the new styles of jazz that were then emerging. Yet, bebop could be considered as a nostalgic element itself in a later noir such as "Dead End for Delia," from the 1993 series *Fallen Angels*.

Body Heat makes use of jazz in both its nondiegetic score by John Barry and its diegetic source music. Set in a small Florida town in 1981, *Body Heat* takes place during a heat wave in which criminal lawyer Ned Racine (William Hurt) becomes obsessed with Matty Walker (Kathleen Turner), a femme fatale who deceives him. Written and directed by Lawrence Kasdan as a deliberate return to the themes of classic film noir, and *Double Indemnity* in particular, the film received considerably mixed reviews. *Monthly Film Bulletin* acknowledged the film's merits, but was not convinced by its status as an original film noir:

> Ultimately, any response to Kasdan's film involves contradiction. The pleasures it offers are undeniable. . . . But with regard to the generic area being plundered, it is equally obvious that nothing new is being offered beneath the gloss. Even the explicit sexual frenzy is already familiar from Rafelson's [*The Postman Always Rings Twice*]. As a critical rather than an industrial genre, *film noir*, if it is to be successfully reworked, needs to be approached with a sense of analysis, rather than simple excess.[75]

Time magazine was impressed with Kasdan's recreation of film noir, however, and noted the parallels between *Body Heat* and its predecessors:

> It is 1946; it is 1981. Overhead fans languidly attempt to rearrange the air. Late afternoon heat seeps through the Venetian blinds. A tenor sax investigates the upper registers of despair. Ned Racine drags voraciously on a nonstop series of cigarettes. He wears a Clark Gable mustache and a Zachary Scott hat. And one night, as a Dorsey-style orchestra plays "That Old Feeling," a sleek, tanned woman in white emerges from the darkness of the band shell and into the rest of Ned's life.[76]

Again, the critic, in this case Richard Corliss, refers to jazz as being evocative of 1940's film noir. Similarly, Michael Stephens suggests that John Barry's "jazz laden score" helps to bring a "sense of 1940's *noir* ambience to the film."[77] The score features solo saxophone, trombone, a rhythm section of bass, piano and drums, in addition to a full symphony orchestra.

Although the saxophone predominates, the score is very much of its own time, marked by Barry's distinctive orchestration, and does not seek to nostalgically re-create the sound of 1940's film noir. The instrumentation of saxophone, muted trombone and rhythm section creates a feeling of jazz that could be related by the listener to the 1940s, but, as with *Farewell, My Lovely*, nothing like Barry's score would have been heard in a film of that time.

The film does consciously seek to evoke the music of the 1940s in one key scene through a diegetic source. Ned's first encounter with Matty takes place at night as a big band performs in an open-air concert. Matty's entrance is steeped in film noir iconography. Blonde and clad in a white dress, Matty is modeled on the classic image of the femme fatale. The presence of the swing band playing "That Old Feeling," a tune and style of the 1940s, also acts as a clue to the origins and nature of Matty's character. Ned is consumed with sexual desire for Matty, a desire that will bring about his destruction, and the appearance of Matty to the sound of a big band could be read as a conventional use of jazz to imply sex and the fallen woman. Kasdan's script suggests, however, that the intention was to use the jazz in a nostalgic way, as the sound of "innocence," and as a contrast with the obvious sexual attraction between Matty and Ned. Ned is described as leaning at the entry door to the Fifth Avenue Pavilion where the Neptune High School Band is playing to a nighttime audience sweating in the oppressive heat. The atmosphere is described as "innocent and informal," an ambience reflected by the music, but this is broken by the appearance of an "extraordinary, beautiful Woman" (Matty) clad in a white dress, who rises up and walks past Ned, instantly drawing him to her without making eye contact or touching him while the band continues to play.[78] The intention in this scene seems to be to draw on the innocence of an older style of music. Yet, the audience's awareness of the standard function of jazz in Hollywood film music is such that, arguably, the scene still plays as if the big band jazz is being used to confirm Matty as a focus for sexual desire. The big band music functions as parallelism, instead of working against the implication of sex, as counterpoint.

The inclusion of the 1940s-style big band is only one of a number of references that Kasdan makes to the period of classic film noir. The use of the band appears to have been made because of its historical compatibility with film noir. Had Barry's nondiegetic score continued these allusions to the music of the original noirs, then *Body Heat* would have been even more open to the charge of unoriginal imitation. Barry contributed, however, a distinctive score that, as Brown notes, consists of "sultry moods" that "help carry that film well beyond the film noir pastiche it could have been."[79] Yet the score maintains the relationship of jazz with sexual desire and deceptive women through its featuring of the solo saxophone. Echoing Brown's observation, Philip Kemp comments that "the sensual mood is heightened by John Barry's bluesy, saxophone-rich score."[80] The film noir saxophone is still associated with sex.

David Lynch's *Blue Velvet* (1986) also employs snatches of jazz, alongside particular imagery and narrative devices, in order to suggest film noir. Lynch's artificial, genre-hopping world is perfectly accompanied by the score of Angelo Badalamenti, which, as Fred Pfeil has observed, is equally restless in its use of idioms, shifting from the Hitchcockian chords of Bernard Herrmann to the walking bass-dominated jazz of Henry Mancini style television noir.[81] When the film's teenage protagonist, Jeffrey Beaumont (Kyle MacLachlan), is introduced, he is underscored by a walking bass that signifies the music of Henry Mancini and private investigator heroes such as Peter Gunn, Johnny Staccato and Richard Diamond. The jazz is used to assert Jeffrey's noir credentials as he fantasizes about investigating and takes pleasure in being "in the middle of a mystery." Yet Jeffrey is no Philip Marlowe, and when he enters into a forbidden world of crime and sadism, the reality of his fantasies proves terrifying. The cod-detective music that introduces Jeffrey is appallingly ineffective for the nature of the crimes that he will discover: the brutal and obscene behavior of the film's psychopathic "villain," Frank Booth (Dennis Hopper). Drawing on the work of Michael Moon, Pfeil argues that Lynch and Badalamenti's conscious artifice functions to reveal "the fragility of the symbolic."[82] The symbolic association of "finger popping" jazz with crime and the investigator hero is made by *Blue Velvet* only to be horribly undermined.

The only character to escape Lynch's satirical artifice is Dorothy Valens (Isabella Rossellini), a singer who fronts a jazz band in a local nightclub. Frank, who has abducted Dorothy's son, subjects her to extreme verbal and physical abuse. Frank screams orders at her throughout the film, and she has little choice but to comply. The one scene where Frank can exercise no control over Dorothy is when she sings on stage at the nightclub, ironically when she is presenting herself on stage as the object of the gaze for a whole audience, within the club and the spectators in the cinema. Frank is seen in the audience, from the point of view of Jeffrey, in tears and occasionally unable to look at Dorothy as she sings "Blue Velvet." Powerless to stop her, the best that Frank can do is to telephone her later, when Dorothy is heard defending her choice of song. An earlier draft of the film's screenplay indicates that Dorothy's rendition of the song is directed at Frank, and that he is under her spell. Frank is described as being completely entranced by Dorothy, simultaneously working a small piece of blue velvet in his hand, as Dorothy sings "Blue Moon," then "Blue Velvet," singling Frank out with her performance of the latter song. Frank is unable to stop watching her when she finishes, and the rest of the audience applaud.[83]

Frank's inability to cope with Dorothy's performance arguably exists because she is momentarily out of his control and possibly because it expresses to the club audience the pain he has put her through. The lighting on the nightclub stage shifts between black, blue and red, suggesting the literal black and blue of Dorothy's body and soul as a result of Frank's cruelty. Barbara Creed suggests that Frank's aversion to Dorothy's gaze is because she "holds the key to male pleasure and happiness and she knows it. This is why Frank screams at her not to look at him. He cannot bear to see that she ultimately holds the power."[84] Dorothy's performance on stage has a purity and honesty of expression that is unique in a film that deals in pastiche and cliché.

The most obviously synthesized character is Sandy Williams (Laura Dern), Jeffrey's girlfriend who seems too good to be true and full of naive dreams. When Jeffrey first encounters Sandy, late at night, Lynch sets her up as a femme fatale, only for that expectation to be confounded. Sandy emerges out of the shadows, and the nondiegetic music underscores her appearance with a sinister cue for the strings. She is soon established as anything but fatal, and her musical theme, which is used for the account of her dream of robins bringing love to the world and her growing romance with Jeffrey, is realized as synthetic, slowly building new age, ambient chords. This manufactured, computerized theme is included in Pfeil's discussion of the film's ending, which, as Jeffrey and Sandy watch an animatronic robin eating a worm, is:

> . . . on the one hand . . . about the ironic relation of the amorally predatory robin to the goopy speech Sandy gave earlier in the film. . . . On the other, though, given the bird's obvious artificiality, the music's clichéd goopiness, and the hypercomposed flatness and stiffness of the mise-en-scène, it is also about the anxious and delightful possibility that Aunt Barbara—and Jeffrey and Sandy . . . are robots too.[85]

Dorothy achieves her freedom from artificiality largely through her performance on stage, which, illuminated in honesty, is disturbing for the man in the audience to watch as he looks at the living embodiment of the injuries he has inflicted on her. In her stage role of the "blue lady," Dorothy indicates that she is not the exotic femme fatale that Jeffrey and the audience might have expected. The script describes the "SLOW CLUB" as a sleazy venue on the edges of town, complete with a sleazy maitre'd and a fat comic telling jokes that are aimed at the club's "kind" of working-class audience.[86] Dorothy's rendition of "Blue Velvet" is described as being a very sexy and slow interpretation, but her performance is fragile and vulnerable, and she rises above her surroundings and the suggestion that she is another spider woman. The effect is similar to that of Rita Hayworth's singing of "Put the Blame on Mame" in the classic film noir *Gilda* (1946). Hayworth, also playing a nightclub chanteuse, is able to transcend her femme fatale casting through her quiet rendition of the song. The script describes the song as a rhythmic and typically American "lowdown tune."[87] Although "Put the Blame on Mame" is a song about men who attribute natural disasters to women's sexuality, Richard Dyer argues that Hayworth's reflective version suggests that her violent treatment by the male protagonist, Johnny, is due more to his pathological character than her "fatality."[88]

Dorothy's response to the horrors of *Blue Velvet* is the most natural one. She is emotionally tortured, and an earlier draft of the script followed the scene of Jeffrey and Sandy's "happy ending" with Dorothy committing suicide and jumping, naked, to her death.[89] There is embarrassment instead of eroticism for the male spectator looking at Dorothy. When Jeffrey spies on Dorothy from her closet, her undressing is accompanied by a mournful lone clarinet hovering in the lower register—hardly coding for an unauthorized, salacious "peep show." It is significant that Dorothy's public "honesty" about the pain in her life comes through the live performance with the jazz band. Jazz musicians frequently refer to a soloist as "telling a story" and the solo as a means of personal expression. For Russell Lack, it is when jazz has functioned as a character's "secret and internal voice" that the music has yielded its most effective partnerships with film:

> What closer form of personal expression can there be than everyday speech with all its stuttering imperfections and what closer form of musical equivalent can there be to everyday speech than jazz with all its uncertainties, semantic "mistakes" and creative individuality? Jazz in film works in a similar way to speech within a film. Both are apparently spontaneous expositions where the main goal is self-expression and communication rather than any kind of "genre fulfillment."[90]

Frank uses a strip of blue velvet as a sex aid during his sadistic intercourse with Dorothy. By singing "Blue Velvet" in public, Dorothy reveals her and Frank's secret life of abuse, and Frank can only sit, momentarily powerless, in the audience.

The nostalgic use of jazz has tended to favor its more mainstream and "popular" styles such as swing. "Dead End for Delia," a short film included in the *Fallen Angels* television series of films noir, however, makes significant use of recordings by Stan Getz, a white saxophonist who came to prominence in the late 1940s as an exponent of what was labeled West Coast cool jazz. The film does not specify in what year it is set, but the mise-en-scène and use of bebop and cool jazz source recordings suggest that it is the late 1940s or early 1950s (despite the Getz recordings being made in 1960).

Delia (Gabrielle Anwar) is the wife of Sgt. Pat Kelley (Gary Oldman), and the film opens with the discovery by Kelley of her corpse. Kelley learns that before she was killed, Delia was about to "settle down" with a man she really loved. Obsessed with tracking down her lover, Kelley's investigations lead him to Dreamland, a black jazz club that Delia frequented. The manager informs him that the man Delia really loved was Kelley himself, and that she was going to return to him. Kelley breaks down in shock, and the film ends with his voice-over reading a suicide message and confessing that he killed Delia because he could not bear the thought of another man being with her. As the police rush into Kelley's apartment, a flashback of Delia is underscored by the Stan Getz recording, "The Folks Who Live on the Hill." Delia says, "Do you hear that? They're playing our song." The camera cuts back to a shot of Kelley raising a gun to his mouth, then a cut to black and a single gunshot. The closing credits are underscored by the Getz recording.

"Dead End for Delia" is able to use styles of jazz and themes that were not available to the first wave of film noir. Because of the restrictions of the PCA, it would not have been possible for post-war film noir to portray the Dreamland club, possibly an allusion to the famous jazz club Birdland named after Charlie Parker, as a venue under black management. Delia goes to the club so that she can dance with men, specifically "coloreds" and "zoot suiters," and Dreamland is suggested as being a location where transgressive sexual relations take place. Significantly, Dreamland is never shown during its opening hours, apart from a brief flashback to the first meeting between Delia and Kelley. The inference that it is a site of forbidden sexual relationships, namely miscegenation, is made by Kelley and his police colleagues, possibly reflecting the assumptions that were made about jazz clubs at the time. In the opening sequence, the camera tracks around the scene of Delia's murder before settling outside the Dreamland club, where a brief burst of up-tempo bop can be heard being played by a tenor saxophonist. The camera then cuts to a shot of Kelley arriving at the scene of the crime. At this point Kelley has not been revealed as Delia's killer. When he looks up to the Dreamland club, the link between jazz and crime, in this case murder, is made, apparently suggesting to Kelley and the audience that the reason for Delia's death is connected with the jazz club. "Dead End for Delia," however, plays on those assumptions, perpetuating them only to reveal them as being misguided. For it is Kelley's assumption that Dreamland is a "seedy" jazz club and that Delia had (black) lovers there that results in him killing Delia.

The function of the recording of "The Folks Who Live on the Hill," a tender ballad ravishingly played by Getz, is to evoke Kelley's memories of Delia and his love for her. It also helps to suggest that Delia is not the woman that Kelley and his colleagues assume her to be. The recording is heard twice in the film, discounting its use to underscore the closing credits. Its first use is when Kelley goes into a flashback of Delia and himself eating breakfast. The two begin to dance, as the recording plays, despite Kelley's protestations that he has two left feet, before they kiss on the sofa. The Getz recording stops, and the scene cuts to a shot of one of Delia's Dreamland dancing partners, a white composer, playing the same tune, "The

Folks Who Live on the Hill," on the piano. Kelley is about to enter to question the composer, suspecting that he was Delia's mystery lover.

The pianist's playing of "The Folks Who Live on the Hill," establishes the song as Delia's theme. It is only at the end of the film just before he kills himself that Kelley hears Delia's voice confirming that it is "our song" and not one that she shared with the other men in her life. Delia's friend Lois (who desires Kelley) tells Kelley that Delia was just "trash." The information that we are given about her lifestyle, frequenting black jazz clubs to dance with men, encourages us to believe that Kelley's suspicions are correct and that Delia was indeed a loose woman. When Delia is first heard speaking, in Kelley's flashback, however, she is revealed as being sophisticated and speaks with an upper-class English accent. The knowledge that Delia had a liking for jazz also encodes her as a woman who would be unfaithful to Kelley and not really in love with him. Yet "her song," "The Folks Who Live on the Hill," is a beautiful, lilting performance by Getz and not the sleazy, blues-inflected jazz that possibly would have been used to confirm her as "trash."

The film demonstrates an awareness of differing styles of jazz and how generalizations have been applied to the overall term "jazz" without identifying its many streams. Kelley had the clue to Delia's true feelings for him in the Stan Getz recording, but he only realizes this fact when it is too late and listens to the music as he shoots himself. Yet, despite the perceptive use of jazz in "Dead End for Delia," the music remains linked to murder and sex and is also utilized as a means of indicating the protagonist's nostalgic yearning.

INTELLECTUALIZING THE GROOVE: JAZZ, GENDER AND THE SCORE IN *THE LAST SEDUCTION*

If jazz were simply used in contemporary film scoring as an evocation of the past, as it is in *Farewell, My Lovely* and *Body Heat*, then it would be difficult to foresee a vibrant future for its continued collaboration with film. John Dahl's 1994 film noir, *The Last Seduction*, however, although employing several of the conventional Hollywood uses for jazz, incorporates a score that often uses jazz in a way that would not have been possible during the classic era of film noir. The following section will center on an analysis of the score for *The Last Seduction* and a discussion of its original use of jazz.

The Last Seduction reworks a traditional noir plot, that of the femme fatale, in this case Bridget Gregory (Linda Fiorentino), who manipulates men and brings about their downfall. The film rather obviously acknowledges the inspiration of *Double Indemnity* (Bridget actually uses the phrase and adopts the pseudonym Mrs. Neff, after the earlier film's male protagonist, and her scheming involves the seduction and duping of an insurance company employee). Unlike *Double Indemnity*, and the majority of films in general, however, Bridget is not punished for her crimes and drives away victorious at the end of the film. Bridget is the dominant force of the film. She is introduced as a cold and aggressive professional New York City woman; as Kim Newman describes her, a "contemporary monster heroine who effortlessly eclipses Sharon Stone's Catherine Trammell as villainess of the decade."[91] She convinces her husband Clay (Bill Pullman) to carry out a dangerous drug deal and promptly absconds with the fortune that he received from it. Hiding out in "cow country," Bridget encounters Mike (Peter Berg), a naive claims adjuster who sees Bridget as a way out from his home town, and exploits him entirely for her own ends, ultimately using him as an assassin to kill her husband. Outwitting men throughout the film, Bridget's final plan goes slightly awry, and she has to murder her husband herself before taunting Mike into raping her while she calls the police, framing him for the murder of Clay and enabling her to escape with the money.

The film makes use of a combination of nondiegetic and diegetic music. The diegetic music is predominantly electric blues or blues-rock and is heard during the sequences set in Ray's bar. The nondiegetic music, by Joseph Vitarelli, is a modern jazz score that is closely linked with Bridget and her scheming. Performed by a standard rhythm section of piano, bass and drums, with the addition of trumpet, clarinet, saxophone and vibraphone for particular cues, the score focuses on three themes that are used repeatedly. For the purpose of clarification, I refer to these themes as "Bridget in Control," "Foiling Men" and "Dark Union."

The lengthy opening cue segues between two central themes. The music initially accompanies the film's credits. The stylish white lettering on a black background establishes a sense of elegant, precise cool that is reinforced by the music. Vitarelli's score begins with the rhythm section of piano, bass and brushed drums setting up a swinging groove. The piano plays a vamp figure, and the style of jazz is modern and cool. Like the titles, the music is precise and has an air of restraint. There are no "hot" solos, and the music is controlled, never cutting loose. The use of brushes by the drummer, which are employed for the majority of the score with certain notable exceptions, adds to the music's feeling of restraint. Avoiding the traditional bluesy aspects of most noir jazz, this music reflects Bridget's character, who remains emotionally detached throughout the film, never allowing her feelings to obscure her vision and only pretending to consider Mike as something other than her "designated fuck" when it suits her purposes.

This first musical theme, which I will call "Bridget in Control," becomes associated with Bridget, suggesting her forward momentum from which she will not be deflected. After thirty seconds of the rhythm section setting up the theme's groove, the first statement by the horns is made with the clarinet to the fore. The melody is then played by a trumpet, again in a cool style that largely confines itself to the middle register, confirming the lack of excessive emotional expression that will be a feature of Bridget's personality. The upbeat rhythm and melody is light and, as it is heard increasingly in the wake of other characters' misfortune, almost anempathetic in its lack of concern for the criminal activities of Bridget.

Just before the first minute is over, the black background fades to the film's first camera shot. The sounds of the city fade in to join the music, which continues on the soundtrack. This opening shot is from behind a stone statue of a bird of prey, looking down on a city street with its tiny cars and pedestrians bustling about. The image is a metaphorical one for Bridget and her heart of stone, preying on the city; swooping down to take who and what she wants. The camera tracks back and up to reveal the cityscape of New York and its office blocks and skyscrapers.

The camera cuts to the offices where Bridget works. Bridget is heard before she is seen, glacially distributing orders and insults to several rows of telephone solicitors under her control. "I can't hear you, people; you maggots sound like suburbanites," she menaces. Her power-dressed body is seen until her face finally comes into shot. There is then a cut to her husband, Clay, meeting the clients for a drug deal under a bridge. Clay is trading pharmaceutical cocaine, but is clearly not used to these kinds of proceedings. The music continues, but changes to a second theme that I call "Foiling Men." This theme uses the same instrumentation as "Bridget in Control," namely the rhythm section and the clarinet and trumpet, with the addition of a vibraphone. It is, however, more comic, and its main use in the film is at those points when a male character is being duped or has just realized that they have been fooled, usually by Bridget. The "Foiling Men" theme consists of fast runs up and down a scale, suggesting a process that is too fast and dizzying for the men who are not fully aware of what is going on until it is too late. In this first instance, the "Foiling Men" theme is heard as the camera cuts back and forth between Bridget being successful and in control at work and Clay almost bungling the drug deal.

One of the clients puts a gun to Clay's head, as he melodramatically sinks to his knees, reduced to a pathetic figure, under the impression that he is about to be killed. The clients, however, empty all the money for the drugs onto the ground and walk away. At this point the "Foiling Men" theme incorporates a device that is used whenever realization of their foolishness is about to dawn on the male character in question. The piano strikes a chord repetitively creating a ringing, chiming effect that rouses the men from their stupidity. The cool jazz of the "Foiling Men" theme is firmly associated with the thought processes of Bridget and her outmaneuvering of the men she encounters, particularly her telephone conversations with Clay. Here, the piano chords begin to chime as the dealers deposit the money and depart and Clay eventually realizes he is not going to be shot. With the deal completed, Bridget's plan is able to go ahead, and the band immediately switch back to playing "Bridget in Control," with its bass, drums and piano vamp. The trumpet states the melody at the point at which the camera cuts to a shot of Bridget clad in black, striding out of her workplace onto the street. The precise editing of the trumpet to Bridget's appearance and actions confirms this music as being Bridget's theme. Bridget is linked with the soloist—effectively Bridget is the film's soloist. As Jonathan Romney writes, it is "entirely Bridget who carries us along on her joyride."[92] Like the jazz musicians on the score, Bridget coolly improvises her plans, constantly adapting to whatever situation she is in without ever appearing to be rushed for a phrase or response.

These two themes soon feature again, further underlining their established function: "Foiling Men." Clay returns home with the money from the deal stuffed down his shirt. Bridget tells him that he is an idiot for carrying the money in such a way on the streets, and Clay lashes out and strikes her face. Although he apologizes, he is not particularly sympathetic, and Bridget only comes round when she sees, feels and smells the money. "You're a criminal mastermind," says Clay, and they begin to make plans about how they will celebrate. Clay goes to take a shower, leaving Bridget alone with the money. The bass, drums, piano and vibraphone of the "Foiling Men" theme begins to fade in on the soundtrack. The camera closes in on Bridget as she smells the money again. As Clay talks to her from the shower about their celebration night, she tells him that he can have "whatever you want," but the music and her face suggests that she is thinking of other things and plotting her scam. As it was under the bridge, Clay's naiveté and stupidity is underscored with the quick, rising and falling motif of the "Foiling Men" theme that emphasizes his slow wits. Bridget departs with the money, leaving a note, written back-to-front, which reads, "how are we supposed to celebrate?" Clay comes out of the shower and reads the note in the mirror. When his suspicions grow, the ringing, repeated piano chord device is heard. He goes to where the money should be and finds it gone. His realization complete, the piano chord stops, and Clay shouts out of the window, "You better run!" as Bridget makes off in a car. Immediately, the cue segues to the "Bridget in Control" theme as the camera cuts to Bridget, in her car, discarding her wedding ring.

This theme continues as Bridget drives away from New York. Her lengthy journey through the night is underscored by her theme, the rhythm section pressing on. The choice of music again serves to highlight Bridget's character. This journey is effectively a flight to freedom. Bridget is on the run, escaping from her husband, but the music suggests no fear or tension, no panic on the part of Bridget. She is doing exactly what she has to do in order to win. Bridget's night journey with a stash of stolen money contrasts with that of Marion in *Psycho* (1960). Marion is on edge, voices swirling round her head as she tries to predict responses to her actions, and her sense of guilt and desperate escape is perfectly reflected by Bernard Herrmann's pounding strings, which underscore the sequence. Bridget, however, trav-eling in remarkably similar circumstances, betrays nothing and neither does the score. It is in this use of the cool jazz of "Bridget in Control" that the detached, anempathetic qualities of her theme are first made particularly evident. A montage of Bridget's journey ends with her arriving in Beston. It is night and raining, and as Bridget drives past a large sign that says "Welcome to Beston: Home of the Bulldogs" (a sign that announces the testosterone-fuelled cowboy mentality of the men that Bridget will encounter here) there is a roll of thunder. It is a traditional device, creating an omi-nous feeling, but Dahl and Vitarelli turn it on its head through the persis-tence of the cool jazz on the soundtrack. Conventionally, Bridget should feel the sense of foreboding as she enters the "strange place." A standard horror or film noir score might emphasize the impending threat with a musical theme that would drown out the music of the intruder. Yet Bridget's theme continues as she drives into Beston; she is making inroads into the town and it does not swamp her cool jazz with its heavy blues and rockabilly. The terms of this encounter are set. Bridget is unstoppable, there is nothing in Beston for her to fear and the role of thunder on the sound-track as she enters the town is more likely a warning of her arrival and the threat that she is bringing to Beston.

The "cow country" town of Beston is musically identified through the diegetic music heard coming from and in Ray's bar. The tracks heard here are predominantly slow, heavy blues-rock pieces with a male vocalist. This style comes as a striking contrast with the light, clinical cool jazz that has dominated the music track until now. The men's conversations are domi-nated by the topic of sex, and the bar is established as a "man's domain," the heavy blues music being a constant feature. Again, Bridget is undaunted by these surroundings and takes control of the situation in the bar. It is here that she picks up Mike and begins to mould him into the pawn for her plans.

In a later scene at Ray's, Mike appears to win Bridget's respect by dem-onstrating some mental prowess, and she congratulates him with the words, "That's quite good." The reward for Mike is sex, and he and Bridget have intercourse outside the bar and at Mike's home. Bridget takes the domi-nant role in both instances. The diegetic blues-rock continues throughout the scenes of their lovemaking, thus becoming nondiegetic when they re-turn to Mike's house. The association of electric blues with sex is confirmed in this sequence in contrast to the intellectual associations of the cool jazz. At this point in their relationship, Bridget treats Mike as nothing more than a sex tool.

Later there is a notable change in the music used to underscore Bridget and Mike's sexual relationship. Bridget persuades Mike to join her in a credit roll exploitation scheme with the promise of sex in her place. As Mike agrees, he tells Bridget that she is "sick." The soundtrack fades in the sound of a trumpet playing in the lower and middle register. The camera then cuts to Mike and Bridget having sex in her house, thunder and lightning raging outside. Significantly, it is only at this point, when Bridget knows she has to play the role of Mike's lover if she is to ensure his support for her plan to succeed, that Bridget allows Mike to take the dominant position. Their sex is now seen as being sensitive instead of aggressive. The music continues on the soundtrack throughout the scene of their lovemaking, but, significantly, it is a theme that is new to the score. Gone is the cool jazz that has represented Bridget and her mind games. Yet neither is the music for this scene the electric blues that has been associated with Ray's and the sexual discussion and activity that takes place there. Instead, there is a fusion of the two.

The instrumentation is drawn from the jazz group heard on the non-diegetic score (trumpet, piano, drums), but the music is much darker in tone. The trumpet plays bluesy phrases that are very much in the style of Miles Davis' score for Louis Malle's *Ascenseur pour l'echafaud* (1957), which uses similar instrumentation. Notably, the drummer no longer plays with the brushes, finally creating a sense of release. The softer restraint of the brushes is replaced by the more varied and tactile, fizzing qualities of the sticks, rustling and probing the cymbals. This melding of the musical styles that represent the two characters on-screen (cool, urban jazz for Bridget and looser, emotionally charged blues for Mike) underscores the images of their tender lovemaking. The suggestion is that they have finally achieved the "commonality" that Bridget says is essential if they are to be friends and lovers. This use of jazz is a conventional one, but not a lazy return to an established tradition, as Turan points out:

> Helping to counteract the plot's dizziness is Dahl's feel for the genre and his skill in making scenes that sound like clichés, for instance passionate sex on a rainy night to a muted jazz score, play like they're supposed to.[93]

The style of jazz here, although rooted in the blues and drawing on that music's perceived sexual connotations, is not, for example, the sultry kind that John Barry works into the score for *Body Heat*. The music in this cue is slow, dark and brooding. It is heard later in the film when Bridget and Mike, en route to New York, discuss their plans to murder "Cahill," who is in fact Clay. This theme is used for Bridget's sinister intentions. For much of the film Bridget has been almost admirable in her forthrightness and refusal to let men take advantage of her. The audience has been encouraged to derive pleasure from her outwitting her male opponents. Now, however, her intention is murder. This theme, which I will refer to as the "Dark Union" theme, both supports and plays against traditional expectations of the music for the sex scene. The jazz might appear "appropriate" at first, but attention to its style reveals that it is not romantic or passionate. It is dark and ominous; for it is by offering Mike this sexual encounter that Bridget knows she will be able to manipulate him to commit murder on her behalf. This dark jazz is last heard when Bridget goads Mike into raping her, an act that will seal his fate. The use of the "Dark Union" theme for this scene, therefore, looks ahead to the malevolent direction that Bridget will take. The visual image may suggest a couple finally consummating their mutual love and respect for each other, but the music tells the audience that all is not well.

The final musical cue continues into the end credits and emphasizes Bridget's escape from the standard film noir practice to punish the dangerous and independent woman in the closing reels. Bridget has killed Clay and successfully framed Mike for the murder. A shot of Bridget, smiling triumphantly in her car as she burns the last piece of evidence against her, cuts to a shot of the car driving away from the camera through the gray, raining city streets. A brief drum roll is heard, and the nondiegetic score breaks into the "Bridget in Control" theme, which fully develops as this shot fades to the closing credits. The music briefly segues to the slow piano theme before returning to "Bridget in Control." The final shot and the music used to underscore it sums up Bridget's character. There is no victorious image of Bridget driving off into the sunset or a triumphant musical theme. Even at the end, when she has won, Bridget's emotions do not break loose, and the cool jazz plays out her exit just as it introduced her. It is business as usual.

RESPONSES TO *THE LAST SEDUCTION* AND DISCUSSION OF ITS SCORE

Reviews of *The Last Seduction* tended not to refer to the contribution of the film's score. The interest for many critics was, as with *Body Heat*, the comparison between Dahl's contemporary noir and established film noir classics of fifty years ago. One of the few critics to comment on Vitarelli's score, albeit briefly, John Anderson noted that the music acted as a counterpoint to the film's plot and was in keeping with the director's approach to the conventions of film noir:

> Dahl, who creates a cool, jazzy atmosphere for a steamy story line, clearly loves the genre, and constantly plays with his audience's expectations regarding gender and plot.[94]

Dahl and Vitarelli's use of jazz also plays with the audience's expectations, both confirming and subverting them, as, for example, with the dark jazz that underscores the sex scene between Bridget and Mike. Jazz might appear to be an unoriginal choice of music to score a film noir, but the style chosen and its application in the film is innovative for noir jazz. When scoring *The Man with the Golden Arm*, Elmer Bernstein had turned to jazz because he felt it contained certain sounds "blues, wails, trumpet screeches—that are perfect for expressing anguish."[95] Vitarelli's score largely dispenses with these aspects of jazz, however, and opts for a cool style that does not reflect the despair or threat that characterize so much of film noir or the "anxiety jazz" that occasionally underscored it in the 1950s. The music almost entirely reflects Bridget's character and psychology. There is little expression by the nondiegetic music of the anguish and defeat experienced by the male characters in the film, as if they are not worthy of the music's attention, and so the music does not encourage the audience to sympathize with the men Bridget eliminates. This lack of music to represent the perspectives or emotions of the male characters heightens the dominance that Bridget has over her victims. As Romney observes:

> You can't help feeling that Bridget deserves some opponent who's actually on her level. That's what makes the film almost tragic; she's so much smarter than anyone else that victory seems futile—there can't be that much fun in it for her. The fun's all ours, watching her prey squirm.[96]

The control that Bridget exercises throughout the film is extended to the music. This privileging of a female character, especially one as ruthless and amoral as Bridget, by the score of a Hollywood film is rare. The musical score, as I have discussed, does not punish Bridget or suggest that her actions are wrong. This bias in favor of the "criminal woman" is atypical of standard Hollywood scores. Pauline MacRory has discussed the neo-noir *Basic Instinct* and the attitude of its score, by Jerry Goldsmith, toward the film's "criminal" female protagonist, Catherine Trammell. MacRory notes that the film keeps the audience guessing as to the killer's identity. The "truth" is never revealed because the rational male character never discovers it, and the women who control it are not to be trusted. MacRory argues that the jazz-inflected score unequivocally denounces Catherine throughout the film, however, coding her as evil. The opening theme is closely associated with Catherine and her seductive powers. MacRory notes Goldsmith's description of his score as being "erotic and evil."[97] The music thus presents Catherine as being guilty when the actual truth is never known. *The Last Seduction* is radically different to *Basic Instinct,* in that its score never denounces Bridget and coolly permits her to escape triumphant at the end.

Although jazz has often been used to suggest the "otherness" of female sexuality, Hollywood films have tended to present the music as being the preserve of male practitioners and fans. The association of jazz with a female protagonist is unusual, Barbara Graham's love for modern jazz being another rare example. As we have seen, jazz has traditionally been linked to male characters such as Rick Martin, Pete Kelly or Frankie

Machine. The jazz world itself reflects this lack of female representation, Gene Lees noting that it has "severely discriminated against women even while its practitioners have been in the forefront of the demand for racial equality."[98] As Miles Kington comments:

> Jazz is still a home to prejudices. It is pro-black, pro-American, pro-hetero-sexual and pro-male (the rare incidence of homosexuals in jazz is astonishing). To come into jazz as a white, English, lesbian woman would be outrageously difficult, in other words.[99]

Hollywood films have frequently presented jazz musicians or jazz fans as being unable to reconcile their musical passion with a successful hetero-sexual relationship. The independence of these characters is often high-lighted through their interest in jazz, as, for example, with James Stewart's bachelor lawyer in *Anatomy of a Murder* (1959), which features a score by Duke Ellington. Alain Silver argues that jazz is used in Robert Aldrich's *Kiss Me Deadly* (1955) as a signifier of the central character's modern and unpleasant masculinity. In the film's opening sequence, the "hero," Mike Hammer, is driving alone at night as his radio plays "Rather Have the Blues," sung by Nat "King" Cole, before a woman, Christina, signals him to pull over. Silver suggests that Hammer's choice of music reveals some-thing of his character:

> What kind of man is Mike Hammer? *Kiss Me Deadly's* opening dialogue types him quickly. Christina's direct accusation of narcissism merely confirms what the icons suggest about "how much you can tell about the person from such simple things": the sports car, the curled lip, the jazz on the radio. Aldrich and writer A.I. Bezzerides use the character of Christina to explain and re-inforce what the images have already suggested, that this is not a modest or admirable man.[100]

Silver's summary of Hammer's character, "egocentric, callous and brutal," could also be applied to Bridget. Does the association of modern jazz with Bridget suggest her lack of traditionally "feminine" characteris-tics, or is it an attempt to redefine the gendering of musical traits? Gabbard refers to Susan McClary's writing on the perceived effeminacy of music and how male musicians have sought to prevent their masculinity from being called into question by emphasizing the rational qualities of music:

The charge that musicians or devotees of music are "effeminate" goes back as far as recorded documentation about music, and music's associa-tion with the body and with subjectivity has led to its being relegated in many historical periods to what was understood as a "feminine" realm.[101]

The Last Seduction applies the "emotional" qualities of the blues to the spaces occupied by the male inhabitants of Beston. Both Mike and Clay allow their feelings to get the better of them. Modern jazz is reserved for

Bridget and her schemes. Yet the typical use of jazz in American film noir has not corresponded to McClary's argument. Chapters 3 and 4 discussed how the modern forms of jazz were seldom featured in films of the 1940s and 1950s because their perceived intellectual pretensions were considered potentially threatening to the masculinity of male characters. Instead, Hollywood focused on the physical, emotional elements of jazz. When it was used, jazz was almost exclusively associated with seediness, sex, violence and immorality, whether directly, as in *Phantom Lady*, or indirectly, as in *The Sweet Smell of Success*. Vitarelli's jazz is not used so obviously.

In *The Last Seduction*, Bridget's victory is achieved through her mental prowess. Moving away from the traditions of noir jazz, cool jazz is used in the film to underscore the intellectual qualities of Bridget and the lack of such qualities demonstrated by Mike and Clay. Less strikingly, the blues and country music are left to suggest the sexual and the unsophisticated, as evidenced in the scenes set in Ray's, all of which are scored with electric blues source music. When jazz does underscore a sex scene, it is notably no longer in the cool style, but shifts to the blues. Admittedly, there is still a relationship between jazz and criminality in that Bridget's scheming is amoral and, ultimately, murderous. In this sense, *The Last Seduction* could be cited as evidence that jazz remains rooted in the associations and assumptions, discussed by Kathryn Kalinak, that films have applied to it ever since the two forms began to collaborate.[102] The film's use of jazz as something other than anguished and sexual underscore is original, however, particularly for film noir. Dahl and Vitarelli seem to have been aware of the themes that jazz has traditionally signified and recast them. Like jazz musicians, they have not completely dispensed with established standards, but used them as the basis for fresh interpretations. As long as the jazz score is able to do that, rather than simply recreating the past, then future collaborations between jazz and film noir need not be exercises in pastiche and preservation.

NOTES

1. Humphrey, H. 1958. *Mirror News*. October 27. Hal Humphrey Collection, Special Collections, USC Cinema and Television Library. Interview and report on Henry Mancini by Humphrey.

2. Holly H. 1957. *Down Beat*. vol. 24, no. 1, January 9, p. 47.

3. Ibid.

4. Holly, H. 1955. *Down Beat*. vol. 22, no. 22, November 2, p. 46. Interview with Otto Preminger and preview of *The Man with the Golden Arm*.

5. Lack, R. 1997. *Twenty Four Frames Under: A Buried History of Film Music*. London: Quartet Books. p. 207.

6. Advertisement for *The Man with the Golden Arm*. 1956. *Down Beat*. vol. 23, no. 1, January 11, p. 16. In the same issue, Bernstein was also featured in an advertisement noting his role as composer and conductor.

7. Ibid., p. 17.

8. Ibid., p. 41.

9. *Down Beat.* vol. 23, no. 6, March 21, 1956, p. 39.

10. Thomas, T. 1977. *Music for the Movies.* South Brunswick, N.J., and New York: A.S. Barnes. p. 200. Interview with Henry Mancini.

11. NBC Press Department biography of Henry Mancini. 1960. February 12. Special Collections, USC Cinema and Television Library.

12. Humphrey, H. 1958. *Mirror News.* October 27. Hal Humphrey Collection, Special Collections, USC Cinema and Television Library. Interview and report of Henry Mancini by Humphrey.

13. Burlingame, J. 1996. Crime to a beat. In *TV's Biggest Hits: The Story of Television Themes from Dragnet to Friends.* New York: Schirmer Books. pp. 29–70. A more detailed account of the changing policy of the American musician's union.

14. Humphrey, H. 1958. *Mirror News.* October 27. Hal Humphrey Collection, Special Collections, USC Cinema and Television Library. Interview and report on Henry Mancini by Humphrey.

15. David Meeker, interviewed by the author, October 27, 1999.

16. Botticelli, J. 1997. Liner notes. In *Crime Jazz: Music in the First Degree.* Rhino/BMG Special Products. R2 72912/DRC1 1669.

17. Ursini, J. 1996. Angst at Sixty Fields per Second. In A. Silver and J. Ursini, eds. *Film Noir Reader.* New York: Limelight Editions. p. 281.

18. Humphrey, H. 1958. *Mirror News.* October 27. Hal Humphrey Collection, Special Collections, USC Cinema and Television Library. Interview and report on Henry Mancini by Humphrey.

19. Ibid.

20. Thomas, T. 1977. *Music for the Movies.* South Brunswick, N.J., and New York: A.S. Barnes. p. 195. Interview with Henry Mancini.

21. Brown, R.S. 1994. *Overtones and Undertones: Reading Film Music.* Berkeley and Los Angeles: University of California Press. p. 303.

22. Ibid., pp. 184–85.

23. Letter to John Lewis from Robert Wise, March 11, 1959. Robert Wise Collection, Special Collections, USC Cinema and Television Library.

24. Ibid.

25. Letter to Joseph Gould from Gabe Sumner, July 22, 1959. Robert Wise Collection, Special Collections, USC Cinema and Television Library.

26. Memo to Mort Nathanson from Gabe Sumner, July 20, 1959. Robert Wise Collection, Special Collections, USC Cinema and Television Library.

27. Olofson, B. 1995. Original liner notes. In *More Music from Peter Gunn.* 1995. RCA and Victor/BMG Music. 74321 29857 2.

28. Ibid.

29. Liner notes. In *Crime Jazz: Music in the First Degree.* Rhino/BMG Special Products. R272912/DRC1 1669.

30. Silver, A., and Ward, E., eds. 1980. *Film Noir.* London: Secker & Warburg. pp. 333–36. Figures taken from Appendix B, which seeks to display the "predominant years, studios, and personnel involved in film noir."

31. Newman, K. 1997. *Murder My Sweet/Farewell, My Lovely.* In P. Hardy, ed. *The BFI Companion To Crime.* Berkeley and Los Angeles: University of California Press. p. 235.

32. Stephens, M. 1995. *Film Noir: A Comprehensive, Illustrated Reference to Movies, Terms and Persons.* Jefferson, N.C.: McFarland & Company. p. 137.

33. Reid, D., and Walker, J.L. 1993. Strange pursuit: Cornell Woolrich and the abandoned city of the forties. In J. Copjec, ed. *Shades of Noir.* London: Verso. p. 88.

34. Grant, B.K. 1995. Purple passages or fiestas in blue? Notes toward an aesthetic of vocalese. In K. Gabbard, ed. *Representing Jazz.* Durham, N.C.: Duke University Press. p. 291.

35. Chion, M. 1994. *Audio-Vision: Sound on Screen.* New York: Columbia University Press. pp. 193–94.

36. Ibid.

37. Smith, S.C. 1991. *A Heart at Fire's Center: The Life and Music of Bernard Herrmann.* Los Angeles: University of California Press. p. 313.

38. David Meeker, interviewed by the author, October 27, 1999.

39. Laurie Johnson, interviewed by the author, October 1,1999.

40. Ibid.

41. Smith, S.C. 1991. *A Heart at Fire's Center: The Life and Music of Bernard Herrmann.* Los Angeles: University of California Press. p. 351.

42. Laurie Johnson, interviewed by the author, October 1, 1999.

43. Ibid.

44. Ibid.

45. Telegram from Bernard Herrmann to Martin Scorsese, June 15, 1974. Martin Scorsese Collection, Special Collections, American Film Institute.

46. Smith, S.C. 1991. *A Heart at Fire's Center: The Life and Music of Bernard Herrmann.* Los Angeles: University of California Press. p. 219.

47. Interoffice communication from music director Dick Berres to Lew Rosso, October 1, 1975. Martin Scorsese Collection, Special Collections, American Film Institute.

48. Fhaner, B., ed. 1998. *Magill's Cinema Annual 1997.* Detroit: Gale Research. p. 610.

49. Polunsky, B. 1976. Review of *Taxi Driver.* In *San Antonio Light.* May 2.

50. Shales, T. 1976. *Washington Post.* April 25.

51. Scorsese, M. 1998. Liner notes for *Taxi Driver.* Arista 07822-19005-2.

52. Chion, M. 1994. *Audio-Vision: Sound on Screen.* New York: Columbia University Press. p. 193.

53. Polunsky, B. 1976. Review of *Taxi Driver. San Antonio Light.* May 2.

54. Scorsese, Martin. 1998. Liner notes for *Taxi Driver.* Arista 07822-19005-2.

55. Music Timing Notes for *Taxi Driver.* Martin Scorsese Collection, Special Collections, American Film Institute.

56. Music Timing Notes for *Taxi Driver*, p. 2. Martin Scorsese Collection, Special Collections, American Film Institute.

57. Bliss, M. 1985. *Martin Scorsese and Michael Cimino: Filmmakers*, no.8. Metuchen, N.J: The Scarecrow Press Inc. p. 104.

58. Friedman, L.S. 1997. *The Cinema of Martin Scorsese.* Oxford: Roundhouse. p. 75.

59. Chion, M. 1994. *Audio-Vision: Sound on Screen.* New York: Columbia University Press. p. 8.

60. Friedman, L.S. 1997. *The Cinema of Martin Scorsese.* Oxford: Roundhouse. p. 79.

61. Ibid., p. 82.

62. Smith, S.C. 1991. *A Heart at Fire's Center: The Life and Music of Bernard Herrmann.* Los Angeles: University of California Press. p. 352.

63. Scorsese, M. 1998. Liner notes for *Taxi Driver.* Arista 07822-19005-2.

64. Stern, L. 1995. *The Scorsese Connection.* London: BFI Publishing. p. 53.

65. Smith, S.C. 1991. *A Heart at Fire's Center: The Life and Music of Bernard Herrmann.* Los Angeles: University of California Press. p. 351.

66. Ibid.

67. Bordwell, D., and Thompson, K. 1993. *Film Art: An Introduction* (4th ed.). London: McGraw-Hill. p. 296.

68. Polunsky, B. 1976. Review of *Taxi Driver. San Antonio Light.* May, 2.

69. Friedman, L.S. 1997. *The Cinema of Martin Scorsese.* Oxford: Roundhouse. p. 74.

70. Bliss, M. 1985. *Martin Scorsese and Michael Cimino: Filmmakers,* no.8. Metuchen, N.J: The Scarecrow Press Inc. p. 94.

71. Taubin, A. 1999. God's lonely man. *Sight and Sound.* April, pp. 16–19.

72. Ibid.

73. Gabbard, K. 1996. *Jammin' at the Margins: Jazz and the American Cinema.* Chicago: University of Chicago Press. p. 266.

74. Undated Production Notes for *Young Man with a Horn* from Warner Bros. Studio. Folder 665, Jack L. Warner Collection, Special Collections, USC Cinema and Television Library.

75. Jenkins, S. 1982. Review of *Body Heat. Monthly Film Bulletin,* January 19, p. 3.

76. Corliss, R. 1981. Review of *Body Heat. Time.* August 24, p. 62.

77. Stephens, M. 1995. *Film Noir: A Comprehensive, Illustrated Reference to Movies, Terms and Persons.* Jefferson, N.C.: McFarland & Company. p. 137.

78. Kasdan, L. 1980. Original Screenplay for *Body Heat.* February 19, p. 7, Arts Special Collections, UCLA.

79. Brown, R.S. 1994. *Overtones and Undertones: Reading Film Music.* Berkeley and Los Angeles: University of California Press. p. 322.

80. Kemp, P. 1990. *Body Heat.* In N. Thomas, ed.) *International Dictionary of Filmmakers: Vol. 1, Films* (2nd ed.). Chicago: St. James Press. p. 124.

81. Pfeil, F. 1993. Home fires burning: Family noir in *Blue Velvet* and *Terminator 2.* In J. Copjec, ed. *Shades of Noir.* London: Verso. pp. 235–36.

82. Ibid., p. 238.

83. Third Draft Screenplay for *Blue Velvet,* August 9, 1984. p. 57. Arts Special Collections, UCLA.

84. Creed, B. 1988. A journey through *Blue Velvet. New Formations.* no. 6, Winter, p. 113.

85. Pfeil, R. 1993. Home fires burning: Family noir in *Blue Velvet* and *Terminator 2.* In J. Copjec, ed. *Shades of Noir.* London: Verso. p. 237.

86. Third Draft Screenplay for *Blue Velvet,* August 9, 1984. p. 36. Arts Special Collections, UCLA.

87. Final Draft Screenplay for *Gilda* by Virginia Van Upp, August 29, 1945. Arts Special Collections, UCLA.

88. Dyer, R. 1978. Resistance through charisma: Rita Hayworth and *Gilda*. In E.A. Kaplan, ed. *Women in Film Noir*. London: BFI. p. 95.

89. Third Draft Screenplay for *Blue Velvet,* August 9, 1984. Arts Special Collections, UCLA.

90. Lack, R. 1997. *Twenty Four Frames Under: A Buried History of Film Music*. London: Quartet Books. pp. 201–2.

91. Review of *The Last Seduction* by Kim Newman. *Sight and Sound*. August 1994, p. 44.

92. Review of *The Last Seduction* by Jonathan Romney. *New Statesman & Society*. August 5, 1994, p. 33.

93. Review of *The Last Seduction* by Kenneth Turan. *Los Angeles Times*. October 26, 1994.

94. Review of *The Last Seduction* by Jonathan Romney. *New Statesman & Society*. August 5, 1994, p. 33.

95. Elmer Bernstein interviewed by Tony Thomas. Thomas, T. 1977. *Music for the Movies*. South Brunswick, N.J., and New York: A.S. Barnes; London: Tantivy Press, p. 190.

96. Review of *The Last Seduction* by Jonathan Romney. *New Statesman & Society*. August 5, 1994, p. 33.

97. MacRory, P. 1998. "*Basic Instinct:* Music and Violent Women." Paper given at a Film Music Conference, held at the University of Leeds, July 11.

98. Lees, G. 1991. *Waiting For Dizzy*. Oxford: Oxford University Press. p. 131.

99. Kington, M. 1993. *The Jazz Anthology*. London: Harper Collins. p. 185.

100. Silver, A. 1996. *Kiss Me Deadly*: Evidence of a Style. In A. Silver and J. Ursini, eds. *Film Noir Reader*. New York: Limelight Reader. p. 210.

101. Gabbard, K. 1996. *Jammin' at the Margins: Jazz and the American Cinema*. Chicago: University of Chicago Press. p. 187.

102. Kalinak, K. 1992. *Settling the Score: Music and the Classical Hollywood Film*. Madison, Wis.: University of Wisconsin Press. p. 167.

6

Reminiscing in Chiaroscuro

Concluding Comments

"Noir" has long since broken free from its origins in film. The noir essence can be found in all manner of settings, ranging from literature, photography and music, to television and computer games. As James Naremore acknowledges in his discussion of the noir "mediascape," noir is a "much more flexible, pervasive and durable mood, style or narrative tendency than is commonly supposed and . . . embraces different media and different national cultures throughout the twentieth century."[1] In fact, Naremore demonstrates how even at the time of its original production in the films of the 1940s and 1950s, noir "spread across every form of narrative or protonarrative communication."[2] Noir has entered the cultural consciousness even though we may not always be aware of the original artifacts or how to accurately define them. Both jazz and film noir are similar in this respect, and the two idioms have found all-encompassing definitions to be elusive. The difference between Louis Armstrong's 1927 recording of "West End Blues" and Miles Davis' *Bitches Brew*, from 1969, is phenomenal. *Bitches Brew*, with its electronic and rock textures, was accused of pandering to commercialism and pursuing mass audiences, the same charges that Davis would make about Armstrong. Above all, many critics claimed that the album was not jazz, as if Davis was duty-bound to correspond to their idea of what jazz was supposed to be. Yet there is something—a thread that runs through each recording and ties them to the same family. The same is true of film noir. Both noir and jazz are defined by something other than their agreeing with an established checklist of requisite features. As I noted in the previous chapter, later or contemporary noirs, such as *Farewell, My Lovely* (1975), have been criticized for their lack of a noir sensibility despite their faithful recreation of the visual style and iconography of classic film noir. To offer a more extreme example, the noir parody, *Dead Men Don't Wear Plaid* (1982), which actually uses inserts from classic noirs, has tended to avoid the attention of even the most eccentric writers seeking to establish a noir canon, despite the fact that it features all the expected noir motifs and stylistics. Neither does it necessarily follow that jazz, good or bad, will be produced by a group of musicians playing the instrumentation of a standard bebop unit. While it is often difficult, therefore, to define jazz and film noir, it is less problematic to state when they are taking place.

The majority of my focus has been on the presence of jazz in film noir. In this closing chapter, however, I want to consider instead the reverse of this relationship, or the wider "mediascape," and discuss the way that film noir has been incorporated into jazz projects. In recent years a number of contemporary musicians have used film noir as a source of inspiration for several of their respective albums. Two of the most prominent musicians to do so are Charlie Haden and John Zorn. Both have consistently referred to film noir in their recordings, but with a contrasting emphasis and to strikingly different effect.

Haden, one of the most important bassists in jazz, beginning with the "free jazz" experiments of Ornette Coleman's band in the late 1950s, has used film noir as a frame of reference for his Quartet West group. Debuting in 1987, the band's albums consciously evoke the atmosphere of the 1940s and 1950s by blending samples of musicians of the day with their own contemporary playing. The band's recording of *Haunted Heart* (1992) was intended to "pass along the feeling of standing in Philip Marlowe's office looking out at the neon lights blinking off and on in the night."[3] This mood of film noir is drawn upon even more extensively for their 1994 album, *Always Say Goodbye*. Featuring a cover with a still of a silhouetted Humphrey Bogart and Lauren Bacall in *The Big Sleep* (1946) and an extract from Raymond Chandler's novel, the album is book-ended with the opening and closing music and dialogue from the film itself. The new music on the album is frequently interrupted by flashbacks, furthering the relationship with film noir, to older recordings by musicians who include Coleman Hawkins, Jo Stafford, Django Reinhardt, Stéphane Grappelli, Duke Ellington and Chet Baker, as well as fresh performances of compositions by Charlie Parker and Bud Powell, both exponents of bebop who died young in the 1950s. Haden's stated intention in making the album would appear to be nostalgic, in a similar vein to the use of classic jazz styles and recordings in much contemporary film noir. In the liner notes to the album, Haden notes his desire to have been present during the making of *The Big Sleep*, or to have actually played with the older musicians sampled on the record. The result, says Haden, is an album that virtually transports him to Los Angeles in the 1940s and 1950s.[4]

Despite this emphasis on looking back, Haden has explained in an interview about the earlier *Haunted Heart* that his Quartet West group is not simply interested in retrospectively recreating a bygone age:

> It's not about the past, because improvisation is really about being in the moment ... I'm talking about the past inspiring the present. That's what's so special about jazz. It teaches you to appreciate the moment you're in now.[5]

It is difficult, however, not to hear the Quartet West recordings as anything other than affectionate kisses to the past, and as a result they lack the sense of threat and despair that pervades the films noir to which they allude. Similarly, the renditions of classic noir themes by the Jazz at the Movies Band for its 1994 recording, *White Heat: Film Noir*, are sleek without really capturing the breadth of the films from which they are taken. Yearning melodies abound in *White Heat: Film Noir*, with an emphasis on lonely siren songs that are seemingly chosen to underscore the femmes fatale who dominate the album's packaging. Haden's evocation of film noir through the music of the period, the music that rarely found its way into the films themselves, does help to confirm and perpetuate the notion of jazz as being the true sound of film noir. Haden is, perhaps, an unlikely musician to contribute to the continuation of this notion, having commented about the tendency of jazz films to focus on tales of drugs, doom and self-destruction.

The noir-related projects of John Zorn are more directly connected to their source of inspiration. Zorn's musical output, as composer and alto saxophonist, takes in a staggering range of genres and styles. Although he is often associated with jazz, usually for the convenience of critics and retailers who do not know where else to place his music, describing Zorn as a jazz musician is to reveal only a fraction of his musical interests. Zorn has turned his attention to idioms as diverse as classical composition, thrash-metal, rockabilly, surf, ambient, bebop and free improvisation, often within a single piece. Zorn has composed a number of scores for film, radio and animation, and his own work displays a great love for film music. Ennio Morricone, Bernard Herrmann, Henry Mancini, John Barry, Nino Rota, Jerry Goldsmith and Johnny Mandel have all been acknowledged in Zorn's music.

One of the film styles to be frequently referenced by Zorn is film noir. The most open homage to noir is his 1987 piece, "Spillane," which re-creates the world of Mickey Spillane's detective and anti-hero, Mike Hammer. Lasting over twenty-five minutes, "Spillane" is an aural journey through Hammer's landscape, punctuated by Hammer's voice-over and jumping from scene to scene with sudden shifts in musical style and natural sound. "Spillane" opens with the screams of a woman, which are followed by an introductory theme in the style of the crime jazz that flourished in the television noir of the late 1950s and early 1960s. It is this crime jazz that predominates in Zorn's musical interpretation of film noir. "Spillane" cuts from the scene of a murder to boxing rings, nightclubs, strip bars, pool halls and the interior of Hammer's car as the wipers struggle to keep back the rain. Snatches of dialogue and sound are interspersed with free improvisation, diegetic music from the various establishments visited by Hammer and more conventional film scoring styles.

"Spillane" effectively demonstrates a trademark Zorn technique: the use of "jump-cuts" between seemingly incompatible styles of music. This approach is best exemplified by Zorn's now-defunct band, Naked City, which perfected real time jumps from reggae to country, punk, jazz and back again in the space of a minute, while maintaining the structure of the composition in question. The jump-cut is particularly well suited to Zorn's evocation of film noir in "Spillane." Inevitably, the piece references *Kiss Me Deadly* (1955), the Robert Aldrich-directed noir adaptation of Spillane's Mike Hammer novel of the same name. Both Zorn and Aldrich express similar intentions in their interpretation of Spillane's work. As Silver has discussed in his analysis of Aldrich's film, the "core" of *Kiss Me Deadly* consists of "speed and violence" with the film swerving "frenziedly through a series of disconnected and cataclysmic scenes."[6] Similarly, in much of Zorn's music, particularly during the period in which "Spillane" was recorded, there has been an emphasis on speed. In the notes that accompany "Spillane," Zorn acknowledges his extremely short attention span and that his music is perfect for the impatient listener as it is full of information that is rapidly and constantly transforming (speed, comments Zorn, is taking control of the world).[7]

The sudden stylistic changes in Zorn projects such as "Spillane" and Naked City are well suited to film noir. As Janey Place and Lowell Peterson have identified, in their study of noir's visual motifs, sharp cutting is a notable feature:

> More common are bizarre, off-angle compositions of figures placed irregularly in the frame, which create a world that is never stable or safe, that is always threatening to change drastically and unexpectedly.... *Noir* cutting often opposes such extreme changes in angle and screen size to create jarring juxtapositions, as with the oft-used cut from huge close-up to high-angle long shot of a man being pursued through the dark city streets.[8]

Aldrich's disorienting visual style and use of jump-cuts is paralleled by Zorn's audio jump-cuts in "Spillane," which further help to re-create the violent and confusing world of the noir protagonist.

Several later Zorn projects have underlined his penchant for film noir. The eponymously titled 1990 debut recording of Naked City featured cover versions of the themes from *I Want To Live!* (1958) and *Chinatown* (1974). Perhaps most suggestive of film noir were the band's title and cover art. "Naked City" refers not only to the 1948 Jules Dassin film noir and the television crime series that followed a decade later, but is also the title of a book by WeeGee, the New York photographer who specialized in capturing on camera the scene of a crime, often before the police arrived themselves. WeeGee's photojournalism provides an account of the reality of noir that was New York in the 1940s and '50s. Zorn's *Naked City* uses as its cover a 1940 WeeGee photograph, titled "Corpse with Revolver," that clearly announces its relationship to film noir. The earlier pieces for *The Bribe* (1998) feature music for three 1986 radio plays by Terry O'Reilly that expand upon many of the themes in "Spillane." Zorn acknowledges that many of the tracks for *The Bribe* convey a film noir ambience, and he specifically cites the pieces "The Bridge," "The Hour of Thirteen," "Midnight Streets," "Skyline" and "Victoria Lake" as examples.[9] These pieces reflect a strong Herrmann influence, whose orchestration Zorn confesses was an "obsession" at the time, with harp glissandi and low woodwinds repeatedly playing short, sinister phrases, as well as the Mancini-style crime jazz of loping bass, steady pulse on the hi-hats and cool flute (particularly prominent on "Midnight Streets"). Yet, Zorn does not simply pastiche or nostalgically re-create his sources, such as crime jazz and dissonant "Hitchcock chords," but imbues his audio films noir with a contemporary edge and avant-garde impulse. The use of extreme noise (another of Zorn's passions), jarring industrial sounds and wrenching jump-cuts ensures that Zorn's audio noir does not simply become an affectionate tribute, but keeps the spirit alive.

Not all of Zorn's film noir-related projects have been cover versions of themes and styles used in the original films. *Thieves Quartet* (1993), directed by Joe Chappelle, prompted Zorn to bring together a band that included himself on saxophone and piano, Dave Douglas on trumpet, Greg Cohen on bass and Joey Baron on drums. Zorn's reasoning might at first appear to have been another acknowledgment of the past of film noir. He notes how, as a contemporary noir, *Thieves Quartet* seemed an ideal project for a jazz score in the same established vein of the Miles Davis quintet's score for Louis Malle's *Ascenseur pour l'echafaud* (1957).[10] The resultant score for *Thieves Quartet*, however, is very much the product of four of the finest and most adventurous improvisers in contemporary music. While drawing upon the "tradition" of a small modern jazz band providing an improvised score for a film noir, Zorn and his colleagues do not simply re-create the style of the Miles Davis Quintet's music for *Ascenseur pour l'echafaud*, but deliver improvisations on compositions that would not have been heard in jazz styles of the late 1950s, and certainly not films noir of that time. Zorn's explanation for using an acoustic jazz combo to score *Thieves Quartet* is interesting, however, for the purpose of this book. Zorn confirms the perceived mutual compatibility of jazz and film noir by noting that *Thieves Quartet* was the "perfect opportunity" for a small band jazz score. The "tradition" that he refers to, however, Miles Davis' 1957 score, is one that does not originate with American film noir, but with a French interpretation. Tellingly, there is no tradition of small band jazz scores in American film noir. Johnny Mandel combines a small band with a larger ensemble in *I Want To Live!* (1958), as does John Lewis in *Odds Against Tomorrow* (1959), whereas *Sweet Smell of Success* (1957) divides its music between the small band of Chico Hamilton and the big band-tinged orchestrations of Elmer Bernstein. Nowhere in classic film noir is a small jazz band entrusted with the entire scoring duties. The use of such an approach was pioneered in France, possibly reflecting not only the French identification of the darkness in American films (that led to the term film noir), but also the kind of American music that they felt best evoked it. Zorn's score for *Thieves Quartet*, therefore, helps to continue a tradition that was never actually established in the films themselves.

SUMMARY AND FINAL THOUGHTS

I have sought to demonstrate in this book that it is problematic to continue to speak in generalized terms about the use of jazz in film noir. Both jazz and film noir are unwieldy labels, consisting of various styles and phases of development. This book has identified three distinct phases for the intersection of these idioms.

First, during the 1940s (the initial decade of the classic period of film noir) there are no distinctly jazz-inflected scores. Chapter 3 explored how jazz was heard diegetically through jukeboxes or the use of a jazz sequence, as in *Phantom Lady* (1944). The jazz that is used in the 1940s favors the blues and hot, rhythmic aspects of the music and is firmly in the swing and mainstream styles. As Chapter 2 discussed, this use of jazz was founded on the prevalent Eurocentric equation of rhythm with sex and the association of early styles of jazz with brothels and gangsters. Rooted in imperialist ideologies and dualisms, these connections were founded on a racist understanding of black culture that considered it inferior and primitive in relation to white cultural forms. Prevailing racial attitudes determined which styles and exponents of jazz could be incorporated in this period of film noir. As I suggested in Chapter 3, the modernist styles of jazz developed in the 1940s, particularly bebop, were not utilized in film noir of the same time. Bebop's origins as a fundamentally black music and its uneasy relationship with the entertainment industry made it a problematic music for mainstream Hollywood to accommodate. The theme of anti-intellectualism, identified in Chapter 3, as a feature of much film noir, was an additional factor in the exclusion of bebop from Hollywood films of this time.

In 1940s film noir, the intensity of jazz is used as a metaphor for sex and immorality. This is the most conventional use of jazz, relating to Eurocentric perceptions of black music and ensuring the authority of the classical Hollywood score. Jazz is representative of the city's threat, an aural expression of the noir protagonist's alienation, characteristically depicted through film noir's visual style of chiaroscuro lighting and distorted camera shots. This association is not confined to film noir. Jazz appears diegetically in non-noir films, but its presence often "noirs" the scene or sequence in which it is heard. A notable example of this use of jazz to "noir" a film is the nightmare sequence in *It's a Wonderful Life* (1946). In this noir passage, *It's a Wonderful Life* uses diegetic jazz to suggest the protagonist's anxiety and alienation: the central themes of film noir originally identified by Borde and Chaumeton.[11]

Immorality and urban threat continue as themes for the use of jazz in the 1950s. *The Big Combo* (1955) utilizes the radio broadcast of a bop drum solo as a weapon, blasted into the ear of the hero by the criminal overlord and his gay henchmen. As Chapter 4 demonstrated, however, styles of jazz are used less as a threat directed at the protagonist. Increasingly, jazz is used in the 1950s as an expression of the protagonist's own attempt to transcend the urban menace in which they are caught. Chico Hamilton's music stands against the corrupt empire of J.J. Hunsecker in *Sweet Smell of Success* (1957), and Barbara Graham's love of Gerry Mulligan's music serves to reveal her character as being more than a worthless dissolute in *I Want To Live!* (1958). It is significant that during the 1950s, jazz began to establish itself as a legitimate aspect of the nondiegetic score instead of being simply heard through the usual means of a jukebox, record player or band in a club. Bernard Herrmann has described one of the prime functions of the film score as being its potential to reveal a character's inner thoughts and psychology.[12] With jazz featuring on the nondiegetic score, it could now be used as something coming from a character rather than being directed at them, attacking and penetrating their personal space from a radio or club.

This book has suggested four potential reasons for the increased presence of jazz in film scores of the 1950s. As the composers Laurie Johnson and Lennie Niehaus have observed, the move of a number of jazz performers into the concert hall, particularly Duke Ellington and Stan Kenton, helped jazz to acquire a more respectable status.

Significantly, it was in the 1950s that a number of white arrangers also came to the fore in the fields of modern jazz. When bebop first emerged in the mid-1940s, its leading exponents were predominantly black. Modern jazz lacked white musicians who could serve as figures for a wider white audience to identify with. In Chapter 2 I noted how Hollywood films had showcased the swing bands and begun to consider an art discourse for jazz only while there were white bands with strong popularity among white audiences. I would suggest that a similar practice was at work in the increased presence of modern jazz in films of the 1950s. White musicians such as Shorty Rogers, Stan Getz, Stan Kenton and Gerry Mulligan provided modern jazz with an "acceptable" face for white audiences.

Chapter 4, however, notes that this respectability was not extended to the films that jazz was permitted to score. The music remained rooted in associations of crime and immorality. The films noir and social problem films of this period were also seeking a grittier and more realistic approach. The debate between Robert Wise and Walter Wanger concerning the use of jazz in *I Want To Live!* demonstrates that jazz was considered to lend naturalism to a film that the large symphonic score undermined. Yet, as David Meeker identified, the most compelling argument for the use of a jazz score was its economic benefits. The large-scale symphonic scores were proving increasingly expensive. The use of a jazz or jazz-inflected score meant the hiring of far fewer musicians. In later years, financial concerns have resulted in film scoring being predominated by the use of synthesizers. As Meeker notes, "Why should they hire an orchestra? Do it all by a single machine."[13] The brief potential of a commercially released recording of a jazz score, such as the enormous success of Henry Mancini's music for *Peter Gunn* (1958–1961), has since been replaced.

The third phase of collaborations between jazz and film noir concerns the music's use in contemporary noir. These films have tended to use jazz in a less dynamic way, utilizing the music in order to create a sense of nostalgia and an evocation of the original period of film noir in the 1940s and 1950s. There are notable exceptions, such as Joseph Vitarelli's cool jazz score for *The Last Seduction* (1994). This retrospective use of jazz can still suggest the sense of alienation that is fundamental to film noir, as the anachronistic jazz melody used in *Taxi Driver* (1976) disturbingly demonstrates. This psychological approach to using jazz is less important in contemporary film noir, however, than the music's ability to act as a signifier of the period in which film noir flourished. As Chapter 5 proposes, this use of jazz is founded on a retrospective illusion of the classic period of film noir.

In Chapter 1 I suggested, through cross-referencing Silver and Ward's work on film noir with Meeker's directory of appearances by jazz in films, that it would be difficult to assert that jazz has been a dominant musical idiom in film noir. Jazz becomes widespread in the television noir of the late 1950s and early 1960s. Something of a middle ground needs to be taken therefore between Orr's claim that African American music, jazz, was "conspicuously absent" from film noir and those writers who have suggested that jazz became a dominant musical presence.

In spite of the relatively small number of films noir to turn to jazz, it is still a significant amount in terms of the overall use of jazz in Hollywood films at the time. It is only in mid- to late 1950's film noir and its offshoots, such as the social problem film, that music was commissioned from modern jazz musicians such as Chico Hamilton, John Lewis, Johnny Mandel, Gerry Mulligan and Shorty Rogers. In that sense film noir does make a significant use of jazz. It is not the overall quantity that should be considered, but the fact that a precedent was established. Orr's claim that African American music, specifically jazz, has been conspicuously absent from film noir should not be rejected, however. The jazz that has been used most consistently in film noir has been that of white musicians and arrangers. As I hope to have demonstrated, racial attitudes and pressures have determined when and how black musicians have been able to work in Hollywood. Yet they have not been wholly absent from film noir. The unnamed bands in *They Live by Night* (1949), *D.O.A.* (1950) or *Kiss Me Deadly* (1955), the appearance of Louis Armstrong in *The Strip*, Chico Hamilton in *Sweet Smell of Success* and Art Farmer in *I Want To Live!* ensures that there is something of a presence of black musicians in film noir of the classic period, albeit a small one. What marks all of these appearances, however, and the general use of jazz in film noir, are the racially informed myths and Eurocentric understanding of jazz that have enabled it to be considered appropriate for the music to appear in these tales of urban decay and immorality.

The contemporary perception that jazz was the sound of the classic period of film noir suggests that the music still remains associated with sex and crime. How deeply rooted is the relationship between film noir and jazz for contemporary audiences? Would the use of a certain style of jazz to underscore a film inevitably bring with it noir associations? The example provided by the composer David Burnand in Chapter 1 suggests that it possibly would. In the Introduction, I referred to Peter Martin's observation that the meaning of certain music can become "taken for granted." Similarly, in her analysis of the hero story that has flourished in Western culture and implies that culture's innate superiority, Margery Hourihan notes Roland Barthes' discussion of the way in which myths "create a perception of the 'falsely obvious.'"[14] For Hourihan, the hero story has been told so many times that its meaning "goes without saying," and "we have come to believe that what it says about the world is true."[15] The same effect is evident in the association between jazz and film noir.

The perception that jazz, and most erroneously bebop in particular, thrived in film noir is not solely expressed in recent American noir such as the series *Fallen Angels* (1993). In March 1998, the BBC launched *Jazz 606*, a series that, as producer Andy King announced, sought to present "the extraordinary diversity of acts currently playing the UK."[16] The mise-en-scène of the program's set, a smoky cellar club, and the interludes provided by a resident bohemian character talking about legendary musicians were widely criticized. The noir-derived club was not an accurate reflection of the jazz scene in 1990s Britain:

> The problem with *Jazz 606* is that it looks far more out of touch with the real jazz scene and mired in irrelevant jazz-lifestyle nostalgia than *Jazz 625*, its 1960s predecessor, ever did. . . . The music takes place in a wide variety of settings from attractive summer festival locations through friendly pubs to arts centres—not all ideal for sure, but very rarely down a flight of stairs guarded by a dungeon-like door, opening out into what can only appear to the casual viewer as a smoke-filled cellar full of "unusual" people.[17]

The key to jazz's ongoing relevance and vitality is its diversity, its ability to change and mutate while still building on the lessons and values of its tradition. The murky club and bohemian hipster of *Jazz 606* is a self-parody of a mythical past and rests uneasily in a program that seeks to present jazz in its current and potentially future forms. An analogy would be for an actor in a teddy boy, or greaser, costume to interrupt an edition of *Top of the Pops* or a slot on MTV and discuss the activities of Bill Haley or Buddy Holly. Such a tactic would almost certainly not be attempted for fear of alienating and losing the audience. *Jazz 606*, as is the case with *Fallen Angels,* draws on the myth of the relationship between jazz and film noir. I would propose that the persistence of this myth ensures the continuation of the same thinking, identified in Chapter 2, which considers black cultural forms as being in some way deviant or inferior to those of white culture. As Lola Young suggests in her discussion of British cinema in the 1980s, established patterns of racist thought adapt instead of dissipating and thus ensure "continuity with deeply entrenched notions of racial difference consolidated during the eighteenth and nineteenth centuries."[18]

It may seem that I am being unduly harsh in my interpretation of the association between jazz and film noir. I would return again to my comments in the Introduction and Chapter 1, where I readily acknowledge the appeal of such guilty pleasures as the cultural stereotype of the smoky jazz club steeped in noir iconography. The media emphasis on "sound bites" and stereotypes as a means of making sense of jazz, however, can only increase while the music receives minor coverage and support and remains beyond the general public's awareness. Film noir provides an alluring range of images, situations and meanings with which a potential audience for jazz can attempt to interpret the music. It is an oft-quoted claim that jazz is music best experienced live. Certainly, the visual information provided by the performers through their expressions and interplay with each other can help to assist an audience in interpreting the sounds that they are hearing. The potential of film in making unfamiliar and "difficult" music familiar and accessible to a wider audience is not an unusual phenomenon, as

Gorbman has argued.[19] Ligeti's unsettling choral music used in *2001: A Space Odyssey* (1968) or Jerry Goldsmith's atonal score for *Planet of the Apes* (1968) are notable examples of non-mainstream music reaching a larger audience through its association with film. The veteran jazz pianist and composer, Dave Brubeck, observed that jazz is being kept alive by the same institutions that "condemned it fifty years ago," namely the educational system, but that younger generations are "unaware that the music they have heard all their lives on radio and TV in commercials, or as background music in movies and TV dramas, actually stems from a jazz source."[20] In this sense, the association of jazz with film noir might be seen as beneficial. The extraordinary success of Henry Mancini's crime jazz for the *Peter Gunn* series was followed with an album of interpretations of Mancini's cues by drummer Shelly Manne's band. Manne, who had worked on the original recordings with Mancini, defended the inevitable criticism that he was "selling out" by arguing that the increased awareness in jazz generated by the project made it a justifiable undertaking:

> It was important that the album was successful because it started the whole show-tune trend for jazz groups. It gave other jazz groups a chance to get across to the public, and it gave the public a chance to form a nodding acquaintance with jazz. . . . The vital thing is to do these things without sacrificing integrity.[21]

The "noiring" of jazz, therefore, could be interpreted as an effective means of explaining and selling the music to a wider audience. Yet, such an acceptance is dangerously limiting for a music as diverse as jazz and brings with it a host of associations rooted in a racially prejudiced misunderstanding of the music. Who is the true beneficiary of the "noir jazz" myth? Does it really assist an increased understanding and appreciation of jazz and, at a deeper level, black culture? As Edward Said advises, it is necessary to demonstrate how "all representations are constructed, for what purpose, by whom and with what components," and it is this task that I have sought to undertake throughout this book.[22]

The negative associations applied to jazz have almost certainly influenced the music's lack of support from official arts organizations in both Britain and America. Peter Martin draws attention to the Arts Council of Great Britain's 1991 survey, which revealed the bias toward "serious" forms of music, such as opera, despite jazz performances receiving similar attendance figures.[23] Since the publication of a Jazz Green Paper in 1996, the Arts Council has increased its support for jazz, yet there remains a "continuing massive discrepancy in the amount of public money made available to classical music and opera, as opposed to jazz."[24] The support available for jazz musicians in America is not particularly improved. As a character in the 1999 Broadway play *Side Man* puts it, while explaining the theory of "jazzeconomics," "Classical musicians have the National Endowment for the Arts. We have New York State unemployment."[25] The question of whether jazz can escape its noir associations with crime and immorality, however exciting they may be, is one that many jazz musicians have to contend with throughout their careers.

NOTES

1. Naremore, J. 1998. *More Than Night: Film Noir in Its Contexts*. Berkeley and Los Angeles: University of California Press. p. 261.

2. Ibid., p. 258.

3. Cooks, J. 1992. Experimental time trip: Jazz bassist Charlie Haden. *Time*. vol. 140, no. 15, October 12, p. 81.

4. Liner notes from the CD *Always Say Goodbye* by Charlie Haden and Quartet West. Verve: 521501-2.

5. Cooks, J. 1992. Experimental time trip: Jazz bassist Charlie Haden. *Time*. vol. 140, no. 15, October 12, p. 81.

6. Silver, A. 1996. *Kiss Me Deadly*: Evidence of a style. In A. Silver and J. Ursini, eds. *Film Noir Reader*. New York: Limelight Editions. p. 209.

7. Liner notes from the CD *Spillane* by John Zorn. Elektra Nonesuch: 979172-2.

8. Place, J., and Peterson, L. 1996. Some visual motifs of film noir. In A. Silver and J. Ursini, eds. *Film Noir Reader*. New York: Limelight Editions. p. 68. Originally published in 1974.

9. Liner notes from the CD *The Bribe* by John Zorn. Tzadik: TZ 7320.

10. Liner notes from the CD *Film Works, vol. 3, 1990–1995* by John Zorn. Tzadik: TZ 7309.

11. Borde, R., and Chaumeton, E. 1996. Towards a definition of film noir. In A. Silver and J. Ursini, eds. *Film Noir Reader*. New York: Limelight Editions. pp. 17–25. Originally published in 1955.

12. Listen, for example, to Herrmann's comments from the excerpt of an interview included on the CD *Elmer Bernstein Conducts the Royal Philharmonic Orchestra: Bernard Herrmann Film Scores*. Milan: 74321 14081-2.

13. David Meeker, interviewed by the author, October 27, 1999.

14. Hourihan, M. 1997. *Deconstructing the Hero: Literary Theory and Children's Literature*. London: Routledge. p. 12.

15. Ibid., p. 1.

16. "Not The Nine O' Clock News," *Jazz UK*. no. 20, March/April 1998, p. 5.

17. A Bohemian View. *Jazz UK*. no. 21, May/June 1998, p. 5.

18. Young, L. 1996. *Fear of the Dark: 'Race,' Gender and Sexuality in the Cinema*. London: Routledge. p. 154.

19. Gorbman, C. 1987. *Unheard Melodies: Narrative Film Music*. London: BFI. p. 153.

20. Brubeck, D. 2001. *Down Beat* First-Person Project—Jazz's evolvement: As an art form, revisited. *Down Beat*. vol. 68, no. 2, February, p. 36.

21. Shelly Manne, in an interview originally published March 5, 1959, for *Down Beat*. Classic interview: Shelly Manne—The modern Manne. *Down Beat*. vol. 64, no. 11, November 1997. pp. 38–9.

22. Said, E. 1994. *Culture and Imperialism*. London: Vintage. p. 380.

23. Martin, P. 1995. *Sounds & Society: Themes in the Sociology of Music.* Manchester: University of Manchester Press. pp. 11–12.

24. "Flogging a Dead Horse," *Jazz UK*. no. 17, September/October 1997, p. 7.

25. Ervin, Y. 1999. Mood swings: Broadway play *Side Man* shows the ugly side of a jazz musician's obsession. *Down Beat*. vol. 66, no. 4, April, p. 70.

Appendix
Timeline of Key Events in the Development of Jazz and Film Noir

1917: The Original Dixieland Jazz Band makes first jazz recordings.

James Reese Europe's jazz-based band of the 15th Infantry of the U.S. Army plays to great success in France during the First World War.

1920: *The Land of Jazz* is released.

1925: Louis Armstrong begins his series of brilliant small-group recordings with his Hot Fives, followed by the Hot Sevens in 1927.

F. Scott Fitzgerald's *The Great Gatsby* is published, typifying the Jazz Age.

1927: Duke Ellington begins his residency at the Cotton Club in Harlem.

The presound era of cinema ends with the release of *The Jazz Singer.*

1930: *King of Jazz* is released, showcasing Paul Whiteman's band and omitting the presence of black musicians in the development of jazz.

1931: Bix Beiderbecke dies.

1933: Prohibition ends.

1935: The Swing Era of big bands flourishes. Benny Goodman is crowned "King of Swing."

1938:   Benny Goodman performs at Carnegie Hall.

1941:   Jam sessions at Minton's, a club in New York, where bebop be-
        gins to take shape.
        The Maltese Falcon is released, generally considered the beginning
        of the classic period of film noir.

1942:   Cornell Woolrich's *Phantom Lady* is published.
        Street of Chance, based on a Cornell Woolrich story, is released—
        an early noir to make diegetic use of jazz.

1943:   Ellington premieres *Black, Brown and Beige* at Carnegie Hall.
        Detroit witnesses a major race riot—Twenty-five blacks and nine
        whites are killed, $2 million in damage.

1944:   Coleman Hawkins makes the first proto-bop recordings after a
        two-year recording ban ends.
        Phantom Lady is released, featuring a striking jazz sequence.

1945:   The Second World War ends—disillusionment generated by it con-
        tributes to the mood of film noir.
        Charlie Parker and Dizzy Gillespie make the first fully fledged and
        groundbreaking bebop recordings.

1946:   Dizzy Gillespie forms his bop big band.

1947:   Stan Kenton's Progressive Orchestra tours.

1949:   The Miles Davis Nonet records *Birth of the Cool*.

1950:   *Young Man with a Horn* is released.
        Louis Armstrong's All-Stars take to the road, reflecting the reviv-
        alism of earlier jazz styles.
        The Swing Era of big bands is virtually at an end.
        Stan Kenton forms his Innovations in Modern Music Orchestra . . .

1951:   . . . and dissolves it the following year.
        Alex North provides the first extensively jazz-inflected score for
        A Streetcar Named Desire.
        The "cool school" of jazz flourishes on the West Coast of America.

1955:   Charlie Parker dies.

1956:   The civil rights movement increases.

1957:   Miles Davis provides an improvised score for the French film
        Ascenseur pour l'echafaud.

1958: Ornette Coleman's first recordings give rise to the term "free jazz."

Johnny Mandel's score for *I Want To Live!* makes the most extensive use of jazz in a Hollywood film during the classic period of film noir.

Touch of Evil is released, featuring Henry Mancini's big band and rock-textured score. The classic period of film noir is generally considered to end.

Filmography

Only those films discussed at length in the book are listed here.

Accattone (Italy, 1961)
Director: Pier Paolo Pasolini
Music: Johann Sebastian Bach

Anatomy of a Murder (USA, 1959)
Director: Otto Preminger
Music: Duke Ellington

Ascenseur pour l'echafaud (France, 1957)
Director: Louis Malle
Music: Miles Davis

The Asphalt Jungle (USA, 1950)
Director: John Huston
Music: Miklós Rózsa and André Previn

Basic Instinct (USA, 1992)
Director: Paul Verhoeven
Music: Jerry Goldsmith

The Big Combo (USA, 1955)
Director: Joseph H. Lewis
Music: David Raksin

Bird (USA, 1988)
Director: Clint Eastwood
Music: Lennie Niehaus (featuring the solos of Charlie Parker)

Blue Velvet (USA, 1986)
Director: David Lynch
Music: Angelo Badalamenti

Body Heat (USA, 1981)
Director: Lawrence Kasdan
Music: John Barry

Citizen Kane (USA, 1941)
Director: Orson Welles
Music: Bernard Herrmann

D.O.A. (USA, 1950)
Director: Rudolph Maté
Music: Dimitri Tiomkin (jazz sequence features Illinois Jacquet)

A Day at the Races (USA, 1937)
Director: Sam Wood
Music: Walter Jurmann and Bronislau Kaper

Detour (USA, 1945)
Director: Edgar G. Ulmer
Music: Leo Erdody

La dolce vita (Italy/France 1960)
Director: Federico Fellini
Music: Nino Rota

Double Indemnity (USA, 1944)
Director: Billy Wilder
Music: Miklós Rózsa

Fantasia (USA, 1940)
Director: James Algar, Samuel Armstrong and others
Music: J. S. Bach, Ludwig van Beethoven, Paul Dukas, Modest Mussorgsky,
    Amilcare Ponchielli, Franz Schubert, Igor Stravinsky, and Peter Ilyich
    Tchaikovsky

Farewell, My Lovely (USA, 1975)
Director: Dick Richards
Music: David Shire

Gilda (USA, 1946)
Director: Charles Vidor
Music: Hugo Friedhofer (uncredited), Doris Fisher and Allan Roberts
(songs)

I Want To Live! (USA, 1958)
Director: Robert Wise
Music: Johnny Mandel (featuring Art Farmer, Pete Jolly, Shelly Manne,
Gerry Mulligan, Frank Rosolino and Bud Shank)

Jammin' the Blues (USA, 1944)
Director: Gjon Mili
Music: Illinois Jacquet, Jo Jones, Barney Kessel, Lester Young and others

Jazz Dance (USA, 1954)
Director: Richard Leacock and Roger Tilton
Music: Jimmy McPartland, Pee Wee Russell, Willie "the Lion" Smith and
others

King of Jazz (USA, 1930)
Director: John Murray Anderson
Music: Paul Whiteman

Kiss Me Deadly (USA, 1955)
Director: Robert Aldrich
Music: Frank DeVol

The Land of Jazz (USA, 1920)
Director: Jules Furthman
Music: Composer not known

The Last Seduction (USA, 1994)
Director: John Dahl
Music: Joseph Vitarelli

The Man with the Golden Arm (USA, 1955)
Director: Otto Preminger
Music: Elmer Bernstein (featuring Shorty Rogers, Shelly Manne and
others)

Mildred Pierce (USA, 1945)
Director: Michael Curtiz
Music: Max Steiner

Mo' Better Blues (USA, 1990)
Director: Spike Lee
Music: Terence Blanchard

Murder at the Vanities (USA, 1934)
Director: Mitchell Leisen
Music: Howard Jackson and Milan Roder (featuring Duke Ellington)

Odds Against Tomorrow (USA, 1959)
Director: Robert Wise
Music: John Lewis

Paris Blues (USA, 1961)
Director: Martin Ritt
Music: Duke Ellington and Billy Strayhorn

Pete Kelly's Blues (USA, 1955)
Director: Jack Webb
Music: Arthur Hamilton and Ray Heindorf

Phantom Lady (USA, 1944)
Director: Robert Siodmak
Music: Hans J. Salter

A Song is Born (USA, 1948)
Director: Howard Hawks
Music: Hugo Friedhofer and Emil Newman (jazz sequences featuring
    Louis Armstrong, Harry Babasin, Charlie Barnet, Louie Bellson,
    Tommy Dorsey, Benny Goodman, Lionel Hampton, Alton
    Hendrickson and Mel Powell)

A Streetcar Named Desire (USA, 1951)
Director: Elia Kazan
Music: Alex North

The Strip (USA, 1951)
Director: Leslie Kardos
Music: Pete Rugolo (jazz sequence featuring Louis Armstrong, Barney
    Bigard, Earl Hines and Jack Teagarden)

The Sweet Smell of Success (USA, 1957)
Director: Alexander Mackendrick
Music: Elmer Bernstein, Chico Hamilton and Fred Katz

Taxi Driver (USA, 1976)
Director: Martin Scorsese
Music: Bernard Herrmann

Touch of Evil (USA, 1958)
Director: Orson Welles
Music: Henry Mancini

Young Man with a Horn (USA, 1950)
Director: Michael Curtiz
Music: Ray Heindorf (featuring Harry James)

Bibliography

Adorno, T. 1992. On Popular music. In A. Easthope and K. McGowan, eds. *A Critical and Cultural Theory Reader*. Buckingham: Open University Press. pp. 211–23. Originally published in 1941.

Ahnert, S. 1995. Klang der dunkelheit: Der film noir und seine musik. Translated by Susie Hird. *Neue Zeitschrift furMusik*. vol. 156, no. 4, July-August, pp. 40–43.

Alkyer, F. 1993. On the beat: Corn vision. *Down Beat*. vol. 60, no. 10, October.

Althusser, L. 1992. Ideology and ideological state apparatuses. In A. Easthope and K. McGowan, eds. *A Critical and Cultural Theory Reader*. Buckingham: Open University Press. pp. 50–58. Originally published in 1970.

Atkinson, M. 1995. Long black limousine: Pop biopics. In J. Romney and A. Wootton, eds. *Celluloid Jukebox: Popular Music and the Movies since the 1950s*. London: BFI. pp. 20–31.

Baraka, A. 1993. Spike Lee at the movies. In M. Diawara, ed. *Black American Cinema*. New York: Routledge. pp. 145–53.

Barnes, M. 1996. Invisible jukebox: Barry Adamson. *The Wire*. no. 150, August, pp. 40–42.

Bazin, A. 1978. *Orson Welles: A Critical View*. New York: Harper & Row.

Becker, H.S. 1963. *Outsiders: Studies in the Sociology of Deviance*. New York: The Free Press.

Berland, J. 1993. Sound, image and social space: Music and video and media re-construction. In S. Frith, A. Goodwin and L. Grossberg, eds. *Sound and Vision: The Music Video Reader*. London: Routledge. pp. 25–43.

Berliner, P. 1994. *Thinking In Jazz: The Infinite Art of Improvisation*. Chicago: The University of Chicago Press.

Bernstein, E. 1956. The Man With The Golden Arm. *Film Music.* vol. 15, no. 4, Spring, p. 3.

Blackburn, D. 1996. Opening flourish: The spectacular credits of Saul Bass. *The Guardian: The Guide.* February 17, p. 4.

Bliss, M. 1985. *Martin Scorsese and Michael Cimino: Filmmakers* no. 8. Metuchen, N.J: The Scarecrow Press, Inc.

Bogle, D. 1994. *Toms, Coons, Mulattoes, Mammies and Bucks: An Interpretive History of Blacks in American Films.* Oxford: Roundhouse.

Boorman, J. 1985. *Money Into Light: The Emerald Forest.* London: Faber & Faber Ltd.

Borde, R. and Chaumeton, É. 1996. Towards a definition of film noir. In A. Silver and J. Ursini, eds. *Film Noir Reader.* pp. 17–25. Originally published in 1955.

Bordwell, D., and Thompson, K. 1993. *Film Art: An Introduction.* London: McGraw-Hill, Inc.

Brady, F. 1989. *Citizen Welles: A Biography of Orson Welles.* London: Hodder & Stoughton.

Brophy, P. 1997. Oscillating in outer space: The secret history of film music. *The Wire.* no. 158, April, pp. 32–33.

Brown, R.S. 1994. *Overtones and Undertones: Reading Film Music.* Berkeley and Los Angeles: University of California Press.

Bruce, G. 1982. *Bernard Herrmann: Film Music and Narrative.* Ann Arbor, Michigan: UMI Research Press.

Bruzzi, S. 1997. *Undressing Cinema: Clothing and Identity in the Movies.* London: Routledge.

Burlingame, J. 1996. *TV's Biggest Hits: The Story of Television Themes from Dragnet to Friends.* New York: Schirmer Books.

Burt, G. 1994. *The Art of Film Music.* Boston: Northeastern University Press.

Buss, R. 1994. *French Film Noir.* London: Boyars.

Bywater, M. 1997. If Only the King Were Dead. *Independent on Sunday.* August 17.

Cameron, I., ed. 1992. *The Movie Book of Film Noir.* London: Studio Vista.

Campbell, J., ed. 1996. *The Picador Book of Jazz and Blues.* London: Picador.

Canham, K. 1973. *The Hollywood Professionals,* vol. 1. London: Tantivy Press; New York: A.S. Barnes & Co.

Carner, G. 1996. *The Miles Davis Companion: Four Decades of Commentary.* New York: Schirmer Books.

Chion, M. 1994. *Audio-Vision: Sound On Screen.* New York: Columbia University Press.

Christopher, N. 1997. *Somewhere in the Night: Film Noir and the American City.* New York: The Free Press.

Collier, J.L. 1993. *Jazz: The American Theme Song.* New York: Oxford University Press.

Comito, T., ed. 1985. *Touch of Evil: Orson Welles Director.* New Brunswick, New Jersey: Rutgers University Press.

Comuzio, E. 1985. Cinema e jazz: Una gloria del passato? *Cineforum.* vol. 25, no. 241, January, pp. 9–16.

Conover, W. 1980. Jazz in the media: A personal view. *Jazz Forschung*. vol. 12, pp. 35–40.

Cook, P. 1978. Duplicity in *Mildred Pierce*. In E.A. Kaplan, ed. *Women in Film Noir*. London: BFI. pp. 68–82.

Cook, P., ed. 1993. *The Cinema Book*. London: BFI.

Cook, R., and Morton, B., eds. 1996. *The Penguin Guide to Jazz on CD*. London: Penguin.

Cooks, J. 1992. Experimental time trip: Jazz bassist Charlie Haden. *Time*. vol. 140, no. 15, October.

Copjec, J., ed. 1993. *Shades of Noir*. London: Verso.

Cordle, O. 1994. *Down Beat's* 59th Annual Readers Poll: Charlie Haden/Quartet West Jazz Acoustic Group of the Year. *Down Beat*. vol. 61, no. 12, December.

Cowie, E. 1993. Film noir and women. In J. Copjec, ed. *Shades of Noir*. London: Verso. pp. 121–65.

Crease, R.P. 1995. Divine frivolity: Hollywood representations of the lindy hop, 1937–1942. In K. Gabbard, ed. *Representing Jazz*. Durham and London: Duke University Press. pp. 207–28.

Creed, B. 1988. A journey through *Blue Velvet*. *New Formations*. no. 6, Winter, pp. 97–115.

Crowther, B. 1988. *Film Noir: Reflections in a Dark Mirror*. London: Columbus Books Ltd.

Dauer, A. 1980. Jazz und film. Ein historisch: Thematischer uberlick. *Jazzforschung*. vol. 12, pp. 41–57.

DeVeaux, S. 1996. What Did We Do To Be So Black and Blue? *The Musical Quarterly*. vol. 80, no. 3, Fall, pp. 392–429.

DeVeaux, S. 1997. *The Birth of Bebop: A Social and Musical History*. Berkeley and Los Angeles: University of California Press.

Diawara, M., ed. 1993. *Black American Cinema*. New York: Routledge.

Dyer, G. 1995. Tradition, influence and innovation. In J. Campbell, ed. *The Picador Book of Jazz and Blues*. London: Picador. pp. 370–90. Originally published in 1991.

Dyer, R. 1978. Resistance through charisma: Rita Hayworth and *Gilda*. In A.E. Kaplan, ed. *Women in Film Noir*. London: BFI. pp. 91–99.

Dyer, R. 1993. *The Matter of Images: Essays on Representations*. London: Routledge.

Dyer, R. 1997. *White*. London: Routledge.

Easton, C. 1973. *Straight Ahead: The Story of Stan Kenton*. New York: Da Capo Press.

Emge, C. 1950. Good jazz film will be made when story found. *Down Beat*. vol. 17, no. 2, January 27, p. 8.

Emge, C. 1951. MGM's 'Strip' is adjudged best jazz film to date. *Down Beat*. vol. 18, no. 22, November 2, p. 6.

Emge, C. 1953. Little of jazz interest in 25 years of sound films. *Down Beat*. vol. 20, no. 17, August 26, p. 3.

Emge, C. 1956. 'Arm' depressingly good with effective jazz use. *Down Beat*. vol. 23, no. 1, January 1, p. 41.

Enright, E. 1998. Perpetuating the groove: Clint Eastwood's latest evokes drama through jazz. *Down Beat.* January.

Erickson, T. 1996. Kill me again: Movement becomes genre. In A. Silver and J. Ursini, eds. *Film Noir Reader.* pp. 307–29.

Eshun, K. 1995. From blaxploitation to rapsploitation. In J. Romney and A. Wootton, eds. *Celluloid Jukebox: Popular Music and the Movies since the 1950s.* London: BFI. pp. 52–59.

Fhaner, B., ed. 1998. *Magill's Cinema Annual 1997.* Detroit: Gale Research.

Firestone, R. 1993. *The Life and Times of Benny Goodman.* London: Hodder & Stoughton.

Flatley, G. 1976. Martin Scorsese's gamble. *The New York Times.* February 8.

Flinn, C. 1990. Male nostalgia and Hollywood film music: The terror of the feminine. *Canadian University Music Review/ Revue de musique des universites canadiennes.* vol. 10, no. 2, pp. 19–26.

Flinn, C. 1992. *Strains of Utopia: Gender, Nostalgia, and Hollywood Film Music.* Princeton: Princeton University Press.

Fordham, J. 1993. *Jazz.* London: Dorling Kindersley Ltd.

French, P., ed. 1993. *Malle On Malle.* London: Faber and Faber Ltd.

Friedman, L. 1997. *The Cinema of Martin Scorsese.* Oxford: Roundhouse.

Friedrich, O. 1987. *City of Nets: A Portrait of Hollywood in the 1940s.* London: Headline Book Publishing.

Frith, S. 1996. *Performing Rites: Evaluating Popular Music.* Oxford: Oxford University Press.

Frith, S., Goodwin, A., and Grossberg, L., eds. 1993. *Sound and Vision: The Music Video Reader.* London: Routledge.

Gabbard, K., ed. 1995. *Jazz Among the Discourses.* Durham and London: Duke University Press.

Gabbard, K., ed. 1995. *Representing Jazz.* Durham and London: Duke University Press.

Gabbard, K. 1996. *Jammin' at the Margins: Jazz and the American Cinema.* Chicago: The University of Chicago Press.

Garber, F. 1995. Fabulating jazz. In K. Gabbard, ed. *Representing Jazz.* Durham and London: Duke University Press. pp. 70–103.

Gee, L. 1997. Get rid of the goatee. *The Guardian.* July 25, p. 23.

Giles, J. 1995. As above, so below: Thirty years of underground cinema and pop music. In J. Romney and A. Wootton, eds. *Celluloid Jukebox: Popular Music and the Movies since the 1950s.* London: BFI. pp. 44–51.

Gioia, T. 1992. *West Coast Jazz: Modern Jazz in California 1945–1960.* New York: Oxford University Press.

Gledhill, C. 1978. *Klute*: A contemporary film noir and feminist criticism. In E.A. Kaplan, ed. *Women in Film Noir.* London: BFI. pp. 6–21.

Gomery, D. 1975. They live by night (Nicholas Ray). In T. McCarthy and C. Flynn, eds. *King of the Bs.* New York: E.P. Dutton. pp. 185–96.

Gorbman, C. 1987. *Unheard Melodies: Narrative Film Music.* London: BFI.

Gordon, R. 1986. *Jazz West Coast.* London: Quartet Books Ltd.

Grant, B.K. 1995. Purple passages or fiestas in blue? notes toward an aesthetic of vocalese. In K. Gabbard, ed. *Representing Jazz.* Durham and London: Duke University Press. pp. 285–303.

Greenberg, M., and Waugh, C., eds. 1981. *The Fantastic Stories of Cornell Woolrich*. Carbondale and Edwardsville: Southern Illinois University Press.

Hajdu, D. 1997. *Lush Life: A Biography of Billy Strayhorn*. London: Granta Books.

Hardy, P., ed. 1997. *The BFI Companion to Crime*. Berkeley and Los Angeles: University of California Press.

Harrison, M. 1991. *A Jazz Retrospect*. London: Quartet Books Ltd.

Hasse, J.E. 1993. *Beyond Category: The Life and Genius of Duke Ellington*. New York: Omnibus.

Hentoff, N. 1962. *The Jazz Life*. London: (Lowe & Brydone) Peter Davies.

Higham, C. 1975. You may not leave the movie house singing their songs, but . . . *New York Times*. May 25.

Hisama, E.M. 1993. Postcolonialism on the make: The music of John Mellencamp, David Bowie and John Zorn. *Popular Music*. vol. 12, no. 2, p. 99.

Hopkins, S. 1997. The primer: John Zorn. *The Wire*. no. 156, February, pp. 38–41.

Hourihan, M. 1997. *Deconstructing the Hero: Literary Theory and Children's Literature*. London: Routledge.

Kalinak, K. 1992. *Settling the Score: Music and the Classical Hollywood Film*. Madison: University of Wisconsin Press.

Kaplan, E.A., ed. 1978. *Women in Film Noir*. London: BFI.

Karlin, F. 1994. *Listening to Movies: The Film Lover's Guide to Film Music*. New York: Schirmer Books.

Karlin, F., and Wright, R. 1990. *On the Track: A Guide to Contemporary Film Scoring*. New York: Schirmer Books.

Kemp, A. 1996. *The Musical Temperament: Psychology and Personality of Musicians*. Oxford: Oxford University Press.

Kernfeld, B., ed. 1995. *The New Grove Dictionary of Jazz*. London: MacMillan.

Kernfeld, B. 1995. *What To Listen for in Jazz*. New Haven: Yale University Press.

Kington, M., ed. 1993. *The Jazz Anthology*. London: Harper Collins.

Knee, A. 1995. Doubling, music, and race in *Cabin in the Sky*. In K. Gabbard, ed. *Representing Jazz*. Durham and London: Duke University Press. pp. 193–204.

Knight, A. 1995. *Jammin' the blues*, or The sight of jazz, 1944. In K. Gabbard, ed. *Representing Jazz*. Durham and London: Duke University Press. pp. 11–53.

Krutnik, F. 1989. In a Lonely Street: 1940s Hollywood, Film Noir, and the "Tough" Thriller. Unpublished Ph.D. dissertation, The University of Kent at Canterbury.

Kuhn, A. 1994. *Women's Pictures*. London: Verso.

De Laborerie, R. 1952. A la recherche de l'hypertendu. *Cahiers du Cinema*. no. 12, May.

Lack, R. 1997. *Twenty Four Frames Under: A Buried History of Film Music*. London: Quartet.

Lange, A. 1989. Cool noir. *Down Beat*. vol. 56, no. 3, March.

Lee, W.F., ed. 1980. *Stan Kenton: Artistry in Rhythm*. Los Angeles: Creative Press of Los Angeles.

Lees, G. 1975. Adventures of a black composer in Hollywood. *The New York Times*. March 16.

Lees, G. 1991. *Waiting for Dizzy*. Oxford: Oxford University Press.

Levin, M., and Wilson, J.S. 1994. The classic interviews-Charlie Parker. *Down Beat*. February.

Lipscomb, S. 1997. Perceptual Measures of Visual and Auditory Cues in Film Music. An online transcript can be found at http://www.music.utsa.edu/~lipscomb/JASA97/.

Lipscomb, S., and Kendall, R. 1994. Perceptual judgement of the relationship between musical and visual components in film. *Psychomusicology*. vol. 13, no. 1, pp. 60–98.

Litweiler, J. 1984. *The Freedom Principle: Jazz after 1958*. New York: Morrow.

McClary, S. 1990. Towards a feminist criticism of music. *Canadian University Music Review: Alternative Musicologies*. vol. 10, no.2.

McGee, M.T. 1990. *The Rock and Roll Movie Encyclopedia of the 1950s*. Jefferson, N.C.: McFarland & Company, Inc.

Manvell, R., and Huntley, J. 1957. *The Technique of Film Music*. London: Focal Press.

Maremaa, T. 1976. The sound of movie music. *New York Times*. March 28.

Marks, M. 1997. *Music and the Silent Film: Contexts and Case Studies 1895–1924*. New York: Oxford University Press.

Martin, P.J. 1995. *Sounds and Society: Themes in the Sociology of Music*. Manchester: University of Manchester Press.

Martin, P.J. 1996. *Improvisation in Jazz*. Manchester: Manchester Sociology Occasional Paper, no. 45.

Meeker, D. 1981. *Jazz in the Movies*. New York: Da Capo Press.

Meltzer, D., ed. 1993. *Reading Jazz*. San Francisco: Mercury House.

Mintz, P. 1985. Orson Welles's use of sound. In E. Weis and J. Bolton, eds. *Film Sound: Theory and Practice*. New York: Columbia University Press. pp. 289–97

Naremore, J. 1995. Uptown folk: Blackness and entertainment in *Cabin in the Sky*. In K. Gabbard, ed. *Representing Jazz*. Durham and London: Duke University Press. pp. 169–92.

Naremore, J. 1998. *More than Night: Film Noir in Its Contexts*. Berkeley and Los Angeles: University of California Press.

Nash, J.R., and Ross, S.R., eds. 1986. *The Motion Picture Guide: H-K 1927–1983*. Chicago: Cinebooks, Inc.

Neve, B. 1992. *Film & Politics in America: A Social Tradition*. London: Routledge.

Nevins, Jr., F. 1981. The poet of the shadows: Cornell Woolrich. In M. Greenberg and C. Waugh, eds. *The Fantastic Stories of Cornell Woolrich*. Carbondale and Edwardsville: Southern Illinois University Press. pp. vii–xxvi.

Nicholson, S. 1990. *Jazz: The Modern Resurgence*. London: Simon & Schuster.

Orr, C. 1997. Genre theory in the context of the noir and post-noir film. *Film Criticism*. vol. 22, no. 1, Fall, pp. 21–37.

Orr, J. 1993. *Cinema and Modernity*. Cambridge: Polity Press.

Penman, I. 1996. Review of Barry Adamson's *Oedipus Schmoedipus*. *The Wire*. no. 150, August, p. 46.

Pfeil, F. 1993. Home fires burning: Film noir in *Blue Velvet* and *Terminator 2*. In J. Copjec, ed. *Shades of Noir*. London: Verso. pp. 227–59.

Place, J. 1978. Women in film noir. In A.E Kaplan, *Women in Film Noir*. London: BFI. pp. 35–67.

Place, J., and Peterson, L. 1996. Some visual motifs of film noir. In A. Silver and J. Ursini, eds. *Film Noir Reader*. New York: Limelight Editions. pp. 65–75. Originally published in 1974.

Pleasants, H. 1968. Jazz and the movies. *The World of Music* (UNESCO). vol. 10, no. 3, pp. 38–47.

Porfirio, R. 1980. Among the living. In A. Silver and E. Ward, eds. *Film Noir*. London: Secker & Warburg. p. 11.

Porfirio, R. 1980. Phantom lady. In A. Silver and E. Ward, eds. *Film Noir*. London: Secker & Warburg. p. 226.

Porfirio, R. 1980. When strangers marry. In A. Silver and E. Ward, eds. *Film Noir*. London: Secker & Warburg. p. 307.

Porfirio, R. 1996. No way out: Existential motifs in the film noir. In A. Silver and J. Ursini, eds. *Film Noir Reader*. New York: Limelight Editions. pp. 77–93. Originally published in 1976.

Porfirio, R. 1996. The killers: Expressiveness of sound and image in film noir. In A. Silver and J. Ursini, eds. *Film Noir Reader*. New York: Limelight Editions. pp. 177–87.

Porfirio, R. 1999. Dark jazz: Music in the film noir. In A. Silver and J. Ursini, eds. *Film Noir Reader 2*. New York: Limelight Editions. pp. 177–87.

Prendergast, R.M. 1992. *Film Music: A Neglected Art*. New York: W.W. Norton and Company.

Radano, R.M. 1993. *New Musical Figurations: Anthony Braxton's Cultural Critique*. Chicago: University of Chicago Press.

Raksin, D. 1949. Talking back: A Hollywood composer states case for his craft. *New York Times*. February 20.

Reid, D.W., Walker J.L. 1993. Strange pursuit: Cornell Woolrich and the abandoned city of the forties. In J. Copjec, ed. *Shades of Noir*. London: Verso. pp. 57–96.

Robertson, J.C. 1993. *The Casablanca Man: The Cinema of Michael Curtiz*. London: Routledge.

Romney, J. 1995. Sound of silents. *The Guardian*. October 19, pp. 12–13.

Romney, J., and Wootton, A., eds. 1995. *Celluloid Jukebox: Popular Music and the Movies since the1950s*. London: BFI.

Said, E. 1992. Extract from *Orientalism*. In A. Easthope and K. McGowan, eds. *A Critical and Cultural Theory Reader*. Buckingham: Open University Press. pp. 59–65. Originally published in 1978.

Said, E. 1994. *Culture and Imperialism*. London: Vintage.

Scharf, W. 1988. *The History of Film Scoring*. Studio City: Cinema Songs, Inc.

Schrader, P. 1996. Notes on film noir. In A. Silver and J. Ursini, eds. *Film Noir Reader*. New York: Limelight Edition. pp. 53–63. Originally published in 1972.

Schutze, P. 1996. Screens not heard. *The Wire*. no. 154, December, pp. 44–45.

Seidenberg, R. 1989. At long last, jazz. *American Film*. vol. 14, no. 7, May, pp. 51–54.

Shepherd, J. 1991. *Music as Social Text*. Cambridge: Polity Press.

Shohat, E., and Stam, R. 1994. *Unthinking Eurocentrism: Multiculturalism and the Media*. London: Routledge.

Sidran, B. 1995. *Black Talk: How the Music of Black America Created a Radical Alternative to the Values of Western Literary Tradition*. Edinburgh: Payback Press.

Silver, A. 1996. *Kiss Me Deadly:* Evidence of a style. In A. Silver and J. Ursini, eds. *Film Noir Reader*. New York: Limelight Edition. pp. 209–35.

Silver, A., and Ursini, J., eds. 1996. *Film Noir Reader*. New York: Limelight Editions.

Silver, A., and Ursini, J., eds. 1999. *Film Noir Reader 2*. New York: Limelight Editions.

Silver, A., and Ward, E., eds. 1980. *Film Noir*. London: Secker & Warburg.

Silverman, K. 1988. *The Acoustic Mirror: The Female Voice in Psychoanalysis and Cinema*. Bloomington and Indianapolis: Indiana University Press.

Sinker, M. 1995. Music as film. In J. Romney and A. Wootton, eds. *Celluloid Jukebox: Popular Music and the Movies since the 1950s*. London: BFI. pp. 106–17.

Sloboda, J. 1985. *The Musical Mind: The Cognitive Psychology of Music*. Oxford: Clarendon Press.

Smith, P. 1993. *Clint Eastwood: A Cultural Production*. London: UCL Press. pp. 225–41.

Smith, S. C. 1991. *A Heart at Fire's Center: The Life and Music of Bernard Herrmann*. Los Angeles: University of California Press.

Spence, K.C. 1988. Jazz digest: From big band to bebop. *Film Comment*. vol. 24, no. 6, November/December, pp. 38–43.

Staiger, J. 1997. Hybrid or inbred: The purity hypothesis and Hollywood genre history. *Film Criticism*. vol. 22, no. 1, Fall, pp. 5–20.

Steiner, F. 1976. An examination of Leith Stevens' use of jazz in *The Wild One*. Part 1. *Film Music Notebook*. no. 2, pp. 26–35.

Steiner, F. 1976. An examination of Leith Stevens' use of jazz in *The Wild One*. Part 2. *Film Music Notebook*. no. 2, pp. 26–34.

Stephens, M.L. 1995. *Film Noir: A Comprehensive, Illustrated Reference to Movies, Terms and Persons*. Jefferson, N.C.: McFarland & Company, Inc.

Stern, L. 1995. *The Scorsese Connection*. London: BFI.

Stilwell, R. 1997. Symbol, narrative and the musics of *Truly, Madly, Deeply*. *Screen*. vol. 38, no. 1, Spring, pp. 60–75.

Stowe, D. 1994. *Big Band Jazz in New Deal America*. Cambridge, Mass.: Harvard University Press.

Stratemann, K. 1981. *Negro Bands on Film: An Exploratory Filmo-Discography*. vol. 1. *Big Bands 1928–1950*. Lubbecke: Uhle and Kleimann.

Stratemann, K. 1992. *Duke Ellington: Day by Day & Film by Film*. Copenhagen: Jazz Media.

Straw, W. 1993. Popular music and post-modernism in the 1980s. In S. Frith, A. Goodwin and L. Grossberg, eds. *Sound and Vision: The Music Video Reader*. London: Routledge. pp. 3—21.

Taubin, A. 1999. God's lonely man. *Sight and Sound*. April, pp. 16–19.

Taylor, J.R. 1983. *Strangers in Paradise: The Hollywood Emigrés 1933–1950*. London: Faber & Faber Ltd.

Thomas, N., ed. 1990. *International Dictionary of Filmmakers*. vol. 1. *Films*. (2nd ed.) Chicago: St. James Press.

Thomas, T. 1977. *Music For The Movies*. South Brunswick, N.J., and New York: A.S. Barnes and Company; London: Tantivy Press.

Tiegel, E. 1993. Scoring in Hollywood. *Down Beat*. vol. 60, no. 10, October, pp. 24–28.

Tilton, R. 1956. Jazz dance. *Film Music*. vol. 15, no. 4, Spring, p. 19.

Toop, D. 1995. *Ocean of Sound*. London: Serpent's Tail.

Toop, D. 1995. Rock musicians and film soundtracks. In J. Romney and A. Wootton, eds. 1995. *Celluloid Jukebox: Popular Music and the Movies since the1950s*. London: BFI. pp. 72–81.

Tuska, J. 1984. *Dark Cinema: American Film Noir in Cultural Perspective*. Westport, Conn.: Greenwood Press.

Ulanov, B. 1972. *A History of Jazz in America*. New York: Da Capo Press.

Ursini, James. 1996. Angst at sixty fields per second. In A. Silver and J. Ursini, eds. *Film Noir Reader*. New York: Limelight Editions. pp. 275–87.

Vincent, T. 1995. *Keep Cool: The Black Activists Who Built the Jazz Age*. London: Pluto Press.

Webb, A. 1999. On the road to nowhere. *The Independent*. March 13.

Weis, E. 1982. *The Silent Scream: Alfred Hitchcock's Sound Track*. London: Associated University Presses.

Weis, E., and Bolton, J., eds. 1985. *Film Sound: Theory and Practice*. New York: Columbia University Press.

Weiss, A. 1992. *Vampires and Violets*. London: Butler and Tanner Ltd.

Wells, D. 1991. *The Night People: The Jazz Life of Dicky Wells (as told to Stanley Dance)*. Washington, D.C.: Smithsonian Institution Press.

Welles, O. (with Peter Bogdanovich). Jonathan R., ed. 1993. *This is Orson Welles*. London: Harper Collins.

White, A. 1989. Celluloid songs—Borrowed images: Music. *Film Comment*. vol. 25, no. 2, March/April, pp. 36–39.

Williams, T. 1996. *Phantom Lady*, Cornell Woolrich, and the masochistic aesthetic. In A. Silver and J. Ursini, eds. *Film Noir Reader*. New York: Limelight Editions. pp. 129–43.

Wilson, J.S. 1961. Jazz film maestro. *New York Times*. September 24.

Wilson, J.S. 1994. The classic interviews-Dizzy Gillespie. *Down Beat*. February.

Woolrich, C. 1981. Dark melody of madness. In M. Greenberg and C. Waugh, eds. *The Fantastic Stories of Cornell Woolrich*. Carbondale and Edwardsville: Southern Illinois University Press. pp. 26–66. Originally published in 1935.

Woolrich, C. (as William Irish). 1982. *Phantom Lady*. New York: Ballantine Books. Originally published in 1942.

Yanow, S. 1988. Bird: The movie. *Down Beat*. September.

Young, A. 1993. We jazz June/We die soon: Jazz film thoughts. *Antaeus*, no. 71-2. pp. 122–29.

Young, L. 1996. *Fear of the Dark: 'Race,' Gender and Sexuality in the Cinema*. London: Routledge.

Zabor, R. 1999. *The Bear Comes Home*. London: Vintage.

Zador, L.T. 1986. Interview with Fred Katz. *The Cue Sheet: The Newsletter of the Society for the Preservation of Film Music*. vol. 3, no. 2, April, pp. 18–22.

Index

About the Author

DAVID BUTLER teaches Film Studies at the University of Manchester in the United Kingdom.